# Moral Panics and the Copyright Wars

# Moral Panics and the Copyright Wars

WILLIAM PATRY

OXFORD

UNIVERSITY PRESS

*Oxford University Press, Inc., publishes works that further Oxford University's objective of excellence in research, scholarship, and education.*

Oxford   New York
Auckland   Cape Town   Dar es Salaam   Hong Kong   Karachi   Kuala Lumpur   Madrid   Melbourne
Mexico City   Nairobi   New Delhi   Shanghai   Taipei   Toronto

With offices in
Argentina   Austria   Brazil   Chile   Czech Republic   France   Greece   Guatemala   Hungary   Italy
Japan   Poland   Portugal   Singapore   South Korea   Switzerland   Thailand   Turkey   Ukraine
Vietnam

Published by Oxford University Press, Inc.
198 Madison Avenue, New York, New York 10016

Oxford is a registered trademark of Oxford University Press
Oxford University Press is a registered trademark of Oxford University Press, Inc.

---

Library of Congress Cataloging-in-Publication Data

Patry, William.
  Moral panics and the copyright wars / William Patry.
    p. cm.
  Includes bibliographical references and index.
  ISBN 978-0-19-538564-9 ((hardback): alk. paper)
  1. Copyright—Philosophy. 2. Moral panics. 3. Metaphor.
  4. Property. I. Title.
  K1420.5.P376 2009
  346.04'82—dc22
                                        2009004973

---

1 2 3 4 5 6 7 8 9
Printed in the United States of America on acid-free paper

**Note to Readers**

You may order this or any other Oxford University Press publication by
visiting the Oxford University Press website at www.oup.com

For Rebecca, a book widow no more

# Contents

# Acknowledgments

The publication of this book by Oxford University Press is solely a consequence of Evan Schnittman's keen business sense. Matt Gallaway, legal acquisitions editor at OUP, provided invaluable advice, leading to a much tighter final manuscript. Thanks as well to Joshua Wattles, a veteran entertainment lawyer and good friend, for reading the manuscript carefully twice, and whose decades of experience and commitment to fairness saved me from error and overstatement more than once. As with everything I write, I did all of the research, drafting, and typing myself and thus have no one to thank.

# Disclaimer

Although I serve as Senior Copyright Counsel to Google Inc., the views in this book are entirely mine, and should not be attributed to Google. The book is not Google's book, nor did I write it as a Google employee or to advance Google's interests, as much as I identify with and value those interests. Instead, I wrote the book on my own initiative to make *personal* observations—observations that come from being a full-time copyright lawyer for 27 years, 24 of which occurred before I joined Google. In short, Google does not endorse this book, does not share the views expressed in this book, so *please* don't preface any discussion of this book with: "Google's Senior Copyright Counsel said," or any other variant. It's my book alone.

# Introduction

We use language to perform many tasks, including expressing emotions, imparting or requesting information, and making arguments. In the case of argumentation, we choose language that conveys our views *and* that will be persuasive to others. The italicized "and" reflects the dual purpose served by language: Language is both a vehicle (of words) and the means by which we cognitively understand concepts contained in words. We think with words.[1]

The words we choose in debates may accurately describe the issues, or they may not. When language confuses rather than enlightens, our understanding is impeded. In extreme cases, the language employed is so inapt that it harms our ability to come to a constructive conclusion. Copyright presents such an extreme case. The way we have come to talk about copyright is harmful to the way we think about copyright, harm that has led to bad business and bad policy decisions. As George Orwell wrote, "if thought corrupts language, language can also corrupt thought."[2] In place of reasoned analysis, too often we encounter emotionally laden appeals using ancient, rhetorical devices designed to demonize opponents and to create the impression there is an existential threat to society. In truth, the only threats are to outdated business models. Unless we recognize that the debates over copyright constitute an economic debate about business models, we will never be able to make the correct business and policy decisions. As a federal court in Manhattan held: "Copyright and trademark are not matters of strong moral principle. Intellectual property regimes are economic legislation based on policy decisions that assign rights based on assessments of what legal rules will produce the greatest economic good for society as a whole."[3]

The argument of this book is that bad business models, failed economic ideologies, and the acceptance of inapposite metaphors have led to an unjustified expansion of our copyright laws. To rectify the current imbalance we must be clear-headed about the guiding principles, and have the courage to change our laws so that they may, once again, further those purposes, rather than, as is currently the case, defeat them. The need for clarity about the principles at stake was eloquently made in the greatest speech ever given on copyright, that of Lord Thomas Macaulay[4] in opposing an 1841 bill in the British House of Commons to increase the term of copyright.[5] The bill's supporters argued Parliament should grant the additional period of protection simply because it was "right and just" to do so. Disagreeing, Lord Macaulay regarded the issue as involving "expediency," meaning Parliament should grant the additional rights only if it was determined empirically that doing so would benefit the public, for copyright had been created for the public good, not for the private benefit of authors. Here is the relevant excerpt from Lord Macaulay's lengthy remarks:

> The first thing to be done, Sir, is to settle on what principles the question is to be argued. Are we free to legislate for the public good, or are we not? Is this a question of expediency, or is it a question of right? Many of those who have written and petitioned against the existing state of things treat the question as one of right. The law of nature, according to them, gives to every man a sacred and indefeasible property in his own ideas, in the fruits of his own reason and imagination....
>
> Now, Sir, if this be so, let justice be done, cost what it may. I am not prepared, like my honourable and learned friend, to agree to a compromise between right and expediency, and to commit an injustice for the public convenience. But I must say, that his theory soars far beyond the reach of my faculties. It is not necessary to go, on the present occasion, into a metaphysical inquiry about the origin of the right of property; and certainly nothing but the strongest necessity would lead me to discuss a subject so likely to be distasteful to the House. I agree, I own, with Paley in thinking that property is the creature of the law, and that the law which creates property can be defended only on this ground, that it is a law beneficial to mankind.
>
> ....
>
> The principle of copyright is this. It is a tax on readers for the purpose of giving a bounty to writers. The tax is an exceedingly bad one; it is a tax on one of the most innocent and most salutary of human

pleasures; and never let us forget, that a tax on innocent pleasures is a premium on vicious pleasures. I admit, however, the necessity of giving a bounty to genius and learning. In order to give such a bounty, I willingly submit even to this severe and burdensome tax. Nay, I am ready to increase the tax, if it can be shown that by so doing I should proportionally increase the bounty. My complaint is, that my honourable and learned friend doubles, triples, quadruples, the tax, and makes scarcely any perceptible addition to the bounty.

. . . It is good that authors should be remunerated; and the least exceptionable way of remunerating them is by a monopoly. Yet monopoly is an evil. For the sake of the good we must submit to the evil; but the evil ought not to last a day longer than is necessary for the purpose of securing the good.[6]

The two approaches offered in the 1841 Parliamentary debates are profoundly different. The approach taken by the bill's advocates was of copyright as a right created by God,[7] with the role of the legislature being to merely implement God's will that authors get whatever they wish simply because they are authors, and without any consideration for adverse effects on the public. The approach taken by Lord Macaulay (and which prevailed) was of copyright as a right that exists only by government decree, created for the public good, and which must be regulated by the government to ensure that the public purpose is fulfilled. Lord Macaulay's insistence that the debate be conducted on the actual economic effect of the proposed legislation on the public good, rather than on sloganeering about an alleged inherent right of authors should stand for all times as the template for policy makers evaluating proposed initiatives.

The final paragraph in the quote is not, as is sometimes asserted, an attack on the entire system of copyright—taxes are necessary for many essential, socially useful purposes. Rather, Lord Macaulay is saying, "let's acknowledge that copyright *is* a government mandated tax, but figure out the appropriate rate of the tax"; if increasing the rate will increase the number of books and thereby learning, he would gladly pay the higher rate, as should we. But there is no automatic benefit in paying higher taxes, whether those taxes are copyright royalties or payroll deductions that go to governmental treasuries. This explains Lord Macaulay's rejection of the argument that more is always better because, allegedly, copyright is inherently good. As a tax, copyright is not inherently good: It is only good when the amount of the tax and the expenditures derived from it lead to good results. If increasing the copyright tax does not lead to the creation of new works, and as is the case presently, also leads to the suppression of innovation, we must acknowledge that copyright has become an unproductive tax: the evil of the monopoly is defeating the very good the monopoly was designed to further: just like medicine in proper doses may cure diseases or save lives, an overdose of that same medicine may kill the patient. Copyright is now at fatal strength.

The solution to our current copyright overtaxation is not to throw out the tax entirely but to reform it, reduce it, tailor it so that it can serve its intended purpose. Calls for strong copyright laws, like calls for weak copyright laws, miss the point entirely: the only proper goal is *effective* laws, with "effective" being judged empirically by whether proposed legislation will lead to an increase in the public good.

Alas, Lord Macaulay is not alive today, and as a result of the lack of a modern inheritor of his mantle, copyright debates rarely focus on the only relevant question: Will the proposal actually serve the public good by promoting learning? Instead, debates degenerate into name-calling and the copyright equivalent of the sky is falling. This Chicken Little approach to copyright is a political tactic by which undeserving economic interests are advanced under the guise of false moral imperatives. Although Lord Macaulay easily saw through such false appeals, too often contemporary courts and policy makers do not.

Sociologists call these false appeals "moral panics"; those allegedly responsible for the moral panics are called "folk devils."[8] Conjuring up moral panics and folk devils occurs through metaphors casting the other side in an unfavorable light, in the case of copyright, by painting those who use works without permission as thieves, trespassers, pirates, or parasites. The purported folk devils employ their own rhetorical devices, describing copyright owners as dinosaurs, Luddites, and evil monopolists out to squelch freedom of expression, and out to force corporate culture down the public's throats.

Both sides' mudslinging is often referred to as the "Copyright Wars." There have been a number of copyright wars. The First Copyright War began in the 1730s in the United Kingdom. The war has been called the "Battle of the Booksellers"[9] because it was an internecine fight among book publishers; it lasted from 1735 to 1774. The most recent copyright wars began in 1998, when copyright owners obtained from Congress unprecedented rights to control access to and use of their works. The wars took a decisive step forward the following year, 1999, when record labels sued Napster. The conflict was dramatically ratcheted up in 2003, when record labels began filing what would ultimately be more than 35,000 lawsuits against individual consumers and sending hundreds of thousands of cease and desist letters. When or how the war will end is anyone's guess, but the copyright industries are preparing themselves for Armageddon, seeking ever greater rights and ever more draconian penalties, as if laws are the answer to all of their problems, and as if the more and stronger the laws, the more fully will their problems be solved. As a direct consequence of the copyright industries' decision to rely on laws and litigation rather than the marketplace, many consumers have shifted to other forms of entertainment because those forms of entertainment have as their purpose satisfying consumers' needs, not denying them. Copyright owners may well find themselves armed to the teeth with weapons against consumers who have left the battlefield.

The Copyright Wars usually center on digital issues, such as peer-to-peer file sharing, Internet posting and hosting of content, and digital locks on consumer goods. But the Copyright Wars also raise deep concerns over the length of copyright—in the United States, life of the author plus seventy years for works created after 1977, and 95 years from publication in the case of works first published before 1978. Additionally, the remedies provided for infringement of copyright, including civil statutory damages that can reach into tens or hundreds of millions of dollars without any loss of sales or income, has given the copyright industries dangerous leverage over the existence and functionalities of new technologies: threatening statutory damages so high that they will bankrupt innovative start-up companies has become a new, but perverted business model. From the public's perspective, the Copyright Wars have multiple fronts.

For their part, the entertainment and publishing companies believe the Internet is a Wild West—a "place"[10] where they are powerless to control digital uses of their works, with control representing, in their view, the foundation of their business. According to the copyright industries, once they lose control they lose their ability to lose money. This is simply not true. Control is not an end in itself for those whose business is selling mass-market goods to consumers: "the purpose of a business is to create and keep customers."[11] Businesses create and keep customers by satisfying customers' needs, and thus it is only through satisfying customers that businesses can make money. Focusing on satisfying consumers rather than on controlling them (or suing them *en masse*) requires businesses to devote themselves to figuring out what consumers want and value, and to then cater to those wants and values.[12]

Consumers are king—not control, not copyright, and not content. Without consumers, copyrights and content have no economic value. Copyright is not fairy dust, vesting everything it touches with magical economic value. Rather, economic value is derived from buyers' willingness to pay for a product or service. Accordingly, as Professor Theodore Levitt noted, what businesses offer for sale should be determined "not by the seller but by the buyer. The seller takes cues from the buyer ... and not vice versa. This may sound like an elementary rule of business, but that does not keep it from being violated wholesale. It is more violated than honored."[13] Copyright industries violate these obvious principles with religious fervor. Their fervor stems from an unswerving belief in a business model of vertical monopolization giving them control over every aspect of production, distribution, and consumption. In the "Golden Era" of film (1920s to 1950s), for example, when the studio system held sway, motion picture companies owned the actors, the scriptwriters, the directors, the copyrights, the film prints, and many of the theaters.[14] Little has changed since those days in terms of the copyright industries' ideal business model. It is only the details that are different: the resulting marketing myopia remains. Indeed, the copyright industries' fondest wish is to be able to transform the Internet, through the use of digital locks, into the greatest form of vertical control ever seen.

The sin of copyright—and it is a large and growing sin—is that it provides the legal framework for such an upside-down business model, a model in which the copyright industries may safely engage in anti-consumer, anti-competitive, and anti-innovative conduct. New technologies are vehemently opposed as an existential threat to the business model of vertical control. Rather than adapt to new technologies and the new business opportunities they present, the copyright industries litigate rather than innovate, with a goal of turning new technologies into one more way to preserve the status quo. Such efforts don't make the copyright industries evil, as is often claimed, but they do reflect the fact that too many of the copyright industries are poorly run by executives whose only vision is in the rearview window. Where such businesses succeed, they succeed in spite of themselves, propped up by consumers' innate love of entertainment and the unnatural leverage provided by copyright laws.

Consumers' current antipathy toward copyright owners arises from the correct belief that too many copyright owners are actively hostile to consumers' desires in favor of tightly controlled markets that parcel out a small number of works in a form copyright owners believe they can safely protect *from* consumers.

Once consumers are regarded as the enemy, things go seriously awry. The very metaphor of "the Copyright Wars" is Exhibit 1 in how things have gone awry. "War" evokes violence, committed by dangerous and aggressive people out to hurt or kill us. Such people must be stopped immediately and by all means necessary.

Wars are, as Clausewitz explained, politics by other means. Copyright owners' creation of political opportunities through creating a false sense of war explains why, in April 2002, then-head of the Motion Picture Association of America (MPAA) Jack Valenti submitted testimony to Congress entitled, "A Clear Present and Future Danger."[15] The title deliberately invoked the metaphor "clear and present danger" coined by Justice Oliver Wendell Holmes, Jr. in his 1919 opinion for the U.S. Supreme Court in *Schenck v. United States.*[16] Charles Schenk was criminally convicted and spent six months in jail for distributing leaflets urging men to resist the draft for World War I. His conduct was neither violent nor seditious, and his statements hardly inflammatory: "Do not submit to intimidation," "Assert your rights," "If you do not assert and support your rights, you are helping to deny or disparage rights which it is the solemn duty of all citizens and residents of the United States to retain." Schenck argued his conviction violated the First Amendment. The Supreme Court rejected Schenck's appeal, Justice Holmes writing:

The question in every case is whether the words used are used in such circumstances and are of such a nature as to create a clear and present danger that they will bring about the substantive evils that Congress has a right to prevent. When a nation is at war, many things that might be said in time of peace are such a hindrance to its effort that their utterance will not be endured so long as men fight, and that no Court could regard them as protected by any constitutional right.[17]

Mr. Valenti's purpose in evoking the wartime *Schenck* opinion was to create, metaphorically, the impression of the copyright industries under siege from hostile forces, an impression he had earlier and shamefully associated with the tragic events of September 11, 2001. An indecently short three months after those events, in January 2002, he declared: "We're fighting our own terrorist war."[18] As a bomber pilot in World War II, Mr. Valenti knew the difference between killing large groups of people by flying planes into building or by dropping armaments on them as he had done, and the unauthorized copying of motion pictures. But it is precisely because he *did know*, firsthand, real war and the patriotic feelings it arouses that he chose to employ the metaphors of war in connection with the comparatively trivial issue of allegedly violating economic rights. Through the metaphor of war, he hoped such a trivial issue would become a priority of the government, which would then, on behalf of his wealthy corporate clients, exercise the powers of the State and rally the population as it had during World Wars I and II, and in the aftermath of September 11, 2001.

All wars require enemies, enemies to be vanquished and not accommodated. To vanquish an enemy we need to know not only who the enemy is, but also who the victims and the heroes are. In the Copyright Wars, copyright owners have cast themselves as the victims, with Congress and, on occasion, the courts cast as the heroes—not because those institutions are heroes—they are not—but because Hollywood realizes such roles are politically useful in order to obtain from them the increased rights they seek. The villains, by contrast, are an ever-changing cast of technological innovations, beginning, over a hundred years ago, with piano rolls.[19] In 1906, John Philip Sousa wrote an article in opposition to player piano called "The Menace of Mechanical Music,"[20] a theme later picked up by the American Society of Composers, Authors, and Publishers, which put out a pamphlet decrying the phonograph record as "the murderer of music."[21] In 1923, the music industry asked the federal government deny radio broadcasters' renewal applications, blaming radio stations for the decline in music sales. Later, talking movies, jukeboxes, television, photocopying machines, cable television, videocassette recorders, digital audio tape, digital music storage lockers, and the Internet have been described in similarly apocalyptic terms. Yet, the apocalypse proverbially ends up being beneficial to the copyright industries. Like cats, the copyright industries are always on the wrong side of the door.

Despite the changing cast, assigning roles to villains and victims requires harsh line drawing, setting one group of human beings against another group of human beings. Such line drawing usually involves a process of dehumanizing opponents:

> Dehumanization is . . . an extension of a . . . process of developing an "enemy image" of the opponent. . . . An enemy image is a negative stereotype through which the opposing group is viewed as evil, in contrast to one's own side, which is seen as good. . . . Enemy images are usually black and white. The negative actions of one's opponent are thought to reflect their fundamental evil nature, traits, or motives. One's own faults, as well as the values and motivations behind the actions of one's opponent, are usually discounted, denied, or ignored. It becomes difficult to empathize or see where one's opponent is coming from. Meaningful communication is unlikely, and it becomes difficult to perceive any common ground.[22]

Opponents thus become The Other: those who are, supposedly, not only unlike us but dangerously so. Wars simultaneously unite those on one side in a common cause and divide those deemed opposed to that cause. Vanquishing enemies also requires weapons. In the Copyright Wars, the courts, Congress, and international agreements are weapons but so too is language, especially metaphoric language: "Metaphor is a weapon in the hand-to-hand struggle with reality."[23] There is a considerable scientific literature documenting the use of violent metaphors[24] including these well-established metaphors for arguments as war:

* He attacked every weak point in my argument.
* He shot down all my arguments.
* His criticisms were right on target.
* Your claims are indefensible.
* If you use that strategy, he'll wipe you out.[25]

Professors Lakoff and Mark Johnson explain:

> It is important to see that we don't actually just talk about arguments
> in terms of war. We actually win or lose arguments. We see the person
> we are arguing with us as an opponent. We gain and lose ground. We
> plan and use strategies. If we find a position indefensible, we can
> abandon it and take a new line of attack. Many of the things we do in
> arguing are structured by concepts of war. Though there is no physical
> battle, there is verbal battle, and the structure of an argument—attack,
> defense, counterattack, etc.—reflect[s] this.[26]

And so it is in the Copyright Wars—the creation of misleading discourse
about economic issues using the metaphors and language of war. Not
only is war hell, but as Senator Hiram Johnson said in 1917, "The first
casualty when war comes is truth,"[27] truth about others as well as truth
about ourselves, although we rarely admit this last point. The current
Copyright Wars have all the prerequisites of wars: conjured up enemies,
weapons (language, lawsuits, legislative and international initiatives),
and truth as a casualty.

A loss of faith in our laws has been another casualty in the Copyright
Wars. Laws should be fair, fit for their purpose, and accountable to the
reality of the world we live in. We do not respect, and will not follow, laws
that conflict with the realities of our lives, nor should we. But we also
want our laws to appeal to the best in our nature, not the worst. President
Obama has rightly called for a new declaration of independence, one that
involves independence from "ideology, and small thinking, prejudice and
bigotry—an appeal not to our easy instincts but to our better angels."[28]
Our current copyright laws fail all these requirements. The Copyright
Wars and the recent grotesque expansion of rights and remedies should
be regarded as a legal equivalent of the subprime mortgage crisis: cancers
on our system that were foreseeable and preventable but for greed,
a failed ideology that the unregulated private pursuit of profit is also in
the best interest of the public, and a worldwide lack of political courage
to admit to and take responsibility for the damage caused by copyright
laws that harm rather than serve the public. The first step in copyright
recovery is honesty about where we are and how we got there. The role of
this book is to provide that first step. It is up to the policy makers to take
the next step.

# ONE

# How the Copyright Wars Are Being Fought and Why

Words matter. We use particular words because we want to convince others of our viewpoint. When the topic is copyright law, however, language is rarely employed to persuade, and most often to demonize. The intensity of the debates over copyright has reached the point where the term the "Copyright Wars" need not be explained; it is now part of our common cultural language.[1] The term originated with those who regard enforcement actions by corporate copyright owners as an assault on consumers. One of those corporate copyright owners, Warner Music Group CEO Edgar Bronfman, Jr., acknowledged the aptness of the phrase in a 2007 speech, agreeing that the recording industry had "gone to war with consumers by denying them what they wanted and could otherwise find; as a result of course, consumers won."[2] What consumers supposedly won is unclear: in 2007, Mr. Bronfman's and other record labels (through the Recording Industry Association of America) were still in the midst of suing tens of thousands of individuals.

Nevertheless, if these views represent Mr. Bronfman's current thinking,[3] they would represent a decided shift: eight years before, on December 7, 1999, the record industry sued Napster, a file-sharing network that consumers were using.[4] In a May 2000 speech, Mr. Bronfman likened Napster to both slavery and Soviet communism.[5] Two months later, however, on July 15, top music industry executives, including Mr. Bronfman, met with Napster executives to strike a licensing deal. Napster is reported to have offered a billion dollars to the industry to settle the litigation[6] and to be permitted to operate Napster solely as a licensed subscription service, paying a monthly subscription fee of $10, split fifty-fifty between Napster and the music industry. At that point, there were about 26.4 million Napster users; had half of them signed up for the subscription service, the music industry would have netted, under the fifty-fifty proposal, 792 million dollars a year, in addition to the billion dollar pay-out for past behavior.

The labels refused the offer. There are a number of explanations for why: the labels are reported to have wanted 90 percent, and Napster's executives are said not to have been "exactly open-minded either."[7] The manager for the band Nine Inch Nails and for singer Gwen Stefani gave a different but plausible explanation for the labels' refusal: "Innovation meant cannibalizing their core business,"[8] namely album sales. (Record labels reacted much the same way, it should be noted, to the introduction to compact discs, fearing they would cut into vinyl sales.)[9] We see in the Napster dispute the fundamental clash between innovation as an opportunity for new markets (Napster's view) and as a perceived threat to existing ones (the record labels' view). The same clashes have occurred with the motion picture and book publishing industries; rather than innovate, these industries have chosen to litigate. Litigation is a poor long-term strategy, serving only to delay the inevitable failure of the old business model.

### ✌ The Copyright Wars and Business Models

Copyright owners' concerns over cannibalizing existing businesses are not inherently irrational: Many businesses understandably worry about shifting from a declining volume but still profitable product to a newer product that may or may not become capable of generating substantial revenues. Many new products fail, and it would be irresponsible for business executives to throw overboard existing products simply because a new (and unproven) product comes along. The commercial promise of truly innovative products may also not be apparent at the time. For example, in 1997, Google founders Sergey Brin and Larry Page (then Stanford graduate students) unsuccessfully tried to sell their technology to Excite for $750,000.[10] Thereafter Mr. Brin and Mr. Page

> gave demonstrations of Google to nearly every search company in [Silicon] Valley, from Yahoo to Infoseek. They also showed their technology to several venture capitalists. Everyone found their technology interesting, but each sent the grad students packing. "I told them to go pound sand," recalled Steven Kirsch, founder of the now-defunct portal Infoseek. Jerry Yang and David Filo, the founders of Yahoo, were more encouraging, but they too, took a pass.[11]

The rejections came because the reigning business model at the time was portals such as AOL, walled gardens, designed to keep consumers within your site, and not, as search engines do, send consumers to the most relevant site. It took years for the new business model provided by organic, unpaid click-through advertising generated by search results to catch on. Even in 2002, four years after Google's founding, the *New York Times* ran an article entitled "Google's Toughest Search is for a Business Model," in which the *Times* quoted Uri Panj, an analyst at UBS Warburg: "The Internet advertising model has been shown not to work. We all know in business that free doesn't work. I think Google will realize that they have to go to some paid search capability."[12] The very next year, 2003, Google's revenues shot up to $1.4 billion, up from $400 million in 2002, paying put to Mr. Panj's forecast and his "we all know in business" expertise. Microsoft is reported to have missed two chances to have created an advertiser-supported system similar to the one Google uses. The first missed opportunity occurred in 2000 when "Microsoft had a rudimentary system that did the same thing [as Google's later would] called Keywords. . . . Advertisers began signing up. But Microsoft executives in part fearing the company would cannibalize other revenue streams, shut it down after two months."[13] The next missed opportunity came three years later in 2003, when it was proposed that Microsoft buy Overture, a pioneer in joining search results to advertising. The proposal was rejected by Bill Gates and Steve Ballmer; Overture was then acquired by Yahoo.

Existing and new business models can coexist for many years, and sometimes simply represent supplementary rather than substitutional markets (as is likely to happen in the book publishing world). In the case of compact discs versus digital downloads for example, the record industry thought it could have its cake and eat it too by continuing to sell CDs until the time when, in the industry's judgment, the industry was ready to shift to digital downloads. Left out of the industry's calculations was consumers' clear preference for digital downloads of singles over CD albums. Napster represented "the revenge of the single,"[14] but the record industry thought it could ignore market demand through refusing to supply that market. This was wishful thinking at best. It was also wishful thinking of a type we all engage in. We all suffer from an occasional inability to make rational decisions when faced with multiple choices, one of which involves giving up existing benefits. Even though we need to choose, we delay doing so, often until we have caused ourselves damage that could have been avoided had we acted earlier.[15] This is what occurred with the record industry's refusal to move to MP3 single-song sales, long after it was apparent to rational observers that the CD market was exhausted:

> Easy profits ended up blinding the industry to the threat of MP3s. Throughout the '90s, a handful of insiders warned of the need to get out in front of digital music, but for the most part they were ignored. The big corporations that had snapped up record labels in the '80s and '90s continued to focus on short-term financial results, even as it become amply clear that the advantages of CDs—control, convenience, durability, flexibility—were even more pronounced with digital files. "There's this mentality of always needing to make the numbers for the next quarter," says Ted Cohen, a former exec at EMI and Warner Bros., now managing partner at the consulting firm TAG Strategic. "It kept me up at night. Some of us could see that something needed to be done, but no one wanted to do anything that wouldn't maximize profit for that quarter...."
>
> "The record labels had an opportunity to create a digital ecosystem and infrastructure to sell music online, but they kept looking at the small picture instead of the big one," Cohen says. "They wouldn't let go of CDs."[16]

The motion picture industry is repeating the same mistake with DVD sales, as Brandon Burgess, Executive Vice President, Corporate Business Development for NBC-Universal noted in 2004: "DVD is the wonder drug that is blinding executives to ... the possibility of other, possibly higher margin businesses, like [distribution over] the Internet."[17]

History has proved repeatedly there is no genuine choice when businesses are faced with a new product that gives consumers what they want. Failure to adapt is fatal even to well-managed market leaders that stay in close touch with their customers.[18] In 2003, when the Recording Industry Association of America (RIAA) began filing lawsuits against individual consumers, the music industry had been artificially propped up for approximately twenty years by CDs—a product based on reselling consumers the same product they had already purchased but in a different format. The period in which the Napster suit was being litigated coincidentally overlapped with the natural end of the CD era. MP3 files didn't cause the decline of CD sales: Consumers' willingness to repurchase albums they previously purchased as LPs or as tapes had already run its course. MP3 single-song files fit consumers' desires to a T, but rather than embrace the format, the record industry mounted an all-out war to prevent consumers from getting what they wanted and were willing to pay for, as the later experience with iTunes and other services has proven.

The Napster litigation represented a classic effort to deny the existence of natural product cycles. Just as fiscal and monetary policies cannot eliminate business cycles, as we have learned all too painfully in 2008 and 2009, businesses cannot prop up a product that the public no longer wants. The desire to continue forever a product that at one time was very profitable is as understandable as the desire for eternal life, but neither is possible. As Ruth Handler, co-founder of Mattel and creator of the Barbie doll observed: "Anyone can manage the upside cycle. . . . The secret is managing a product down its life cycle properly."[19] The record industry's failure to adapt to the next product, digital singles, was suicidal.

## 𝄞 The Internet and Push versus Pull Marketing

Copyright owners' extreme reaction to the Internet is based on the role of the Internet in breaking the vertical monopolization business model long favored by the copyright industries. In contemporary marketing lingo, the copyright industries practice "push" and not "pull" marketing. Push marketing is top-down and hierarchical. With push marketing, businesses create products or services based on what they want to sell to consumers and not based on what consumers want to buy, resulting in what Theodore Levitt called "marketing myopia."[20] John Seely Brown, formerly the Chief Scientist of Xerox Corporation and the Director of its Palo Alto Research Center (PARC), explained that the core assumption of businesses that practice push marketing is that they

> can anticipate demand and that mobilizing scarce resources in previously specified ways is the most efficient and reliable way to meet it. But the efficiency of push systems comes at a stiff price, for they require companies to specify, monitor, and enforce detailed activities and tasks. This rigidity necessarily restricts the number and diversity of the participants in push models, thus limiting the innovation and learning

that can take place in them. It also tends to turn workers into mere instruments of management at a time when self-directed effort from a broad range of employees is ever more essential to big corporations . . . .

The highly specified, centralized, and restrictive nature of push systems prevents companies from experimenting, improvising, and learning as quickly as they might, both throughout their own organizations and across others. Push systems not only inhibit product innovation but—even more important—make it much harder to implement incremental process innovations rapidly. In a world where the relative pace and trajectory of capability building are of constantly rising importance, push systems thus hinder companies from participating in the distributed resource networks that are now indispensable to competitive advantage.[21]

Push marketing in the entertainment industries goes well beyond trying to get consumers to buy records by the latest boy band or bubblegum pop star, or to watch the latest movie in an ongoing franchise series; it also encompasses their desire to control all aspects of production, distribution, and consumption. Such an approach requires an extensive command-and-control economy similar to that of the early Soviet five-year plans: consumers will have what the Politburo decides they can have, when they can have it, in what quantities, at what price, where they can buy it, as well as how long it will be available. This approach, based on a top-down bureaucratic structure, is not designed to change course quickly, and is rooted in risk avoidance rather than innovation and customer satisfaction. The approach is also premised on the ability to effectively exercise absolute control. While copyright laws are intended to be the principal vehicle of control, the Internet has largely thrown such control out the window, and with it the ability to impose push marketing.

In place of push marketing, the Internet leads to "pull" marketing, what Theodore Levitt described in 1983 as sellers taking their cue from buyers and not the other way around. Dr. Brown explained in 2005:

Push systems contrast starkly with pull ones, particularly in their view of demand: the former treat it as foreseeable, the latter as highly uncertain. This difference in a basic premise leads to fundamentally different design principles. For instance, instead of dealing with uncertainty by tightening controls, as push systems would, pull models address immediate needs by expanding opportunities for local participants—employees and customers alike—to use their creativity. To exploit the opportunities that uncertainty presents, pull models help people come together and innovate by drawing on a growing array of specialized and distributed resources.

Rather than seeking to constrain the range of resources available to participants, pull models constantly strive to expand it while helping participants to find the most relevant options. Rather than seeking to dictate the actions of participants, pull models give even people on the periphery the tools and resources (including connections to other people) needed to take the initiative and to address opportunities creatively as they arise. Rather than treating producers as passive consumers whose needs can be anticipated and shaped by centralized decision makers, pull models treat people as networked creators even when they actually are customers purchasing goods and services. Pull platforms harness their participants' passion, commitment, and desire to learn, thereby creating communities that can improvise and innovate rapidly.

. . .

In the media business, pull approaches have transformed more than just distribution channels. On the production side, a vibrant "remix" culture has emerged thanks to the availability of widely affordable digital audio-editing tools, which make it possible for DJs in nightclubs and other music fans to pull in tracks from a variety of music sources and to recombine them. "Blogging" tools help users "publish" their own writings, music, or photographs, most often by pulling in content from a broad range of sources and creatively mixing and commenting on it.[22]

Collaboration, not control, is the baseline for pull approaches. Pull approaches to marketing copyrighted works are obviously 180 degrees from the push-vertical monopolization approach favored by the copyright industries, and it is this profound difference, not piracy, that explains the hysteria with which the copyright industries have reacted to the Internet. The Internet renders push marketing and vertical monopolization impossible. The Copyright Wars are an effort to accomplish the impossible, to change the Internet into a vehicle for the greatest form of vertical monopolization ever seen, even though the benefits from a pull approach to marketing are also obvious and are grounded in common, economic sense:

> The benefits of pull systems should by now be clear: enhanced innovation, increased opportunity for collaboration, closer relationships with customers and suppliers, more rapid feedback, richer reflection on the results of distributed experimentation, and greater scalability, for example.... [T]he essential reason to begin implementing pull systems is the fact that they help companies to secure deeper sources of competitive advantage at a time when the traditional sources are disappearing.[23]

Due to their push mentality, the copyright industries view the entirety of copyright as unidirectional: the public is a passive participant, whose role is simply to pay copyright owners, or to stop using copyrighted works. As we shall now see, the record industry's fanatical attachment to push marketing led them to miss an early and perhaps their best chance to take advantage of Internet pull marketing and to eliminate in the process a great deal of unauthorized file-sharing.

## ℳ Appetite for Self-Destruction: The Record Industry's Failure to Offer an Alternative to Napster

On July 2, 2001, Napster was shut down.[24] Following the shutdown, it took the record labels almost two years to offer consumers their own subscription services—PressPlay and MusicNet. PressPlay was owned by Universal Music Group and by Sony. MusicNet was owned by TimeWarner, BMG, and EMI.[25] Those services were predictable failures because they offered songs only from their own label owners.[26] Consumers of music do not have label brand loyalty. Consumers do not want a Universal Music Group song, or a Warner Brothers Music song. Rather, they have performer or genre loyalty. Consumers want the new song by this or that group or performer. Any site that is based on the wrong consumer preferences, as PressPlay and MusicNet were, is doomed to fail. As the *Wall Street Journal* observed at the time: "MusicNet and Press[P]lay are designed in a way that represents the false lesson of Napster—all people are thieves—much more than the true lesson, that there's a business in selling downloadable songs of a modest price."[27]

In his 2009 book *Appetite for Destruction: The Spectacular Crash of the Record Industry in the Digital Age*,[28] journalist Steve Knopper writes that the failure of the labels to agree to a deal with Napster executives was "the last chance for the record industry as we know it to stave off certain ruin," adding that "label chiefs were so bogged down in the file-sharing battleground that they refused to act on the digital future of the business. Many figured they would simply win in the courts and the CD-selling business would go back to normal."[29] Later court proceedings in the Napster case bear this assessment out and point to a possible role for PressPlay and MusicNet in such a plan to stem the digital tide.

Beginning in 2001, the U.S. Department of Justice began investigating the major record labels over allegations that PressPlay and MusicNet were designed specifically to impede the growth of *authorized* distribution of music on the Internet, through refusing to issue licenses and by refusing to offer genuinely attractive services of their own. The Department closed its investigation two years later without bringing changes, but in 2006, in a spin off to the original Napster case, the venture capital firm Hummer Winblad argued in court papers that two of the major labels used PressPlay and MusicNet

> to obtain information about their competitors' content licensing practices and to coordinate the terms of their licenses. . . . Hummer argues that the labels deliberately limited the joint ventures to offering unpopular forms of digital music distribution, such as streaming and "tethered" downloads which do not threaten the market for the distribution of compact discs. Thus, according to Hummer, the joint ventures were a smokescreen designed to obscure the fact that the labels were uniformly refusing to support meaningful distribution of digital music on the Internet.[30]

Hummer Winblad further argued that the Department of Justice's decision to close its investigation was based on the department's verbatim copying of submissions by some of the joint venture labels through their attorneys, and that those submissions were criminally false under 18 United States Code §1001. On April 26, 2000 Judge Marilyn Patel, the trial judge for all the Napster litigation, found "reasonable cause to believe that the attorney's services were utilized in furtherance of the [alleged] ongoing unlawful scheme."[31] Judge Patel required the labels to turn over to Hummer Winblad documents asserted to have been withheld from the Department of Justice concerning the alleged collusion. Perhaps as a result of Judge Patel's ruling, the labels settled their litigation against Hummer Winblad, conditioned, interestingly, on Judge Patel's vacating her opinion and order. She did, on March 20, 2007.[32]

## ✌ The Copyright Wars and the Great Cultural Revolution

In the quote above in which Warner Brothers CEO Edgar Bronfman, Jr., acknowledged the music industry had gone to war with consumers, I omitted a word. Mr. Bronfman actually said the record industry had "inadvertently" gone to war with consumers. Mr. Bronfman's use of the word "inadvertently" was the subject of justifiable derision as it implied the industry's *actions* were unintended, rather than there being unintended *consequences* from intended actions, namely a negative backlash from consumers and the press. It is, after all, difficult to see how more than 35,000 lawsuits could have been filed inadvertently. Cary Sherman, President of the RIAA, which filed the suits on behalf of Mr. Bronfman's company and other record labels, regards such suits as an exercise in youthful character building. In an interview on CNN, he related: "We had one grandfather who had those kids work off the amount that he paid to settle as a way of teaching them a lesson and making this a family event."[33] He also told the press at the time: "The public has been educated, and re-educated, and re-educated again. People now know this is illegal. . . . People can no longer count on just getting a warning."[34] "Inadvertence" seems a poor choice to describe such a campaign.

Mr. Sherman's words evoked the Maoist Great Proletarian Cultural Revolution,[35] especially the December 1968, "Down to the Countryside Movement," in which intellectuals living in cities were ordered to go to the countryside, where their bourgeoisie thinking would be worked out of them and they would be reeducated by the masses. The Great Cultural Revolution was a disaster, its motives suspect from the beginning. In addition to ruined careers, families torn apart, a lost generation of youth, and massive loss of life, millions of ancient cultural artifacts were destroyed as exemplars of the "old ways of thinking." In the Copyright

Wars, the battle is being fought to preserve old business models, closed methods of distribution and restricted consumer experiences, determined and tightly controlled by the copyright industries, rather than being responsive to consumer preferences. Such a closed business method—based on methods of distribution used in the hard copy world—is contrary to the successful business models employed on the Internet. Successful Internet business models are based on satisfying consumer preferences, honed and targeted through information provided by consumers. Such business models offer more choices, more consumer satisfaction (since they are based on consumers' own preferences), and therefore ultimately lead to greater revenue. The Copyright Wars are a losing effort on the part of the copyright industries to reshape the Internet into a closed system in a vain effort to perpetuate vertical monopolization.

## ⅌ The Digital Guillotine

The copyright industries' efforts to reshape the Internet is evident in the December 2008 announcement by the RIAA that it will allegedly begin phasing out its strategy of suing large numbers of individuals, and will instead enter into agreements with Internet Service Providers (ISPs) to institute what has been misdescribed as "graduated response." I say allegedly because of the many caveats in RIAA's announcement: the RIAA has indicated that it will continue to sue those who in its opinion are engaged in substantial downloading, that it will continue to prosecute suits already filed, and that it will file future suits that are in the "pipeline." It is unknown how the RIAA will treat customers of ISPs that refuse to enter into a graduated response agreement: unless the RIAA's cessation of at least some future suits is in fact an admission of failure, with graduated response agreements being a public relations smokescreen, it would be reasonable that customers of ISPs that refuse to sign up would continue to be sued: otherwise what incentive would there be for ISPs to sign up?[36] Finally, RIAA's decision is purely voluntary; it can change its mind and course of action at any time.

Graduated response implies a series of reasonable, proportionate steps taken over a reasonable period of time, carefully tailored to encourage desired behavior; in this case, encouraging individuals to cease downloading and sharing unauthorized versions of copyrighted works. The RIAA's effort to adopt graduated response is part of a global record industry campaign, and is being pushed heavily by copyright owners in France and England, and was adopted in New Zealand.

Graduated response is all stick and no carrot; as such, it can never accomplish its purported goal of encouraging lawful behavior because the industry refuses to respond to consumer demand, and instead insists on suppressing it, even when third party ISPs are willing to do all the work. For example, the UK Virgin Media group, working with PlayLouder MSP, had invested millions of dollars into a planned music service that would have "allowed paying subscribers to continue transferring songs over P2P networks, and would have paid [record labels] for the privilege."[37] The proposed service was cancelled at the last minute "by major-label demands the ISP block transfer of songs outside of computers owned by subscribers."[38] PlayLouder strategy director Paul Sanders is reported to have said: "The music service as it was conceived is on ice. It's incredibly sad for both sides, and even sadder for consumers as the research . . . shows consumers want legal P2P services and want to buy them from their ISP. The project is off and the project team is stood down."[39] The Register Web site reports that record labels declined to comment on the cancellation, but adds: "Speaking off the record, a source close to the recording industry stressed that ISPs must abide by the obligations in [a previous memorandum of understanding] and that government regulation was likely if they didn't. From that unprompted statement, it's possible to infer that major labels still fear losing control, and have pinned their hopes on changing behaviour rather than creating services that generate new revenue streams."[40]

The RIAA announcement does not reflect a change of heart toward the Copyright Wars or a change of heart toward giving consumers what they want and are willing to pay for, but instead reflects a desire simply to find a more effective strategy of obtaining control over consumers *and* ISPs.

Although there is reportedly no one-size-fits-all plan for all ISPs, graduated response proposals have generally involved three strikes and your Internet service is terminated: first, ISP customers will receive an email notifying them that a copyright owner is alleging they have illegally downloaded or shared; the ISP demands the customer stop doing so. If the alleged conduct occurs a second time, another notice is sent, accompanied possibly by a slow down in the customer's Internet connection, or by a temporary suspension of all Internet access. If copyright owners send a third notice, the ISP will terminate the customer's service. (How long the service termination lasts for is not specified; under some proposals service is terminated for a year.) Under a French version of graduated response, customers are blacklisted so that they cannot, during the termination period, sign up with another ISP. For consumers whose landline telephone service is tied to their Internet service, it would appear that loss of their Internet service will lead to loss of telephone, as well as email service.

Among the many flaws in graduated response is the notice system. It is receipt of a notice from the copyright owner that triggers the termination process. Notices of alleged infringement are not, as popularly assumed, the result of copyright owners sitting down at a computer terminal and *directly* detecting infringement. Instead, notices of alleged infringement are generated automatically by the millions, by third-party companies hired by copyright owners. This process, which involves *indirect* detection of alleged unauthorized activity,[41] relies on automated webcrawler technology and databases of digital fingerprints. The process has been notoriously inaccurate, leading to lawsuits against people who don't even have computers or who are dead, as well as takedown notices sent to individuals claiming that wholly original videos created by those individuals are infringing.

Faced with the receipt of hundreds of thousands or millions of such notices under graduated response, ISPs will simply pass the notices along to customers, who will be presumed guilty. Unlike court proceedings, where consumers are presumed innocent, and are afforded due process of law and defenses such as fair use, under private enforcement by ISPs on copyright owners' behalf, there is no guarantee or even reason to believe ISPs' customers will be able to get service restored due to errors or that they will have the ability to prove their use was lawful as fair use. Even more fundamentally, where a notice is sent as a result of a false positive identification by one of copyright owners' third-party investigators, how will customers disprove a negative; that they have *not* been engaged in authorized copying?

The term graduated response should be replaced with the more accurate term "digital guillotine," reflecting its killing of a critical way people connect with the world and in some cases, eliminating their ability to make a living. If proportionately is a hallmark of civilization, the digital guillotine is the hallmark of barbarians. For this reason, the government of Sweden concluded in March 2008 that the approach is disproportionate, adding that corporate copyright owners should "not use the copyright laws to defend old business models" but should rather offer legitimate services.[42] The European Parliament twice rejected the proposal in 2008, as has Germany. In place of *liberté, égalité, fraternité*, the digital guillotine substitutes *la terreur*, the terror. As Robespierre remarked five months before he was executed by the mobs he had incited against others: *La terreur n'est autre chose que la justice prompte, severe, inflexible* (Terror is nothing other than prompt, severe, inflexible justice). This doesn't mean, oddly, that policy makers will shun the digital guillotine: to the contrary, the French Revolution shows that when we are in the throes of a moral panic, harsh, disproportionate measures can be made to appear essential. As Barry Goldwater put it in his speech to the Republican National Convention in 1964: "Extremism in the defense of liberty is no vice. And let me remind you also that moderation in the pursuit of justice is no virtue." But extremism is a vice—a disproportionate, immoderate reaction. Just as Goldwater was trounced by Lyndon Johnson in the 1964 Presidential election, one can only hope that the digital guillotine is defeated by policy makers who genuinely pursue justice, rather than is too often the case, pursue celebrities.

## 🎞 The Copyright Wars and Framing

No side in the Copyright Wars can claim semantic purity or sole virtue. We should accept up front that the various interests will never see eye to eye because conflicting economic interests prevent that, but we should be able to make more progress than we have in being able to resolve those economic conflicts. How do we do that?

The first step is to figure out how we got where we are. One way we got where we are is through the misuse of language, specifically metaphors that characterize the nature of copyright as property and that characterize those who use copyrighted works without permission as thieves or parasites.[43] When a court or legislature is faced with a copyright dispute, there is more than one way to frame that dispute. There is, after all, no Platonic copyright against which we can match the ideal form of copyright. Instead, the outcome is determined by reference to the contesting legal, economic, and social forces. Those forces in turn are defined and understood in terms of the conceptual frameworks employed.[44] As Steven Pinker wrote: "The language of thought allows us to frame a situation in different and incompatible ways."[45] Framing is the reference point from which judgments and decisions are made,[46] and thus can have a dramatic impact on the perceived desirable outcome.

This is hardly a new idea. We readily accept the importance of framing in other areas, and should in copyright. The effect of framing in polls is well documented. In 1982, Richard Wirthlin, pollster to President Ronald Reagan, asked whether people agreed with this very wordy question: "A freeze in nuclear weapons should be opposed because it would do nothing to reduce the danger of the thousands of nuclear warheads already in place and would leave the Soviet Union in a position of nuclear superiority." Fifty-eight percent of the respondents agreed. Later in the same poll, he asked whether the same people agreed with the following equally wordy question: "A freeze in nuclear weapons should be favored because it would begin a much-needed process to stop everyone in the world from building nuclear weapons now and reduce the possibility of nuclear war in the future." Fifty-six percent of the same people agreed with this statement, and 27 percent of the people answered affirmatively to both questions, although the two questions were completely inconsistent with each other.[47]

Framing in the Copyright Wars occurs for the same purposes as in political contests—to get what you want by defining yourself positively and by defining your opponent negatively.


## ✍ The Copyright Wars and Piracy

Listening to the copyright industries' constant kvetching, one would think revenues are at Great Depression levels. To the contrary: Nielsen Soundscan reported overall recorded music sales were at an all-time high in 2008. NDP Group research reported total music consumption in the

U.S. rose by one-third from 2003–2007. In 2008, U.S. movie box office receipts hit record levels for the fourth straight year. Although copyright owners insist they are suffering declines in revenue due to unauthorized copying, the empirical evidence is to the contrary. To the extent that copyright owners actually believe the flawed studies they commission, they are engaging in the logical fallacy of confusing correlation with cause. A classic illustration of the fallacy is a prevalence of bald men wearing hats, from which the conclusion is erroneously made that wearing hats causes baldness. The fallacy of a decline in CD sales being attributable to unauthorized copying serves the record industry's political objectives extremely well, and thus while the correlation is false, it is advanced at every opportunity. The decline is attributable to the industry's inability to force consumers to buy albums.

Although not starting out that way, albums evolved into an anticonsumer tying device, the forced bundling of a great deal of material consumers did not want. More than sixty years ago, the motion picture industry attempted a similar tactic by requiring theater owners to pay to exhibit dozens of terrible films in order to get the one or two blockbusters they did want.[48] This tactic, called "block booking," was a cause célèbre in the 1940s, when it was attacked by the Society of Independent Motion Picture Producers. Block booking has been described this way:

> Block booking meant that a studio would sell its films in packages on an all-or-nothing basis—usually requiring theaters to buy several mediocre pictures for every desirable one. Because the studios made mass-produced films, they also sold them in bulk. . . . Block booking made it difficult for the independents to get their own movies into theaters when exhibitors had already purchased a block of films that would provide the theater with plenty of movies. But even worse, since the independent[s] released their films through the studio-owned exchanges, the independents found that their films were being used by the Hollywood distributors to pawn off low-budget studio B-pictures. The producers believed that block booking encouraged slack filmmaking by forcing inferior films on the theaters and the moviegoers.[49]

Block booking was banned by the Supreme Court in 1948 with the Court relying on the harm done to the purposes of the Copyright Act. In upholding the district court's enjoining the motion picture studios "from performing or entering into any license in which the right to exhibit one feature is conditioned upon the licensee's taking one or more other features," the Court added the following:

> The copyright law, like the patent statutes, makes reward to the owner a secondary consideration.... But the reward does not serve its public purpose if it is not related to the quality of the copyright. Where a high quality film greatly desired is licensed only if an inferior one is taken, the latter borrows quality from the former and strengthens its monopoly by drawing on the other.... As the District Court said, the result is to add to the monopoly of the copyright in violation of the principle of the patent cases involving tying clauses.[50]

Consumers of music had no such luck. Fortunately, other forms of entertainment have come along, such as video games, sparked by exciting new technologies such as Nintendo's Wii, Sony's PlayStation, and Microsoft's Xbox. In 2008, sales of the Wii gave Amazon.com its best winter season ever, despite the severe recession. For many, especially those in the music and motion picture industries' core age groups, video games are more fun and provide a better value than movies and music. In 2007, sales of video games overtook sales of music, a trend that will only accelerate. In 2008, a single video game, *Grand Theft Auto IV* generated more than $1 billion dollars in sales in seven months, selling more than $500 million in its first week. Adjusted for full-year sales, *Grand Theft Auto IV* would have generated approximately $1.93 billion. The highest grossing movie ever is *Titanic*, which over 11 years, grossed less, $1,845,034,188.[51] In the music field, the highest selling album of all time is Michael Jackson's *Thriller*, released in 1982, and which has sold approximately 45 million copies in 26 years. By contrast, *Grand Auto Theft IV* sold more twice that amount, 95 million copies *in its first year.*

In 2008, global sales of video games overtook DVD and Blu-Ray disc sales, accounting for 53% of all packaged entertainment sales.[52] Those involved in entertainment retailing—hardly left-wing fanatics, but rather conservative, establishment businessmen eager to make as much money as possible from as many sources as possible—attribute the ascendancy of video games and the fall of music sales to the music industry's failure to develop content that people are interested in hearing, and not to piracy. Paul Quirk, chairman of the British Entertainment Retailers Association, which represents retailers who sell entertainment products such as recorded music, DVDs, and games, was quoted in a March 2008 interview as saying:

> One thing the music business can learn from the games industry is the way it introduces new and attractive products into the marketplace on a regular basis to stimulate the customers and it is disappointing that during 2007 record companies were slow to create innovative new music products ... ERA will continue to lobby for this during 2008 and we hope to see a greater variety of music products available going forward.[53]

David Byrne, former lead singer for the Talking Heads and founder of the independent label Luka Bop, put the matter bluntly in a December 2007, article in *Wired* magazine: "Major labels aren't doing well because they put out terrible records for years and years and kept raising the price of those terrible records and finally people were like, 'Screw You.'"[54] Simon Wright, CEO of the Virgin Entertainment Group, which owns the Virgin Megastores—one of the few brick and mortar stores left selling music (although no longer in the U.S.) and which therefore is keenly interested in selling as many CDs as possible—agrees: "The record companies have created this situation themselves."[55] Tower Records, now bankrupt, also complained to the labels, to no avail:

> For one stretch, every Christmas, Tower Records' Russ Solomon recalls, CDs went up—from $13.98 to $14.98 to $16 to $17 to $18. "Every year they'd do this and [retailers] would say, 'Goddamnit! People aren't gonna buy it at this price. . . . You *complained*. If you don't mind having a conversation with a wall! They'd *laugh*."[56]

Bono, lead singer of U2, also debunked the claim that piracy was the cause of the record industry's ills: "Don't believe those people. *Crap music* is hurting music. Give people what they want when they want it. The CD is not a fair fight with the download. We want to stop running away from the future, like the music business has."[57] There is no evidence the industry has. Lyor Cohen, a top executive for Mr. Bronfman's label, was quoted in a January 17, 2009, interview in Billboard magazine, asserting that the ability to charge consumers $1.29 on iTunes rather than 99 cents was "important to make sure that the consumer has a choice and that we have the flexibility to give them an offer that makes sense."[58] There is no consumer choice: the consumer has to pay whatever the label charges, whether the price is 99 cents, $1.29, or $9.99; the price is not negotiable. Mr. Cohen is merely using the rhetoric of responding to consumers as a cover to justify the labels' greed, a greed that arose after Steve Jobs insisted on a flat 99 cents for all iTunes downloads.[59] Having weaned consumers off Napster and other free sites, Apple returns to the labels 70 cents out of the 99 cents: three years after opening, iTunes sold its *billionth* download in 2006, to give some perspective on the amount of revenue involved with 99 cent sales and the amount of found money the labels are receiving.

Each year the Entertainment Retailers Association publishes a yearbook that contains sales figures for the previous year. Here is a revealing excerpt from the 2008 Yearbook:[60]

More than two-thirds of sales in the entertainment retail sector are now accounted for by DVD and games, with music sales in 2007 making up the remainder. In 2000 DVD and games accounted for about half the market. Since 2000 music sales have declined in value by more than 30%. In contrast sales of DVD and computer games have grown by around 80%.

Bullish sales of DVD and games in 2007 meant that although music sales declined by 14.4%, the overall market grew by 3.2% thanks to DVD sales up 2.1% and computer games growing by a significant 26.3%.

Retail Values £s

|  | 2005 | 2006 | 2007 | % change 2006/2007 |
|---|---|---|---|---|
| Recorded Music | 1839 | 1651 | 1413 | −14.4 |
| Video (exc. Rental) | 2196 | 2122 | 2167 | 2.1 |
| Games (exc. Rental) | 1345 | 1361 | 1719 | 26.3 |
| Total | 5380 | 5134 | 5299 | 3.2 |

These figures show a modest growth in all entertainment sales (3.2 percent), but a radical realignment within relative market shares, with music sales decreasing in one year alone by 14.4 percent and sales of video games increasing 26.3 percent during that same year.

How has the music industry responded to the plea of retailers for better product? Edgar Bronfman, Jr., quoted in the beginning of this chapter for a purported change of heart in giving consumers what they want, was quoted a year later, in August 2008, as threatening to stop issuing licenses for video games such as *Guitar Hero* and *Rock Band*:

> The amount being paid the music industry, even though the games are entirely dependent on the content we own and control, is far too small. . . . We need to be very careful that [we] do not allow an ecosystem to occur where we are not properly compensated. . . . The industry as a whole needs to take a very different look at this business and participate more fully and in a much more partnership way. If that does not become the case, as far as Warner Music Group is concerned, we will not license to those games."[61]

Recording artists—the actual creators—do not share Mr. Bronfman's view, and for good reason: recording artists make more money off of licensing such games than they do from record sales. Radiohead, for example, when it released its "In Rainbow" album at the end of 2007 on the Internet and allowed consumers to pay whatever price they wanted, made more money off digital downloads for that one album than they had for all of their other albums combined, for the simple reason that the groups' label never paid them a dime for downloads of those other albums. The groups' label didn't pay them a dime because the contracts didn't require them to. Radiohead's contracts were not unique in this respect.

In June 2008, "Guitar Hero: Aerosmith" was released, resulting in more money to Aerosmith than either of the group's recent albums. "Guitar Hero III: Legends of Rock" sold $750 million in its first year. Overall music video game sales were almost $2 billion in 2008. This is the market Mr. Bronfman apparently is willing to walk away from if he doesn't get a lot more of what is found money. An industry analyst observed that "If Warner wants to say we'll take our 20 percent of the market and go away, a lot of bands are going to leave the label if they think they can get better exposure by being on these games."[62] In fact, a number of prominent artists have already left their labels. In October 207, Madonna, formerly signed to Mr. Bronfman's company, signed with concert promoter Live Nation, explaining: "The paradigm in the music business has shifted and as an artist and a businesswoman, I had to move with that shift."[63] Irish mega group U2 followed in March 2008, with a 12 year digital distribution and marketing deal. Hip hop artist and former president of Def

Jam Records Jay-Z signed a 10 year deal with Live Nation in April 2008. Singer Shakira and Canadian rock band Nickelback also signed with Live Nation (in the latter case after Mr. Bronfman's company bought Nickelback's label Roadrunner Records for $73 million in an effort to buy into Nickelback's success).

Other groups, such as Nine Inch Nails, have abandoned their labels in favor of selling directly to the public. Trent Reznor, the group's lead singer, explained: "I have been under recording contracts for 18 years and have watched the music business radically mutate from one thing to something inherently very different."[64] Mr. Reznor is famous for encouraging his fans to copy their CDs in protest over what he regarded as obscenely high prices, but he was also likely referring to record labels' increasing insistence for a share of artists' tour and merchandising revenue. Given that artists make most of their money from such forms of exploitation, it may make more sense to simply sign up with a concert promoter than a record label, or make direct sales to consumers.

When Mr. Bronfman referred to "participating more fully and in a more partnership way" from video game licensing, he was using code words for naked efforts to extract more money, and not to providing extra value for consumers.[65] The value in video games is provided by the design of the hardware, the software, and by the recording artists, not by record labels that act simply as bankers holding their hands out. Mr. Bronfman's statement that video games "are entirely dependent on the content" Mr. Bronfman and others "own and control" is therefore false, but, as Yogi Berra quipped, "It's déjà vu all over again." Whether it is the videocassette industry for the motion picture industry, Napster, iTunes, or video games for the music industry, or the Internet for all types of works, the copyright industries fail to innovate but are saved by others who do. Those others are consumer electronics manufacturers and Silicon Valley (e.g., Apple and the iPod). It is the innovation of these others that creates the demand for copyright owners' works. Far from encouraging innovations that create such demand, the copyright industries proverbially resent the success of innovators and claim that the innovator's success is caused solely by the value provided by the copyright industries. The innovator is described metaphorically as a parasite, fattening itself off of copyright owners. Working themselves up into righteous indignation, copyright owners then insist that the innovator must disgorge a healthy share of its profits to them, even though if the copyright industries were left to their own devices, they would have starved to death decades ago. This cycle of copyright owners shaking down innovators is a central trope in the business of the Copyright Wars and has been repeated over and over again with almost every new innovation.

But it is a trope whose usefulness is waning, as the public has found different ways to spend their time and money than on passively consuming corporate fare. Online video gaming sites draw 200 million players *a week*, a size that led then-senator Barack Obama to include political campaign ads on those sites during the 2008 presidential election. Social networks such as Facebook and MySpace attract more than 120 million visitors. A member of my family who recently started a Facebook page used to watch movies and television at night but now catches up with friends through Facebook, or plays Scramble online with a network of friends. Cell phones, instant messaging, Twitter, and SMS text messaging have revolutionized the way the core young audience spends its day. These services are carefully designed to take advantage of the unique features of the Internet. Monetizing such sites has proved difficult, illustrating the fact that new technologies do not automatically lead to substantial new revenue sources, but none of these sites have made the cardinal mistake of altering the features that make them attractive to consumers in order to conform to an inappropriate business model.

While some in the copyright industries are fighting to preserve their old business model of controlling consumers, consumers, freed by open source systems and the open architecture of the Internet, have voted with their feet for democracy, favoring innovative products that let them create their own experiences. It doesn't take an economist to explain that "time spent on one activity, after all, is time taken away from another."[66]

Innovation is the solution, not the problem. Innovation is the solution because innovation provides the means by which new content can be created and then distributed to consumers in a form and manner consumers desire. The problem lies with those in the copyright industries who are neither innovative nor willing to license those who are. In the hard copy world, the copyright industries' lack of innovation could not be overcome by consumers for practical reasons; copyright owners remained in control, even if remaining in control meant poor sales. The shift of control away from the copyright industries to consumers has occurred uncommonly quickly as a result of the decentralized nature of the Internet. Because of the rapidity of change, some copyright owners have understandably been caught flat-footed. But the process of change, brought about by what economist Joseph Schumpeter called "creative destruction,"[67] is an age-old one, arising from the very essence of capitalism's dynamic nature. The static business models that have been the foundation of the copyright industries for many decades will be replaced, either voluntarily or involuntarily through business failure.

## ⁂ The Copyright Wars and Marketing Myopia

Although usually written about as battles over technology or principles, the Copyright Wars are instead centrally rooted, what Harvard Business School professor Theodore Levitt called "marketing myopia." Professor Levitt argued that corporations are successful only if the entire corporation regards itself as a customer-creating and customer satisfying organism:

> Management must think of itself not as producing products but as producing customer value satisfactions. . . . [T]he organization must learn to think of itself not as producing goods or services but as . . . doing things that will make people *want* to do business with it.[68]

Measured by these principles, the copyright industries are too often abysmal failures, and have been for a very long time. It is not coincidental that Professor Levitt began his *1960* article with Hollywood as an example of a failure to appreciate the foundation of its corporate purpose, in Hollywood's case entertaining and therefore *pleasing* the public. Hollywood is *not* in the business of selling DVDs or stamping out piracy, as it currently believes, no more than record labels are in the business of selling CDs. Here are Professor Levitt's comments on Hollywood:

> Hollywood barely escaped being totally ravished by television. Actually, all the established film companies went through drastic reorganizations. Some simply disappeared. All of them got into trouble because of their own myopia. As with the railroads, Hollywood defined its business incorrectly. It thought it was in the movie business when it was

actually in the entertainment business. "Movies" implied a specific, limited product. This produced a fatuous contentment which from the beginning led producers to view TV as a threat. Hollywood scorned and rejected TV when it should have welcomed it as an opportunity— an opportunity to expand the entertainment business.[69]

Hollywood made the same mistake with VCRs and the home rental market, and it is making the same mistake with online distribution. Motion picture companies—like all copyright owners—are continually looking for a magic and safe solution that will permit them to control consumers and therefore control growth, to smooth out product cycles and innovation so that favored products can continue forever, with incremental changes at best. The CD was supposed to fill this role for the record industry, as the DVD was for the motion picture industry. But as Professor Levitt pointed out:

> There is no such thing as a growth industry. . . . There are only companies organized and operated to create and capitalize on growth opportunities. Industries that assume themselves to be riding some automatic growth escalator invariably descend into stagnation. The history of every dead and dying "growth" industry shows a self-deceiving cycle of bountiful expansion and undetected decay.[70]

Litigation has become the tool by which the copyright industries deceive themselves into thinking they can avoid the inevitable stagnation that occurs when they fail to focus on the essential purpose of their business as a "customer-creating and customer-satisfying organism." How one creates customers by suing them *en masse* is a mystery known only to the copyright industries. Professor Levitt's 1960 observations are as appropriate for the copyright industries in 2009 as they were when made:

> An industry begins with the customer and his or her needs, not with a patent, a raw material, or a selling skill. Given the customer's needs, the industry develops backwards, first concerning itself with the delivery of consumer satisfaction. Then it moves back further to creating the things by which these substitutions are . . . achieved.[71]

Such an approach involves "managerial imaginativeness and audacity"[72] and is the approach advocated by Google CEO Eric Schmidt. In a June 11, 2008 interview with *New Yorker* magazine writer Ken Auletta, Mr. Schmidt stated that "Google's ambition is to solve big problems that impact a lot of people."[73] To fulfill this ambition. Google, and other innovative Silicon Valley companies that have the same philosophy, begin, as Professor Levitt suggested, by determining what problems consumers would like solved. They then work backwards to figure out how to effectively solve those problems. Managerial imagination and audacity is the opposite of husbanding existing markets and products, and being content with controlled, incremental growth.

Too many companies in the copyright industries appear oblivious to the very idea that consumers have needs; to them, consumers are passive purchasers of what those companies decide to sell. In a passage that resonates loudly in the current economic environment, in 1960, Professor Levitt identified the root cause of the American car industry's ills, the same ills that the copyright industries have inflicted on themselves:

> Detroit's vast resources have for a long time failed to reveal what consumers really wanted. . . . Why did research not reveal consumer preferences before consumers' buying decisions themselves revealed the fact? The answer is that Detroit never really researched their preferences between the kinds of things which it had already decided to offer them. For Detroit is mainly product-oriented. To the extent that the consumer is recognized as having needs that the manufacturer should try to satisfy, Detroit usually acts as if the job can be done entirely by product changes.[74]

These words could easily be applied to many copyright industries, in particular record companies which have been regurgitating the same albums in every new format that comes along while denying consumers the one format they wanted, singles. The record industry could get away with ignoring consumer preferences due to physical limitations. The Internet has ended the ability of copyright owners to deny consumers their preferences, but rather than make money by satisfying them, copyright owners have resorted to litigation and technological locks to thwart them. Myopia appears to be, in their case, a congenital disease.

## 𝓂 Control as the Business Model

The myopia stems from corporate copyright owners' adoption of control as their principal business model—closed systems, in which copyright owners tightly control everything connected to their works: which play back devices will be offered to the public; what types of access controls will be interposed before consumers can ever see, hear, or in the case of books or other literary works, even read a snippet of the work; the time period during which consumers will have access to the work; how many times can consumers see, hear, or read the work; in what format will consumers be able to access the work; what will they be able to do with the work once they finally access it: Can they copy reasonable portions for criticism and comment, can they make personal use copies or copies for use on other devices, can they use parts of the work to make other new works, including mash-ups?

Turning the open architectural structure and philosophy of the Internet on its head, too often the copyright industries' business model for the Internet is one even more vertically controlled than it was in the world of physical distribution of copies; the consumer's experience is to be rigorously prescribed and circumscribed: Nothing is left to consumer choice or to innovation. A movie studio lawyer gave an illustration of the idea behind this in explaining the controls built into DVD players: "The first task is to keep consumers from accessing decrypted content during the playback process."[75] To accomplish this, technology and copy protection obligations must apply "to all devices and services that are capable of playing back, recording and/or transmitting protected content. Given the realities of the networked environment and the Internet, all devices and 'way stations' of delivery systems must maintain content as securely as it was received and neither circumvent protections nor release content to the next device or component in the clear."[76] DVD players and DVDs were deliberately crippled at birth in an effort to thwart consumers' desires and the exciting possibilities that motion pictures in a digital format presented: no record button, a forced viewing of advertisements in the form of previews, regional coding that prevents lawfully purchased DVDs in one country from being played on another, and an inability to upload lawfully purchased DVDs to one's video iPod, to name only a few. Such a crippling of a new technology is enough to make one yearn for the good old days of videocassettes.

This desire to control every part of the design of playback machines, to the accessing of works, and their use, is the reverse of the "end-to-end" architecture of the Internet.[77] Such control is usually coupled with the motto that "content is king": As the owner of the content, copyright owners must be absolute sovereigns of their realms, realms protected with a twenty-first century version of medieval moats and armaments. This effort has backfired, as noted by Andrew Currah:

> [T]he deployment of [digital locks] by the Hollywood studios has served to displace, rather than eradicate, disruptive technologies. The emerging result is a bifurcation of a networked environment: . . . [t]he emergence of a closed commercial sphere, and the ongoing expansion of a separate open sphere. The open sphere . . . continues to evolve and is increasingly difficult to regulate. It is now impossible, for example, to prosecute every re-mixed video that appears at YouTube, or every copyrighted file that appears in a peer-to-peer network.[78]

In the world of Internet-based companies, a completely different approach to consumers is taken, a collaborative approach rooted in the customer being king. Open systems are not only consistent with the architecture of the Internet, but—and this is the key dividing line between the copyright industries and Internet companies—open systems are consistent with the experience users want from the Internet: the ability to access and use information when and how you want. The Copyright Wars are an effort to deny the type of experience consumers want on the Internet; they are an effort to deny the very nature of the present by changing it back into the past. In large measure, the divide is generational, in many cases up to two generations difference. Large entertainment corporations are hierarchical, top-down businesses in which the desire to stay at the top severely limits the risks executives are willing to take. As a vice-president of a major studio observed:

> You have to understand the [studio] strategy [for the Internet] in relation to the lifestyle here. . . . Once you reach the top of the hierarchy, you acquire status and benefits that can soon be lost—the nice cars, the home in Brentwood, the private schools. . . . It doesn't make sense to jeopardize any of that by adopting a reckless attitude towards new technologies, new markets. Moving slow, and making clear, safe progress is the mantra.[79]

Andrew Currah, in a series of extended interviews with studio executives observed:

> In the course of my research, I encountered a 'not on my watch' philosophy.... [E]xecutives were unwilling to formulate, pursue or even suggest strategies that would disrupt the status quo and threaten their own well-heeled positions, not least because many were within 5–10 years of retirement.[80]

Not making mistakes by playing it safe entails not departing from the old. Albert Einstein once quipped: "Anyone who has never made a mistake has never tried anything new." David Wertheimer, the former head of Paramount Studios Digital Entertainment noted further institutional constraints: "In the studios, where you have a ton of history and a ton of lawyers and a ton of people whose job it is to say no, you end up doing things that are slow and incredibly safe.... The studios are always going to be followers rather than leaders."[81]

If John Holt is right that "Intelligence is not the measure of how much we know how to do, but of how we behave when we don't know what to do,"[82] then the problem—and it is apparently a huge problem—is for corporate copyright owners to find intelligent leaders. The problem is not unique to entertainment companies, although ubiquity is not an excuse. In 1960, Professor Theodore Levitt wrote: "Every major industry was once a growth industry. . . . In every case the reason growth is threatened, slowed, or stopped is *not* because the market is saturated. It is because there has been a failure of management. The failure is at the top. The executives responsible for it, in the last analysis, are those who deal with broad aims and policies."[83]

Unfortunately at the present, "the executives who guide these firms are generally paid to *avoid* strategies of 'creative destruction.'"[84] In practice, this means that corporate copyright owners live in fear, especially fear of their own consumers. Those consumers are young, tech savvy, and have wrested control over corporations' physical product from them, an unthinkable act 10 years ago. The result is a classical moral panic against youth. Most moral panics (explored in Chapter 7) involve youth: fear of youthful violence, fear of youthful sexuality,[85] and perhaps most of all, the fear of having grown old and facing mortality, a fear that youth so cruelly throw up in our faces simply by being young. The way in which youth interact with each other and with content on the Internet is radically different than the ways that corporate heads have spent their careers: slowly, carefully, and in a risk-averse way, milking proven winners whether those winners be formulaic movies, boy bands, CDs, or DVDs. The response of the heads of these companies to the youthful rebellion of democratizing content on the Internet has been that of many parents worldwide: to fight against the present, to try to ban the future, and to punish those audacious enough to challenge the status quo. The Copyright Wars are a fight against our own children, and it is a fight that says everything about the adults and very little about the children.

They are wars in which copyright owners have badly abused the legal system to intimidate and financially crush poor and middle class families. In *BMW v. Gore*, the U.S. Supreme Court, in throwing out a punitive damage award as unconstitutional, noted that perhaps the "most commonly cited indicium of an unreasonable or excessive punitive damages award is its ratio to the actual harm inflicted on the plaintiff."[86] The Court added: "The principle that punishment should fit the crime 'is deeply rooted and frequently repeated in common-law jurisprudence.'"[87] Wars are not, of course, concerned with proportionality, but instead with visiting destruction on the enemy. As Harvard Law School Professor Charles Nesson wrote in court papers submitted in a suit against student Joel Tenenbaum for downloading seven songs:

> The plaintiffs and the RIAA are seeking to punish him beyond any measure of the damage he allegedly caused. They do this, not for the purpose of recovering compensation for actual damages caused by Joel's individual actions, nor for the primary purpose of deterring him from future copyright infringement, but for the ulterior purpose of creating an urban legend so frightening to children using computers, and so frightening to parents and teachers using computers, that they will somehow reverse the tide of the digital future.[88]

By framing the debate as bipolar, between good (property rights) and evil (immoral youths who steal property), issues are semantically shifted away from the failure of copyright owners to rationally advance their own economic interests, and toward abstract principles, such as rewarding creators and punishing pirates. Unable or unwilling to compete in an innovative capitalist economy, the copyright industries do what those on the ropes always do: attack the character of their perceived opponents. In the case of copyright, those opponents are described as thieves and parasites intent on sucking the blood of America's creativity,[89] intent on destroying our very way of life. War against such enemies is the only option.

The politics of the Copyright Wars are fought out in courts, before legislatures and in international trade forums. Although misleadingly framed in the psychological language of moral panics and folk devils,[90] these skirmishes are, in fact, entirely economic battles. They are battles the copyright industries deserve to lose for the good of the public and for the industries' own good too.

### Chicken Little and False Figures

In the Copyright Wars, the copyright industries portray themselves as the victims in an epic battle to protect their business interests, businesses that are touted as essential to the economic survival of the United States. This explains why the copyright industries throw out figures such as 750,000 jobs and $250 billion lost to piracy, and why they commission economic studies by well-paid consultants who have no scruples about delivering the doomsday analysis requested. As we shall now see, those figures and studies are obviously and fatally flawed. These flawed figures and studies are unfortunately uncritically adopted by members of Congress and the Executive Branch, which recycle them year after year, decade after decade, to justify the next increase in rights that are sought.

Here are a few examples: To support passage of the 2008 Prioritizing Resources and Organization for Intellectual Property (PRO-IP) Act,[91] which contained new criminal penalties and harsh forfeiture provisions, Senator Patrick Leahy, chairman of the Judiciary Committee issued a press release on July 24, 2008.[92] The release quoted Senator Evan Bayh as follows:

> "The global economy is not working as it should when we buy from countries that have a competitive advantage over us, and they steal from us when we have a competitive advantage over them," Bayh said.

"American businesses lose $250 billion every year, and we have lost more than 750,000 jobs because of intellectual property theft."

Senator Bayh's comments were directed toward foreign piracy, but others have used the exact same figures to also include activity in the United States. In an October 10, 2007, interview,[93] Margaret Peterlin, Deputy Under Secretary of Commerce for Intellectual Property and Deputy Director of the United States Patent and Trademark Office, made no distinction between foreign and domestic activity:

Question: How big is the counterfeiting problem?
Peterlin: Counterfeiting and piracy drain about $250 billion out of the U.S. economy each year and 750,000 jobs. No matter what metric you use, there's either loss or harm.[94]

Note that Ms. Peterlin declares the $250 billion alleged loss *and* the 750,000 job loss occur every year; others using the data are vague on this point: In March 2008, the United States Chamber of Commerce sent a letter to members of the House of Representatives indicating the 250,000 figure was cumulative, but asserted that the $250 billion figure was annual:

An estimated 750,000 U.S. jobs have been lost due to counterfeiting and piracy of IP and U.S. companies are deprived of an estimated $250 billion in annual revenue because of this growing problem. Aside from the economic threat posed by IP theft, counterfeit products such as auto and aviation parts, toothpaste, prescription drugs and many others endanger the health and safety of U.S. consumers.[95]

Note here the reference to auto parts counterfeiting as *not* included in these figures. This differs markedly from a statement made in May 2002 by the United States Customs Service, which was very much concerned with auto (and tractor) parts counterfeiting: "The illegal manufacture of counterfeit parts affects U.S. jobs and has safety implications. Customs estimates that businesses and industries lose about $200 billion a year in revenue and 750,000 jobs due to the counterfeiting of merchandise."[96]

Where do the figures come from? Julian Sanchez of the Ars Technica blog undertook a thorough study of the origins of the figures, and published his results in October 2008.[97] First, he contacted the Chamber of

Commerce about where their figures came from. The Chamber said they obtained the figure from "several federal government departments and agencies," including the U.S. Department of Commerce, and provided a link to a September 21, 2005, statement from then-Commerce Secretary Carlos Gutierrez citing the 750,000 figure. But Emily Lawrimore, a U.S. Department of Commerce spokeswoman, stated to Mr. Sanchez in a telephone interview that the "information was provided by the Chamber of Commerce. . . . That's where we received the information from." The Chamber's own Web site states that the U.S. Customs and Border Protection is the source. As quoted above, the Customs statement was made in connection with auto and tractor parts counterfeiting. As it turns out, although Customs had been using the same figures since 2002, six years before their use with the PRO-IP bill, the figures don't come from Customs either. As Mr. Sanchez explains: "[W]hen we contacted [Customs] to determine how they had arrived at that imposing figure, we were informed that it was, in essence, a goof. The figure, Customs assured us, came from somewhere else, and was mistakenly described as the agency's own."

Mr. Sanchez then dug further:

With Customs a dead end, we dove into press archives, hoping to find the earliest public mention of the elusive 750,000 jobs number. And we found it in—this is not a typo—1986. Yes, back in the days when "Papa Don't Preach" and "You Give Love a Bad Name" topped the charts, the *Christian Science Monitor* quoted then-Commerce Secretary Malcolm Baldridge, trumpeting Ronald Reagan's own precursor to the recently passed PRO-IP bill. Baldridge estimated the number of jobs lost to the counterfeiting of U.S. goods at "anywhere from 130,000 to 750,000."

Where did that preposterously broad range come from? As with the number of licks needed to denude a Tootsie Pop, the world may never know. Ars [Technica] submitted a Freedom of Information Act request to the Department of Commerce this summer, hoping to uncover the basis of Baldridge's claim—or any other Commerce Department estimates of job losses to piracy—but came up empty. So whatever marvelous proof the late secretary discovered was not to be found in the margins of any document in the government's vaults. But no matter: By 1987, that Brobdingnagian statistical span had been reduced, as far as the press were concerned, to "as many as 750,000" jobs. Subsequent reportage dropped the qualifier. The 750,000 figure was still being bandied about this summer [2008] in support of the aforementioned PRO-IP bill.[98]

At the time of passage of the 2008 Pro-IP bill, that figure represented 8 percent of the total number of all unemployed, an astonishing statistic indeed. If the figure is assumed to be cumulative, from 1986 to 2008, a period of 22 years, rather than one year, then there was an average of 34,090 loss of jobs a year at the top of the range, or at the low end of the range mentioned by Secretary Baldridge (130,000), a loss of 5,909 jobs a year. We would then have to figure out which jobs are attributable to foreign versus domestic activity, which activity involved copying of things such as auto and tractor parts, and which concerns copying of movies and music. This in turn assumes both that the figures are correct and that there is a correlation to cause, neither of which we should assume. The 750,000 figure is bogus, no matter how it is used.

The $250 billion figure for revenue losses fares no better. As Mr. Sanchez observes, "250 billion is more than the combined 2005 gross domestic revenues of the movie, music, software, and video game industries." The figure is farcical on its face. But where does it come from? Not from the same source as the 750,000 job losses. Mr. Sanchez relates his efforts to track down the origin of the revenue figure:

> According to FBI spokesperson Catherine Milhoan, the figure "was derived through our coordination with industry, trade associations, rights holders, and other law enforcement agencies" at a 2002 antipiracy confab. But neither the Bureau nor the National Intellectual Property Rights Coordination Center, . . . could find any record of how that number was computed.
>
> . . . .
>
> Another group that routinely uses the $200 to $250 billion figure is the International Anti-Counterfeiting Coalition, which (along with the FBI) is often given as the source of the number. That organization's white papers, as recently as 2005, footnote the figure to 1995 congressional testimony urging passage of what became the Anticounterfeiting Consumer Protection Act of 1996.[99]

As it turns out, the origins of the figure, which is stated to be the correct figure for 2008, go back beyond 1995 to 1993. At the 1995 hearings:

> Rep. John Conyers (D-MI) noted that . . . "a more recent estimate by *Forbes Magazine* says that American businesses are losing over $200 billion each year as a result of illegal counterfeiting." Finally, Charlotte Simmons-Gill of the International Trademark Association was kind enough to give a precise citation: the October 25, 1993 issue of *Forbes*.
>
> Ars [Technica] eagerly hunted down that issue and found a short article on counterfeiting, in which the reader is informed that "counterfeit merchandise" is "a $200 billion enterprise worldwide and growing faster than many of the industries it's preying on." No further source is given.[100]

So it is that an unsourced article from 1993 for global counterfeiting (itself not defined) became the source for figures allegedly representing unauthorized infringement of copyrighted works in 2008. The phony 750,000 and $250 billion figures are hardly atypical; to the contrary, they are quite typical. In 2005, the MPAA launched an aggressive campaign against colleges and universities, aided by threats from prominent members of Congress (made at MPAA's request) that their federal funding was in jeopardy unless they cleaned up their act.[101] Members of Congress relied on a study commissioned by MPAA that claimed a breathtaking 44 percent of the industry's domestic losses were attributable to on-campus "piracy" by college and university students. Two years later, the MPAA admitted the study was deeply flawed. The correct figure, the MPAA then claimed, was 15 percent, although it refused to disclose the actual studies or the basis for the 15 percent figure. There is no reason to believe the 15 percent figure bears any resemblance to reality. Indeed, if any of copyright owners' studies or figures bore such a relationship, it would be a first. For example, even taking up the 15 percent figure, MPAA ignored the important fact that nationwide, 80 percent of students live off campus, and therefore, generally use other networks for their Internet connections: Deducting 80 percent of 15 percent gives us 3 percent, hardly a crisis requiring federal regulation of universities or colleges for copyright violations, much less a cut-off of funds used for educational purposes.

The record industry has commissioned its own studies on the alleged effect of campus peer-to-peer (P2P) file sharing, studies that are no more sound than MPAA's. We do have a sound study, however. In 2007, the Canadian government, through the Ministry of Industry, conducted a professional, unbiased study of the effects of P2P file sharing on music sales, both of CDs and of lawful digital downloads. Here is the report's summary of findings:

> The primary objective of this paper is to determine the effects of P2P file-sharing on purchases of CDs and electronically delivered music tracks, using representative survey data from the Canadian population.
>
> In the aggregate, we are unable to discover any direct relationship between P2P file-sharing and CD purchases in Canada. The analysis of the entire Canadian population does not uncover either a positive or negative relationship between the number of files downloaded from P2P networks and CDs purchased. That is, we find no direct evidence to suggest that the net effect of P2P file-sharing on CD purchasing is either positive or negative for Canada as a whole. These inferences are based on the results obtained from estimation of the negative binomial models. . . . However, our analysis of the Canadian P2P file-sharing subpopulation suggests that there is a strong positive relationship between P2P file-sharing and CD purchasing. That is, among Canadians actually engaged in it, P2P file-sharing increases CD purchasing. We estimate that the effect of one additional P2P download per month is to increase music purchasing by 0.44 CDs per year. . . . In the aggregate, we find mixed evidence on the relationship between P2P file-sharing and purchases of electronically delivered music tracks in Canada. Furthermore, our analysis of the Canadian P2P file-sharing subpopulation does not uncover any relationship between P2P file-sharing and the purchasing of electronically-delivered music files.[102]

The point in the Copyright Wars is not to point to real data—quite the opposite, the data is fake—the point is create a sense of siege, of urgency, of a clear and present danger that must be eliminated by either Congress or the courts. To prove this point, even after MPAA's mea culpa over its phony data, Congress, at MPAA's request, went on to pass legislation imposing new obligations on colleges and universities to assist MPAA in stopping a concocted crisis that does not exist.[103] Those obligations not only chill use of new technologies, but they also come at a high financial cost: "Some universities may spend more than $500,000 in cash and personnel time annually on P2P compliance,"[104] unfunded mandates that arose out of copyright owners' repeated use of false data.

## ✻ Copyright, Innovation, and Joseph Schumpeter's "Creative Destruction"

Although it may be said that in the current economic environment in the United States we live under a hybrid, dual economy where there is socialism for the wealthy and raw capitalism for the middle and lower classes, we still rely on the marketplace, rather than patronage or state sponsorship for the creation of works of authorship. The economic conflict at the heart of the Copyright Wars[105] lies in what economist Joseph Schumpeter termed "creative destruction": [106] the introduction of innovative products and business models that displace old ones. Far from being a threat to capitalism, Schumpeter's great insight was that creative destruction "incessantly revolutionizes the economic structure *from within,* incessantly destroying the old one, incessantly creative a new one. This process of creative destruction is the essential fact about capitalism. It is what capitalism consists in and what every capitalist concern has got to live in."[107] Capitalism is, Schumpeter described, "by nature a . . . method of economic change and not only never is but can never be stationary."[108] "Stabilized capitalism is a contradiction in terms."[109] As an inherent fact, "every company [must] prepare the way for its own disruption."[110]

Innovation—the root cause of creative destruction—is thus the way capitalism survives its own inherent tendency toward monopolization and stagnation, even as innovation is regarded as an existential threat to those who benefit from the status quo. In Schumpeter's words, "a new firm's intrusion into an existing industry always entails 'warring' with an 'old sphere,' which tries to prohibit, discredit, or otherwise restrict every advantage afforded to the new form by its innovation."[111] Given the inevitability of such counter-innovative instincts by existing business, in order to ensure the continued vitality of innovation and capitalism itself, we must encourage innovation rather than try to kill it off as the copyright industries do.

Innovation, moreover, presents the opportunity for a win-win situation, rather than the zero-sum game advocated too often by the copyright industries: "The MPAA has . . . portrayed the digital transition, in the press and in policy circles as a zero-sum situation with two possible outcomes: the elimination of control, through piracy; or the perfection of control."[112] Jack Valenti expressed the copyright industries' zero-sum approach before Congress in 1998, stating "for every gain there is a loss and for every loss there is a gain."[113] Under this approach, every defeat of a proposed amendment in the public interest is a gain to the copyright industries, and every failure to grant an increase in protection is a loss to them.

For policy makers and the public, copyright is not a winner-takes-all proposition. Copyright is a system to advance public interests; those interests *can* be furthered by a copyright regime tailored to provide sufficient incentives to create new works. But at the same time, we must recognize that the public interest is genuinely harmed by overprotection. Calls for "strong protection" or "for stronger protection" are absurdly off the mark: just like there is no inherent benefit from steeper taxes, there is no inherent benefit from granting copyright owners more extensive monopoly rights. As Lord Macaulay observed in 1841, in a quote reproduced in the introduction: "it is good that authors should be remunerated; and the least exceptionable way of remunerating them is by a monopoly. Yet monopoly is an evil. For the sake of the good we must submit to the evil; but the evil ought not to last a day longer than is necessary for the purpose of securing the good." The point at which the evil subsumes the good should be determined empirically by evaluating whether any incentive is needed for creation of a work—many works need no incentive, such as private letters, speeches, and business documents—and if an incentive is needed, we must empirically evaluate the actual market conditions for the works in question. Distorted incentives produce distorted conduct, and it is conduct that we should be concerned with: what conduct do we want to encourage and what conduct do we want to discourage? If the theory behind laws is that through proper incentives they will lead to proper conduct it is essential that our copyright laws contain neither too few nor too many incentives.

Regrettably, policy makers (and even many copyright owners) have been taken in by the slogan that stronger rights are somehow not only inherently better but inherently necessary. There is no empirical support for this view, and much evidence to the contrary. If stronger protection is always better, why not make the term of patent protection life of the inventor plus 70 years too? If stronger criminal laws are necessary to deter infringers, why not impose the death penalty, as China has done?

The only type of laws we need are *effective* laws, laws that are effective for their purpose, in the case of copyright, to promote the progress of science, in the words of the U.S. Constitution. Copyright owner's problems are market problems, and they can only be solved by responding to market demands: strong copyright protection cannot make consumers buy things they do not want to buy and, as RIAA's ill-conceived, ill-executed, and ill-fated campaign of suing individuals demonstrates, laws cannot stop individuals from file sharing.

Laws can, though, stifle innovation, and in this respect the copyright industries have been successful, and tragically so, for the public and for authors. Innovation leads to greater consumer demand and therefore greater profits for copyright owners. Genuine support—rather than lip service—for innovation by policy makers can help break us out of the zero-sum dead-end we are currently in. As John Cantwell wrote in "Innovation and Competitiveness," a win-win situation is possible when all involved work together to "develop[] the capabilities for innovation and growth, and not . . . the mutual potential for damaging one another."[114] Innovation can provide new opportunities, rather than fewer, but there must be a willingness to take advantage of those opportunities. The copyright industries have generally shown a willingness only to litigate, not innovate. There is every reason to believe this will continue unless policy makers put the correct goals—furthering innovation, furthering new business models, furthering competition, and furthering consumer choice—front and center where they belong.

Here is an example of how the zero-sum mentality can be replaced with an approach in which both copyright owners and consumers win. At its own expense, and using its own engineers, YouTube[115] developed a prepublication video identification system. Other non-YouTube systems include Auditude.[116] Here's how the YouTube system works: A motion picture studio or other audiovisual content owner provides YouTube with a file of its work. YouTube then encodes the file; when a third party attempts to upload content that provides a match, YouTube contacts the studio and asks the studio what steps it wants to take. The studio can decide to block the upload, let the file be uploaded but tracked, or let the file be uploaded and run either contextual or its own advertisements against it, with the revenues generated being shared. An estimated 90 percent of content owners using video content identification have chosen to monetize their works, resulting in revenues that would not otherwise have been received.[117] Even before the development of its video content identification, YouTube had in place a similar system for audio content contained in consumer-created videos, with an additional feature: Where an audio content owner objects to the use of the music, YouTube offers the user who created the video the ability to engage in an "audio swap." YouTube will, if requested, strip out the objected-to audio and replace it with a song that either is in the public domain or licensed, thereby leaving the user-generated, noninfringing video up for viewing, while respecting copyright owners' rights. These systems are a win-win and were praised in October 2008, by Viviane Reding, Information Society Commissioner for the European Union:

> One innovative business model that has helped reconcile the interest of right holders with those of content is the approach taken by Google for its YouTube platform. It can be summarized as "Track, Monetise or Block": [W]hen confronted with the use of copyrighted content on YouTube, the platform informs the right owner. The right owner can then decide if he wishes to monitor the use of the content; or whether he wishes to make money out of his content at YouTube via advertising revenues; or whether the content should simply be taken down from YouTube. This approach ensures that right owner regains sovereignty over the exploitation of his work.[118]

As Charles Clark, a prominent UK book publisher, copyright expert, and ardent champion of authors' rights, "put it the answer to the machine is in the machine."[119]

## ⚿ The Copyright Wars as a Rearguard Effort to Stave Off Innovation

The Copyright Wars should be seen as a classic and classically wrong response to innovation. It is innovation, not the status quo that keeps the economy fresh. It is innovation that leads to progress and to new learning—the only goals of copyright. The Copyright Wars are an effort to accomplish the impossible: to stop time, to stop innovation, to stop new ways of learning and new ways of creating. The Copyright Wars are wars to ensure that old business models are frozen into place, and innovative approaches are frozen out.

Innovation need not take the form of a superior technology or more bells and whistles. Innovation can take the form of lower-performing products that in novel combinations can be harnessed in more efficient ways. For example, the ever-growing capacity of silicon chips led to faster processing speeds and greater capacity hard drives. The assumption of many in Silicon Valley was that companies would simply keep upgrading to higher-performance chips, and that Moore's Law[120] (the number of transistors that can be placed on a chip doubles approximately every two years) would govern commercial decisions to buy those chips. Yet, that it is not what happened with Google. In a February 2003 article in the *Red Herring* magazine, the story is told of Eric Schmidt, CEO of Google, being asked how the then-new 64-bit processor chip from Intel would affect Google:

> Mr. Schmidt replied that it wouldn't. Google had no intention of buying the superchip. Rather, he said, the company intends to build its future servers with smaller, cheaper processors.
>
> Most who know Google dismissed Mr. Schmidt's words as yet another example of the company's notoriously militant not-invented-here mentality.
>
> . . . .
>
> But few people realized that Mr. Schmidt's announcement was even more far-reaching than that. In essence, what he said was that Google, the hottest young company in technology, had committed the ultimate apostasy: [I]t had declared its independence from Moore's law.[121]

The story of Google and the 64-bit processor chip is reminiscent of what Clayton Christensen, in his book, *The Innovator's Dilemma*, calls "disruptive technologies," that is, "disruptive technologies bring to market a very different value proposition than had been available previously. . . . Products based on disruptive technologies are typically cheaper, simpler, smaller, and, frequently more convenient to use."[122]

Internet delivery of copyrighted works brings precisely such different value propositions than those of the hard copy world, which is based on hierarchical production and distribution systems. Whether those systems were ever efficient, they no longer are: why, for example, should performances of songs be pressed onto CDs, encased in a plastic case with separate artwork and lyrics booklets, shipped from warehouses to retail stores that consumers have to drive to? Ditto for DVDs. Online production and distribution promise higher profit margins than physical copies do as a result of far lower costs of production and distribution.[123] Distribution directly to consumers is a far more efficient system, and it is, moreover the way consumers wish to purchase their music. Yet, it is a system that has been fought tooth-and-nail by record labels and motion picture studios,[124] which, having strangled the online market, then point to the strangled state of that market as a reason not to invest in it. There is a saying in Silicon Valley—"Don't fight the Internet." The reasons are simple; not only can one not fight something that doesn't exist as a place, it is a technology that is here to stay. Seth Godin reminds us:

> [T]he market and the internet don't care if you make money. That's important to say. You have no right to make money from every development in media, and the humility that comes from approaching the market that way matters. It's not "how can the market make me money" it's "how can I do things for this market."[125]

To make money, you have to serve customers, not sue them or control them.

# The Role of Metaphors in Understanding

Understanding one thing by associating it with another is integral to the way we learn. When we ask how a food we haven't tried tastes, the answer is usually, "It tastes like ..."[1] These type of comparisons draw their power from the accuracy of the perceived similarities, even in the presence of dissimilarities: If we say pheasant tastes like chicken, we also know that a pheasant isn't a chicken and won't taste exactly like one either. But we do expect that pheasant will share certain taste characteristics with chicken but not with other meat, say beef.[2]

Associations are also made for rhetorical purposes, such as "lawyers are sharks," in which the message is that lawyers are "swift, powerful, relentless, voracious, and predatory, ... [having] neither conscience nor compassion."[3] Note we are not saying lawyers are *like* sharks (a simile), but rather that lawyers *are* sharks (a metaphor), even as we know that no member of the legal profession is actually a large fish with a fin in the middle of the back, and lots of big, dangerous teeth. Metaphors, by making a direct association, are more powerful than similes,[4] where the association is indirect.[5]

The biggest difference between metaphor and simile was described by Professor Walter Kintsch: "*He eats like a pig* implies that his eating was like that of a pig in most respects, while *He is a pig* ... say[s] something about his behavior, character, even appearance, without disputing the obvious difference in many other respects between man and pig."[6] This explains why in the Copyright Wars, copyright owners do not say, "X acted *like* a pirate," but instead that "X *is* a pirate." The Copyright Wars are an effort to recast someone's character, and for that task only metaphor works.[7]

Both metaphors and similes can be used positively or negatively. As we shall see in Chapter 8, the use of metaphors in the Copyright Wars is almost entirely negative, the result of calculated political strategies to psychologically demonize opponents to make them appear to be "bad" people. Because these bad people are doing bad things, they must be punished the way bad people are: by being sued, by paying exorbitant damages, and in some cases by going to jail. Metaphors are used in the Copyright Wars precisely because they tap into fundamental aspects of how humans feel about themselves and how they feel about others. Metaphors are powerful weapons and are employed in the Copyright Wars as weapons, not as figures of speech. In understanding how metaphors are used as weapons we need to understand the political objectives behind them. In understanding those objectives, we can then reject them because they are not only wrong but dangerously so.

### ✎ Figurative Metaphors

Figurative use of language, particularly metaphors, plays an important role in many aspects of life, in so many different aspects that "metaphor" itself stands for different things.[8] There are image metaphors used in literature ("Juliet is the Sun,"[9] "Aryeh is a Lion"). No one thinks that Juliet actually is the solar entity or that Aryeh is the King of the Jungle. By associating Juliet with the sun, we are meant to appreciate her as a warm person. By associating Aryeh with a lion, we are meant to appreciate him as brave.

Since ancient times, both similes and metaphors have been evoked so that readers can understand one person or one thing through another. (Hence the sometime translation of the Greek word *metaphor* as "carrying something from one thing to another.") Aristotle spoke highly of metaphors,[10] offering that metaphor "is the one thing that cannot be learned from others, and it is also a sign of genius, since a good metaphor implies an intuitive perception of the similarity in dissimilars."[11] Despite this praise, Aristotle regarded metaphors to be merely ornamental, "a happy extra trick with words," as I.A. Richards put it.[12] Aristotle represents the traditional view, a view in which metaphors are not regarded as doing any cognitive work, but are instead poetic devices.[13]

Figurative metaphors do not, however, exhaust the ways in which metaphors are employed. In particular, the Aristotelian view overlooks that much thought is of necessity metaphoric.[14] Neurologists, linguists, and psychologists now believe that "metaphor is not merely a figure of speech but is a fundamental form of cognition."[15] One may in fact question, as Professor Sam Glucksberg has, whether literal meanings are functionally primary:[16] "When one encounters a metaphorical expression, there is no principled reason for a literal interpretation to take precedence over a metaphorical one."[17] Many of the attacks on metaphors—describing, for example, metaphors as "false" or reflecting "deviant" meanings—stem from this view: that all meaning is literal meaning and must be conveyed by literal language.[18] As we shall see in the next section, this view, held by philosophers such as John Searle and Richard Rorty, has never been anything more than a polemical position; empirical evidence is to the contrary.[19]

## ✎ I.A. Richards and the Beginning of Conceptual Metaphors

In February and March 1936, English literary critic and rhetorician I.A. Richards[20] gave six lectures at Bryn Mawr College, later published as *The Philosophy of Rhetoric*.[21] The fifth and sixth of the lectures dealt with metaphor. In the fifth lecture, Professor Richards observed that "metaphor is the omnipresent principle of language [that] can be shown by mere observation";[22] noting that as topics become more abstract, "we think increasingly by means of metaphors that we profess *not* to be relying on. . . . I would hold . . . that our pretence to do without metaphor is never more than a bluff waiting to be called."[23]

Professor Richards went on to propose an analytic tool for thinking about how metaphor transfers meaning from one concept to another. He proposed the term "vehicle" for the concept that is being transferred, and "tenor" for the concept that is to be understood through the vehicle. Professor Richards used these terms as a way to describe generally what happens with our use of metaphors:

> [T]he most important uses of metaphor, the co-presence of the vehicle and the tenor results in a meaning . . . which is not attainable without their interaction. That the vehicle is not merely an embellishment of a tenor which is otherwise unchanged by it but that the vehicle and the tenor in cooperation give a meaning of more varied powers than can be ascribed to either.[24]

### 🎞 Max Black's Theory of Associated Commonplaces

In 1962, Max Black, a professor of philosophy at Cornell University, proposed a division between the subject and predicate of a metaphorical statement similar to Professor Richards' "tenor and vehicle."[25] Professor Black believed that metaphors work by "associated commonplaces," giving the example of "Man is a wolf," in which

> what is needed is not so much that the reader shall know the standard dictionary meaning of "wolf" . . . the important thing for the metaphor's effectiveness is not that the commonplace [associations with wolves] be true, but that they should be readily and freely evoked.[26]

As Professor Colin Turbayne explains:

> [W]hen I say that man is a wolf. . . . Something besides that name is transferred from wolves to men. I do not pretend that man shares the properties of wolves; I intend it. What these properties are I may, but need not, specify. They cannot be all the properties common to wolves, otherwise I should intend that man is actually a wolf. Thus when I say that man is a wolf. . . . I intend that he shares some of the properties of wolves but not enough of them to be classified as an actual wolf—not enough to let him be ranged alongside the timber-wolf and the Tasmanian wolf.[27]

These are good explanations for how metaphors work in the Copyright Wars: It doesn't matter whether people know what pirates were actually like in the Golden Age of Piracy in the seventeenth and eighteenth centuries; rather, it is enough that the term evokes powerful negative associations which are then transferred to the desired folk devils, for example, the manufacturer of VCRs, file-sharers, or Internet service providers (ISPs). In the transference, our attitudes are changed. As Professor Black wrote: "Nor must we neglect shifts in attitude that regularly result from the use of metaphorical language. A wolf is (conventionally) a hateful and alarming object; so to call a man a wolf is to imply that he too is hateful and alarming."[28]

The Copyright Wars routinely rely on such hateful messages to demonize the other side. When we say that man is a wolf, we are aware we are pretending. But when it is said that Internet service providers are pirates, there is no pretense: The statement is meant to be taken as true. As pirates, ISPs will be made to walk a legal gangplank unless they agree to return to the polite ways of society and respect property. Professor Colin Turbayne, in his 1962 book, *The Myth of Metaphor*, noted the shift that occurs when we confuse the pretense with a proposed but false reality:

> [Metaphor] involves the pretense that something is the case when it is not. . . . [O]ften . . . the pretense has been dropped, either by the pretenders or by their followers.[29]
>
> . . . .
>
> When the pretense is dropped either by the original pretenders [or] their followers, what was before called a screen or filter is now more appropriately called a disguise or mask. There is a difference between using a metaphor and being used by it.[30]
>
> There is a difference between using a metaphor and taking it literally. . . . The one is to make believe that something is the case; the other is to believe that it is. The one is to use a disguise or mask for illustrative or explanatory purposes; the other is to mistake the mask for the face. . . . After the disguise or mask has been worn for a considerable period of time it tends to blend with the face, and it becomes extremely difficult to "see through" it.[31]

Metaphors in the Copyright Wars are not an effort to describe reality but are rather an attempt to deny the reality of the copyright industries' repeated failed responses to innovation. These failures are, through metaphors, recast as the failures of others, usually innovators or the public's. Having failed copyright owners, innovators and the public must be threatened and if necessary, punished.

## ✺ The Role of Repetition in Metaphors

Making a metaphoric claim that someone is a pirate doesn't by itself make others regard that person as a pirate, but it does put the claim in play. Repetition is one way to make the claim stick.[32] Repetition of the false metaphor gives it strength it does not deserve: "A story often told— like advertising and propaganda—comes to be believed more seriously."[33]

Repetition not only increases our familiarity with a claim, but as advertisers of products (and politicians) are well aware:

> In the absence of evidence to the contrary, a feeling of greater likelihood that the claim *is* true begins to accompany the growing familiarity. This effect of repetition is known as the "truth effect." We tend to think that if something is not true it would somehow be challenged. If it is repeated constantly and not challenged, our minds seem to regard this as prima facie evidence that perhaps it is true. The effect of repetition is to produce small but cumulative increments in this "truth" inference. It is hardly rational but we really don't think about it.[34]

In his book, *Words that Work*, conservative pollster Frank Luntz explained the role of repetition in the speeches of former president George W. Bush:

> Rarely does the President make official remarks without the topic of those remarks spelled out multiple times on the wall behind him. "Strengthening Social Security" or "Winning the War on Terror" repeated over and over and over for the television cameras to capture and viewers at home to read . . . and read . . . and read.[35]

Repetition of a preexisting concept that has been paired with an unrelated word also serves to change our meaning of the preexisting words. In their book, *Advertising and the Mind of the Consumer*, Max Sutherland and Alice Sylvester explain how this works: "[W]hen a given adjective is repeatedly paired with a given noun, the 'meaning' of the noun . . . undergoes a change in the direction of the adjective. For example, if the noun 'snake' is repetitively paired with the adjective 'slimy,' we begin to think of snakes as slimy creatures (even though they aren't)."[36] With enough repetition (and especially with no rebuttal of contravening facts), the paired associations stick, and thus we will remember Company X as a pirate. Thereafter, when Company X is referred to, it is the negative associations we have with pirates that will be activated: "A central aspect of the art of political persuasion is creating, solidifying, and activating networks that create primarily positive feelings toward your candidate or party and negative feelings toward the opposition."[37] The Copyright Wars are political campaigns to persuade policy makers and courts by precisely such appeals to feelings.[38] As Professor Patricia Loughlan wrote: "It is . . . quite easy to tell a good guy from a bad guy when one of the guys is being called a thief. He is the bad guy. It is in fact quite hard to think of a thief as any sort of good guy at all once you have begun thinking about him, even impressionistically, as a thief."[39] Or, again, from advertising: "For emotion to fulfill its . . . role of ensuring we pay attention to the right things, it must work quickly and simply. . . . [40] At its simplest, all 'emotions' can be analyzed down into one of two basic emotions, which might be described as positive . . . or negative."[41]

## ⅏ Conceptual Metaphors

We frequently use metaphors in discussing legal principles. The "law as a person" metaphor is used when we speak of the "long arm" of the law, the "conscience of equity," a "body" of case law, and when we say that a statute "contemplates" a particular result.[42] Abstract concepts such as copyright can only be understood metaphorically because the rights that comprise copyright do not exist as tangible things: You cannot kiss a copyright or tuck it into bed at night. Professors Lakoff and Johnson call these type of metaphors "conceptual metaphors" to distinguish them from poetic metaphors.[43]

Conceptual metaphors constitute a cognitive process;[44] they are not merely a felicitous turn of phrase.[45] As Professors William Croft and Alan Cruse put it, "metaphors are conceptual structures, and are not merely linguistic in nature, although, of course, they are normally realized linguistically."[46] Unlike similes, the purpose of metaphors is not to make comparisons[47] or to substitute one word or name for another word or name.[48] Rather, metaphors seek to create new meaning in one concept through associating it with the previous understandings we already have of another concept. Cognitive metaphors involving copyright thus *create* conceptual associations that did not exist before.[49] It is not the case that Sony Corporation was a thief by manufacturing the Betamax videocassette recorder: Sony didn't steal anything to make the machine. The Universal City Studios corporation attempted to create a metaphoric thief association by claiming the record button on the Betamax, which permitted consumers to tape, for time-shifting purposes, free, over-the-air broadcasts of television programs made Sony a thief. Of course, Sony did not tape the programs, consumers did. Nor did anyone steal anything: The VCR record button simply stored an over-the-air broadcast that was sent for free to consumers' homes and stored that broadcast for later viewing on a piece of magnetic tape. The physical tape was itself lawfully purchased and owned by consumers; nothing was "taken" from Universal City Studios—no breaking and entering was made of its offices, and nothing that Universal had not already authorized to be seen for free was seen. No law was broken—the Supreme Court held in 1984 that it was lawful for consumers to time-shift using their Betamax machines, and therefore that it was lawful for Sony to manufacture and sell those machines to consumers. The metaphor failed, but the attempt to tag Sony as a thief was made.[50]

Because the root of cognitive metaphors is in concepts, not words, it mattered little, if at all whether Universal City Studios employed the term thief or a pirate.[51] It was the association of illicit and immoral behavior that Universal wished to associate Sony with.[52] Universal employed the metaphor at the institution of its litigation against Sony to frame the way courts and policy makers thought of the VCR. One writer on metaphor noted this tactic:

> Because metaphors can guide our imagination about a new invention, they can influence what it can be even before it exists. The metaphors we use suggest ideas and we absorb them so quickly that we seldom even notice the metaphor, making much of our understanding completely unconscious.[53]

This explains why copyright owners are extremely quick to paint almost every new technology as an instrument of piracy or theft. It is an effort to define the new invention in the minds of legislators or judges. The way such defining is done is through the use of preexisting metaphors that conjure up a desired, negative association with the new innovation.

Memory—the encoding, storage, and later retrieval of experiences, language, and information—plays a central role in that process,[54] a process that includes both emotional memory and what George Lakoff and Mark Johnson refer to as "the cognitive unconscious," that is, those "unconscious mental operations concerned with conceptual systems, meaning and language."[55] According to Lakoff and Johnson, "[a]ll aspects of thought and language, conscious or unconscious, are . . . cognitive."[56] Professors Brian Nosek and Jeffrey Hansen use the term "implicit cognition."[57] Whatever the term used, metaphors serve as fast methods to make these and other processes work, by acting as triggers for a concept that we already know (or think we know), e.g., pirates. The metaphorical concept of pirate is then applied to someone who has not previously been associated with that concept, for example, manufacturers of VCRs. Triggering the concept occurs through resort to our long-term memory,[58] which is why Arnold Modell calls metaphor "the interpreter of unconscious memory."[59] For example, when we say "shark" we have memories of what we think sharks look and act like. We then interpret a new association (say, lawyers) in light of our memory of sharks. The process of interpreting lawyers as sharks occurs instantly: we do not research a shark's actual characteristics before processing the statement "lawyers are sharks." When we say pirates, our memory calls up violent, lower-class criminals who operate in the shadows, physically confront and steal from upstanding members of society, and sometimes kill them in the process.

In the language of cognitive linguistics, metaphorical creation of associations occurs through the process of "mapping," in which elements from one domain are understood in terms of another.[60] The first domain (e.g., pirates) is known as the source domain; it serves as the domain from which we draw metaphorical expressions. The second domain is the target domain (e.g., VCR manufacturers); it is the domain we are led to understand through "mapping" the metaphors drawn from the source domain.[61] A similar process takes place in dreams. In his book, *Internet Dreams: Archetypes, Myths, and Metaphors*, Martin Stefik interviewed a dream analyst who observed:

> When the unconscious speaks, it speaks about what is not known. And it always makes reference to things already known. So there is some framework, some kind of net you can get hold of that can pull the really unconscious thing up into the light where you can see it. So it's not that dreams never make reference to things to what you already know. They always make reference to it, but in my experience, the reference to what is already known is for the purpose of building a foundation upon which the new thing can be placed, so it can be seen.[62]

This also describes the process by which cognitive metaphors work: A preexisting concept is used as a way to automatically transfer understanding about that preexisting concept to a new, different concept or person.[63] It is not surprising, therefore, that both dreams and metaphors are powerful ways by which we come to form new associations.

## 𝍣 Metaphors and Emotion

Metaphors in the Copyright Wars employ powerful words, intended to convey a carefully constructed emotional message and to focus our attention on that message. Every day we come into contact with thousands of stimuli: images, words, sounds, and smells. We forget most of them right away. Very few make their way into our long-term memory.[64] In advertising terms, what is needed to get your message across is an attention-grabbling image or slogan that will "cut through the noise." Metaphors are designed to cut through the noise. The vividness of the stimulus also plays an important role in the possibility of long-term retention (and importantly recall); metaphor is a mainstay in creating vivid stimuli—to call someone an unauthorized user of a copyrighted work is not the same as calling someone a pirate. Saying that VCRs could result in fewer people watching advertisements on television, and that fewer people watching advertisements might lead to a reduction in the amount of money Hollywood can charge TV broadcasters, is not the same as saying, as Jack Valenti did, that the VCR is to the American film producer as the Boston Strangler is to the woman home alone. To create negative associations where they did not exist before, metaphors are impressed into duty. Thus, Jamie Kellner, then CEO of Turner Broadcasting asserted: "Any time you skip a commercial . . . you are actually stealing the program."[65] Both Mr. Kellner and Valenti were using emotion as the maker of meaning and had no concern at all that the meaning was false, as it assuredly was.

The emotional power of our beliefs is often the main determinant in our decision making;[66] "If you're trying to convince people to change course, you generally have to elicit emotions such as anxiety or anger along with enthusiasm for your cause."[67] The Copyright Wars are a continual campaign to change the course of copyright, and as in politics, the more emotional the better.

Metaphors in the Copyright Wars are often a special form of emotion, outrage, intended to conjure up the presence of a clear and present danger that requires national mobilization against an existential enemy. The role of emotion in cognition has gained wide acceptance in many quarters. In 1978, French philosopher Paul Ricoeur, in his article "The Metaphorical Process as Cognition, Imagination, and Feeling,"[68] wrote: "Feeling is not contrary to thought. It is thought made ours."[69] Two hundred years earlier, in 1776, Scottish philosopher George Campbell[70] wrote that emotions "are not the supplanters of reason, or even rivals in her sway; they are [reason's] handmaidens, by whose ministry [reason] is able to usher truth into the heart."[71] Campbell warned, however, that as "handmaids [emotions] are liable to be seduced by sophistry in the garb of reason, and sometimes are made ignorantly to lend their aid to falsehood."[72] Campbell believed that persuasion cannot occur in the absence of emotion,[73] even if the persuasion sometimes conveys a truthful proposition and sometimes not.

Physicians Michael Lewis, Margaret Sullivan, and Linda Michalson propose that "emotion and cognition are neither separate nor independent processes. Rather both are elements of a continuous, inseparable stream of behavior."[74] Psychiatrist Arnold Modell has argued that when we experience a "'raw sensation,' those sensations are interpreted by unconscious processes entailing memory and metaphor, the results of which are then experienced as feelings . . ."[75] "Metaphor mediates, categorizes, and thus organizes the perception of bodily sensations."[76] An expert on advertising has written: "[Emotion] also determines what becomes conscious. Emotion feeds into, shapes and controls our conscious thought."[77] The use of emotion on the reasoning process is well documented in advertising. In a foreword to the book, *The Advertised Mind*, by Erik du Plessis, Nigel Hollis wrote:

Emotion plays a critical role in guiding our instinctive reaction to events happening around us.

. . . .

It is the emotional properties of [our] memories that determine whether we pay attention or not, and how much attention we pay. The more intense the emotional charge of the association memories, the more attention we pay. If the charge is positive, it is likely we will feel attracted to what is happening. If it is negative, we will repelled.[78]

## 𝍚 Emotions and Cognitive Misers

How do emotions serve to persuade? Professor Robin Nabi offered the following two relevant answers:

> First, emotions may serve as heuristics, or cognitive rules of thumb, guiding decisions with minimal information processing or thought.
>
>     . . . .
>
> [Second], emotions may promote selective information processing[;] emotions can be conceptualized as frames or perspectives infused into messages that promote the salience of selected pieces of information over other[] [messages] and thus encourage different problem definitions, causal interpretations and/or treatment recommendations.[79]

Both of these methods by which emotion persuades share a common essence—quick decision making with incomplete information under conditions where there is more than one possible outcome. In 1984, Professors Susan Fisk and Shelley Taylor coined a metaphor, the "cognitive miser" to refer to this process:[80]

> Cognitive Miser refers to the idea that a small amount of information is actively perceived by individuals, with many cognitive shortcuts used to attend to relevant information . . . [a]n idea fundamental in the information-processing model of social cognition that . . . it would be enormously taxing on individuals to attend to all information in the world scientifically (basically, with a high degree of analysis), with individuals' becoming overwhelmed by the confusion and complexity of the social stimuli that they are attending to. As a result, people ignore large amounts of information from the social world, and in doing so, make rapid inferences about information, and use categories to organize information. As a result, people aim to expend the minimum amount of cognitive resources as required.[81]

Although the cognitive miser concept has been criticized for implying intellectual laziness, the criticism misunderstands the thrust of the concept:

> A number of studies conducted within the "cognitive miser" framework over the last decade or so would seem to provide support for the

notion that reliance on categories or stereotypes is likely to increase as a function of mental load.[82]

In the case of members of Congress, I can state from firsthand experience of working for that body that the large number and complexity of subjects and issues frequently renders reliance on shorthand, often metaphors, an absolute necessity. Those who wish to gussy up such theories use the fancy Greek-derived word, "heuristics." A heuristic is sometimes called a shorthand method for deciding something, but this implies that heuristics involve logic, perhaps even a deductive-reasoning process. To the contrary, heuristics are intuitive, subjective,[83] and it is here that emotionally freighted metaphors are pressed into service as a heuristic: to say that X is a pirate is a metaphoric heuristic, intended to persuade a policy maker that the in-depth analysis can be skipped and the desired result immediately attained.[84] As we shall see in the next chapter, the metaphors used in the Copyright Wars are deliberately chosen for their heuristic, emotional punch.

# THREE

# Metaphors and the Law

The reputation of metaphors in the legal literature is mixed: Some judges delight in their usage. British jurist Lord Hoffman wrote in *Designers Guild Ltd. v. Russell Williams (Textiles) Ltd.*: "Copyright law protects foxes better than hedgehogs."[1] Judge Fysh later praised this metaphor with his own metaphor, describing Lord Hoffman's remarks as a "sibylline observation."[2] (Scholars, less generously, have termed the observation "enigmatic."[3])

Others have, however, regarded metaphors with hostility. Jeremy Bentham condemned metaphor as the very antithesis of legal reasoning.[4] Judge Benjamin Cardozo wrote, "[m]etaphors in law are to be narrowly watched, for starting as devices to liberate thought, they end often by enslaving it."[5] As Professor Patricia Loughlan has pointed out, Cardozo himself uses the metaphors of slavery and liberation in warning against metaphors, illustrating the difficulty of avoiding them.[6]

The danger of conceptual metaphors in law is easy to identify. Inferences inherent in the source domain (say, sharks) are automatically mapped onto the target domain (say, lawyers) where they become an inherent part of how we reason about the target domain (lawyers are sharks). This process is not one of comparison, where we merely note similarities and differences between two preexisting categories (like chicken and pheasant); instead, the mapping of inferences from the source to the target domain creates meaning in the target domain that did not exist before. Such mapping, however, may not always be apt; it may in fact be horribly wrong.[7] Lord Palmerston[8] once quipped: "Half the wrong assumptions at which mankind arrive are reached by the abuse of metaphors, and by mistaking general resemblance or imaginary similarity for real identity."[9] In law, the consequence of inapt metaphors is likely to be significant.

The solution to this problem is not to abandon the use of metaphors. If cognitive linguists are correct that much thought is of necessity metaphoric, such a task is impossible. As George Lakoff wrote, "Metaphorical thought, in itself, is neither good or bad; it is simply commonplace and inescapable."[10] Arturo Rosenbluth and Norber Wiener wisely observed, "The price of metaphor is eternal vigilance."[11] We must pay constant attention to how metaphors are used to ensure that the associations made are apt and helpful.

## 🎜 Ideas as Metaphors

Conceptual metaphors play an essential role in law, and law would be impossible without them, given law's many abstract concepts, for example, the "marketplace of ideas," the "wall of separation" between church and state in First Amendment law, and the "color of law" principle used to determine the liability of public officials.[12] The indispensability of metaphors in law is particularly true in copyright law, given copyright's intangible nature. It is black letter law[13] that ideas aren't protectible by copyright, but the original expression of ideas is.[14] Put differently, we protect the particular words authors use to clothe their thoughts in[15] but not the abstract thoughts conveyed by such works. But ideas are also expressed in words, so how do we know whether the material at issue is protected by copyright or not? How one determines in a given case whether the defendant copied an idea or expression is not susceptible of *a priori* tests. Judge Learned Hand stated this forthrightly: "Obviously, no principle can be stated as to when an imitator has gone beyond copying the 'idea,' and has borrowed its 'expression.'"[16]

If we cannot figure out beforehand what is an idea and what is its expression, we can at least appreciate that the dichotomy is grounded in the use of conceptual metaphors. The Supreme Court gave a powerful illustration of this: "The right thus secured by the copyright act is not a right to the use of certain words, because they are the common property of the human race, and as little susceptible of private appropriation as air or sunlight."[17]

The metaphor of ideas as air or sunlight was hardly new with the U.S. Supreme Court. Lord Camden, in the 1774 English Parliamentary debates on copyright, stated that "If there be anything in the world common to all mankind, science and learning are in their nature *publici juri,* and they ought to be as free and general as air or water."[18] Justice Yates made the same point five years earlier in his dissenting opinion in *Millar v. Taylor,*[19] a landmark dispute before the King's Bench about whether copyright is a natural right or is instead solely a creature of positive law. (Courts in the United Kingdom and the United States have taken the latter approach; Australia and Canada legislatively state that copyright is a creature of Parliament.) In 1813, Thomas Jefferson, in a letter to Isaac McPherson, wrote:

> That ideas should freely spread from one to another over the globe, for the moral and mutual instruction of man, and improvement of his condition seems to have been peculiarly and benevolently designed by nature, when she made them, like fire, expansible over all space, without lessening their density at any point, and like the air in which we breathe, move, and have our physical being, incapable of confinement or exclusive appropriation. Inventions, then cannot, in nature, be a subject of property.[20]

Those who argue in favor of owning ideas also treat ideas metaphorically as objects, by employing the "mind is a container" metaphor.[21] In this metaphor, the mind is a container holding ideas. Those who wish to own ideas reify them; ideas are spoken of as if they have a physical state. Ideas are said to be "thin" or "weighty." They may be "crafted" or "shaped," and have "sides." We "toss" them around. Regarded as an object, ideas may be inspected, physically manipulated, or controlled. Because one is metaphorically said to be capable of exercising dominion "over" them, it makes sense, the argument goes, to be able to own rights "in" them.

The Supreme Court, however, rejected the argument that ideas can be owned, and therefore it also rejected that argument's idea-as-physical-object metaphor. According to the Court, ideas are "as free as air or sunlight";[22] that is, ideas are without physical substance, and hence cannot be controlled. The metaphors used by the Court evoke concepts that can, at best, be evanescently perceived but can never be captured or controlled, and therefore can never be owned. You can breathe the air and feel the sunlight, but you cannot take them with you, and therefore you cannot exercise dominion over them.[23] If you cannot exercise dominion over them, you cannot own them because, under traditional views of property, owning property means being able to exercise dominion over an object.[24]

# FOUR

# The Mythical Origins of Copyright and Three Favorite Copyright Metaphors

## ☰ The Mythical Origins of Copyright

Despite the constitutional basis for copyright in the United States as rooted in the objective of promoting learning, there are a number of different origin theories advanced for why we have copyright.[1] No theory, however, commands majority agreement. The lack of an agreed-on foundational theory justifying copyright is a considerable embarrassment for advocates of such extra-constitutional theories.[2] As Joanne Wright observed, origin stories are "narratives that do more than simply uncover beginnings; they authorize implicitly particular solutions."[3] Like historical writing, origin stories are an effort to influence the present and not to objectively unearth the past. In the case of copyright, Majid Yar asserts:

> [M]yths serve to naturalize what are in fact historically, culturally and politically contingencies and represent[] them as something simply given in *natura rerum*, in the nature of things and, as such enduring and inviolable. The conception of individual property rights promulgated in the copyright industries' claims is just such a myth.[4]

Like metaphors, origin stories in copyright serve to frame the debate; they are not descriptive of reality and do not rely on empiricism to make their case. As Professor James Galbraith observed: "A governing myth hides an underlying reality, and any attempt to govern through the myth is bound to be short-lived."[5] For this reason, unless laws are grounded in the Constitution, decisions will be ad hoc, and therefore likely short-lived as well. We shall now review the various origin stories because they continue to be asserted in the Copyright Wars as grounds for policy makers to base their decisions on.

## The Utilitarian/Consequentialist Origin Story

The utilitarian/consequentialist origin story is based on the assertion that only by providing copyright protection will there be sufficient incentives for authors to distribute their works to the public. The public will then benefit from having available works that would not have been produced but for copyright.[6] Without the ability to exclude provided by copyright law, Judge Posner and Professor Landes worry there will be a decline in investment in copyrighted works.[7] Because the creation of some copyrighted works involves substantial up-front costs, to recoup that investment, the author must be able to charge for copies of the work but cannot do so unless there is a legal right that allows him or her to control unauthorized copying. Failing such a legal right, economically minded authors will not make the initial investment, and fewer works will be produced. Under this approach, copyright addresses an excludability problem not present with real property, where the owner can build a fence to keep intruders out.

Among the many difficulties with this origin story is that it is not used as a practical guide to legislating. We protect numerous types of works that require no incentive at all, including private letters, business documents, speeches, designs of useful articles, much academic writing, and works of architecture. Indeed, the approach we utilize is to protect virtually everything that can constitutionally be protected, except typeface, and only then because of objections from book publishers and authors. Even when the issue is the level of incentive, in my 27 years of practicing copyright law, I have never seen a study presented to Congress that even makes a stab at demonstrating that if the proposed legislation is passed, X number of works that would not have been created will be. Indeed, in the case of extending the term of protection all the evidence is to the contrary. In 1998, when Congress extended the general term of protection from life of the author plus fifty years to seventy years postmortem, it would have been absurd to claim that there was a single author in the entire world who said, "I will not create unless the term is my life plus seventy years after I die; fifty years postmortem is not enough." On top of this, the extended term was given to the works of dead authors, who are decomposing and not composing. A brief presented to the Supreme Court in the *Eldred* case by 12 economists, including 5 Nobel Prize winners (such as Kenneth Arrow, Ronald Coase, and Milton Friedman),[8] demonstrated that the extra 20 years was simply a windfall to copyright owners, a redistribution of money from consumers to copyright owners, and which will result in far fewer derivative works being created as the cost of clearing rights to use works that would otherwise be in the public domain is prohibitive.

### Competition and IP Rights

The incentive argument is not only inconsistent with actual practice, it also ignores that the end goal of a market economy is efficiency and that efficiency occurs through competition, not through monopoly power. As Professor Mark Lemley wrote: "It is competition, not the skill or incentives of any given firm, that drives the market to efficiency."[9] The great jurist and scholar Sir Hugh Laddie wrote:

> Competition is the whip which drives traders to offer more or less to their customers. . . . If they don't they will lose market share and profits to competitors who do. In our system, competition is king. It is the enemy of complacency.[10]

Sir Hugh then asked:

> So where do IP rights fit into this? After all, they appear to undermine the very basis of our economic success. They hinder by creating areas of exclusivity. What are they supposed to deliver which justifies this subversion of the free market?

Sir Hugh's answer was this:

> The function of IP rights is to provide an economic incentive to goods and services, which, absent them would not exist or would take many more years to reach the market. They make up for a defect in the competitive system by supplying an incentive where otherwise there would be none.
>
> . . .
>
> IP rights are the carrot to competition's stick. Their purpose is not to displace competition but to modify it, to create sufficient economic incentive to justify the labour and investment in new products or art, but, after that incentive has worked its magic, to allow the normal

forces of competition to have their way. . . . [O]nce the incentive has had its effect there is no further justification for its retention. It has done its work and competition should be allowed to return.

. . .

We should be trying to hone the system so that the greatest rewards and encouragement go to those industries which need and deserve them the most. Where IP rights perform their function of advancing the science or arts, they should be encouraged to do so. Where or to the extent that they do not, they have no justification and the normal discipline of competition should apply. The gluttony which has resulted in the growth of completely unnecessary or excessively long IP rights undermines the system itself. As Shakespeare wrote in Richard II,—"With eager feeding food doth choke the feeder."

Because far greater incentives than are necessary have been given to copyright owners, the end result is that market inefficiency as monopoly power is used to stifle competition and innovation. Distorted incentives lead to distorted behavior, usually in the form of anti-competitive behavior. Professor Joseph Stiglitz, who was awarded the Nobel Prize for economics in 2001, has pointed out that the monopoly power provided by intellectual property rights has an inherent bias against competition and innovation:

[I]ncentives for innovation are less with monopoly than in a more competitive marketplace. There are several reasons for this. First, monopolists produce less—because they charge higher prices. Because they produce less, the benefit from reducing the cost of production by a given amount is less. Moreover, monopolists do not have the spur of competition. They may realize, in addition, that an innovation may lead to a decrease in the value of their existing capital.

Not only do monopolists have a diminished incentive for engaging in research themselves, but monopolists can also increase their profit by discouraging innovation by rivals and raising rivals' costs.[11]

If we truly want innovation and competitive behavior, we must first retrofit our rights so that they accomplish those goals. Calls for strong intellectual property rights falsely assume that strong monopoly rights lead to better competition; the opposite is true.

### The Labor Origin Story

The labor origin story is a variant of "don't reap what you haven't sown." Under this theory, copyright exists as recognition of the labor that went into its production; we should, it is often said, protect the fruits of mental labor for the same reasons and in the same way we protect the fruits of manual labor. Among the faults with this theory are that copyright is not, in fact, based on the degree of labor or time spent in creating a work, but instead on the presence of originality, a different concept altogether.[12] As a court of appeals held on June 17, 2008, rejecting a claim of copyright in complicated computer modeling of a Toyota car:

> In reaching this conclusion, we do not for a moment seek to downplay the considerable amount of time, effort, and skill that went into making Meshwerks' digital wire-frame models. But, in assessing the originality of a work for which copyright protection is sought, we look only at the final product, not the process, and the fact that intensive, skillful, and even creative labor is invested in the process of creating a product does not guarantee its copyrightability.[13]

Twenty-three years before, Judge Easterbrook of the Seventh Court of Appeals in Chicago, a staunch advocate for regarding copyright as property, similarly wrote for the court:

> The input of time is irrelevant. A photograph may be copyrighted, although it is the work of an instant and its significance may be accidental. In 14 hours Mozart could write a piano concerto, J. S. Bach a cantata, or Dickens a week's installment of Bleak House. The Laffer Curve, an economic graph prominent in political debates, appeared on the back of a napkin after dinner, the work of a minute.[14]

But most fatal to the labor basis for copyright is the fact that, in 1991, the United States Supreme Court rejected it as unconstitutional.[15]

### Natural Rights and Geniuses

Finally, there is a natural rights origin story, which asserts copyright is a fundamental human right that preexists legal recognition in a statute.

The role of the legislature is merely to confirm the preexisting right. Under this approach, copyright is like life and liberty, the protection of which is a fundamental obligation of all civilized societies, perhaps ordained by God. The natural rights approach conveniently ignores that exclusive rights exercised by one person involves taking away the liberty interests of others.

The origin story told by copyright owners is based on the alleged natural justice of recognizing and rewarding geniuses. Because it is only in Lake Wobegon that "all the women are strong, all the men are good looking, and all the children are above average,"[16] geniuses are by definition not like the rest of us. It is their singularity that copyright is supposed to protect. In one hyperbolic version of the genius origin story, it was declared: "[C]opyright is, after all, about authorship, about sustaining the conditions for creativity that enable an artist to create out of thin air and intense devouring labor an *Appalachian Spring*, *A Sun Also Rises*, a *Citizen Kane*."[17]

Here are a few salient facts about the works in question: (1) *Appalachian Spring* was composed by Aaron Copland. The work was a collaboration with ballet great Martha Graham, who wrote the narrative underpinning the ballet—the story of a wedding in rural Pennsylvania. Copland followed Graham's scenarios in writing the score. Copland's music was influenced by jazz and Postimpressionist French music. He was said to be "insatiable in seeking out the newest European music,"[18] and called Igor Stravinsky his hero: "Stravinsky's rhythm and vitality is apparent in most of his work."[19] The seventh section of the piece, which is the most well-known part of the work, did not originate with Copland and is instead a set of variations on a nineteenth-century Shaker melody called "Simple Gifts."[20] (2) The novel, *A Sun Also Rises*, written by Ernest Hemingway, was not only influenced by Hemingway's prior reading of a manuscript version of F. Scott Fitzgerald's *The Great Gatsby*, but Fitzgerald, a far more experienced writer, heavily edited Hemingway's book before publication.[21] (3) Describing *Citizen Kane*, Orson Welles' classic motion picture. as being created of thin air is the most shocking of all, given its nature as a roman à clef of the life of William Randolph Hearst and other figures.[22]

Unfortunately for those of the thin-air, genius persuasion, the United States Supreme Court has rejected the natural rights theory,[23] forcing copyright owners to rely on whatever laws Congress decides to enact. Until quite recently those laws were parsimonious. Our first Copyright Act, in 1790, provided very limited protection and then only for books, maps, and charts, contingent on copyright claimants complying with a thicket of formalities to obtain and keep copyright. The approach of the 1790 Act, drafted by members of Congress who had also drafted the Constitution, is fatally in conflict with the Romantic, sun-drenched thin-air view of copyright. Instead, the origins of copyright are, as Thomas Hobbes put it in his *Leviathan* (describing humanity in its natural state), "poor, nasty, brutish, and short."[24]

## Copyright Has Historically Been Unimportant to Authors

People are willing to take almost anything for free; if it later turns out to have value, all the better; if not, nothing is lost. By contrast, if you have to do something to get something, people will weigh the costs and benefits of exerting themselves. Even though the costs of obtaining copyright were almost non-existent for the first 222 years of our copyright laws—a filing fee that was $2 from 1909 until 1977, and $10 in 1978—plus filling out a short, simple government, historically, few copyright owners bothered to take even these minimal steps. In 1992, copyright became fully automatic and devoid of formalities: in other words, authors now have the equivalent of a free lunch. This new world has transformed the way copyright is regarded by corporations: paradoxically, something given away for free has come to be regarded as more valuable than when there was a de minimis toll.

Amnesia has set in: copyright has historically been unimportant to most authors. Although there has been a steady increase in the scope of copyright in the United States since the 1790 Act, for the first 119 years, the expansion was extremely modest. The 1909 Copyright Act expanded the scope of copyright further and increased the term of protection but still in a relatively small way: from 42 years of possible copyright to 56 years. Further expansion occurred in 1978 with the next revision, especially in the term of protection, which switched from a set number of years based on the date of publication to life of the author plus fifty years. It was not until the final quarter of the twentieth century, when compliance with formalities such as mandatory notice and renewal was done away with, that copyright was automatically given without authors having to do anything to claim it. Before this time, authors and publishers voted with their feet in either not claiming copyright at all or in only claiming it for a very short period of time.

We can see proof of this in government records. Records assembled by the Library of Congress and private researchers indicate that more than 21,000 works were published in the United States between 1790 and 1800, but that only 648 copyright registrations were made in this same period, resulting in a registration rate of 3.28 percent, at a time when registration was mandatory to get protection.[25] Of this paltry 3.28 percent, an unknown percentage was renewed, but if we apply the equivalent percentage to those, only 0.9 percent of the works eligible for protection received the 28 years provided for in the act. When the number of works that weren't eligible for protection is included, the number shrinks even more.

Nor has the picture changed appreciably in the intervening 200 years. Mandatory renewal remained a requirement of U.S. law until 1992, when it was abolished for works first published from 1964 to 1977.[26] The records for works first published before 1964 reveal a low renewal rate. On top of this, one can also look to other indicia of the rapidly depreciating value of copyrights, indicia demonstrating that a very long term of protection and extensive rights impose enormous costs on the public without any offsetting revenues going to copyright owners. A study by Jason Schultz of 10,027 books published in the United States in 1930 and therefore still under copyright until 2025,[27] showed only 174 books, or 1.7 percent are still in print. The tiny number of books still in print does not mean the public is free to use such works: to the contrary, the threat of infringement suits renders use of them economically unfeasible.

Here are other data: In a survey of renewal rates from 1910 to 2001, Judge Posner and Professor Landes found a range from 3 percent in 1913 to 22 percent in 1991.[28] Project Gutenberg, a nonprofit organization that makes public domain works available to the public for free (and which thus must be quite sure about the public domain status of works on pain of being sued), has estimated that 90 percent of works published between 1923 and 1963 were not renewed.[29] In 1960, the Copyright Office did a study of renewals in 1958 through 1959, and found an average rate of 15 percent. Even more significant is the breakdown by subject group:

Copyright Renewal Rates 1958–1959

| Type of Work Renewal Percentage | |
| --- | --- |
| Books | 7% |
| Periodicals | 11% |
| Lectures, Sermons and other oral works | 0.4% |
| Dramatic Works | 11% |
| Music | 35% |
| Maps | 48% |
| Works of Art | 4% |
| Technical Drawings | 0.4% |
| Art Prints | 4% |
| Movies | 74%[30] |

Metaphors serve to create a different, happier fantasy for copyright owners, one in which copyright has allegedly served as a vital incentive. The data recited above prove otherwise: When it counted, most authors and publishers ignored copyright, or claimed rights only for a short period of time.

## ⁂ Three Favorite Copyright Metaphors

The power of metaphors lies in their tapping into fundamental cultural beliefs or fears, beliefs and fears that antedate conceptions of intellectual property by many centuries. In this chapter, we shall see how three of the favorite copyright metaphors are designed to instill in us unthinking associations with such beliefs and fears.

### Authors as the Parents of their Works: The Birth Metaphor

A powerful metaphor employed to argue that authors (or, more usually their corporate assignees) should have extensive control over the works they create is the metaphor evoking the relationship between an author and the author's works as that of a parent-child. The metaphor is known as the creation-as-birth metaphor and is used in many areas besides copyright. Here are some examples:

Our nation was born out of a desire for freedom.
Her experiment spawned a host of new theories.
Your actions will only breed violence.
He hatched a clever scheme.

And most on point for us:

Her writings are products of her fertile imagination

The creation-as-birth metaphor posits an intimate connection between an author and his or her work. Under the metaphor, it is a violation of the author's personhood to use his or her work without permission.[31] The author, having given birth to the works, should have the right to raise and protect them as if they were the author's children. Those who copy from the author's work without permission are kidnappers, the vilest form of thief.

In asserting the birth metaphor as a justification for a strong copyright regime, proponents of the metaphor hearken back to pre-copyright days, because for any metaphor to work in a new context, it has to be based on preexisting associations. The birth metaphor is quite ancient. In his "Symposium," Plato had Diotima describe poems created by Homer and Hesiod as their intellectual children, even greater than actual children.[32]

Later authors such as Cervantes[33] and Milton also referred to their literary creations as their children.[34] James Joyce, writing to Nora Barnacle, described his then unpublished work, *The Dubliners*, as a "child which I have carried for years and years in the womb of imagination as you carried in your womb the children you love."[35] Daniel Defoe, in urging passage of what became the world's first general copyright statute, the 1710 UK Statute of Anne, declared:

A Book is the Author's Property, 'tis the Child of his Inventions, the Brat of his Brain; if he sells his Property, it then becomes the Right of the Purchaser; if not, 'tis as much his own, as his Wife and Children are his own—But behold in this Christian Nation, these Children of our Heads are seiz'd, captivated, spirited away, and carry'd into Captivity, and there is none to redeem them.[36]

(Parenthetically, for Defoe, the brain was regarded as the womb of thought,[37] thereby metaphorically overcoming the obvious biological objection to Defoe metaphorically birthing anything.[38]) Nor is use of the metaphor limited to literary authors. Graphic artist Gary Larson, known for his "Far Side" comic strip, sent out a letter to a fan site that had digitized his works without permission, asking the site to delete the copies. The end of the letter read:

> These cartoons are my "children" of sorts, and like a parent, I'm concerned where they go at night without telling me. And, seeing them on someone's website is like getting the call at 2:00 a.m. that goes, "Uh, Dad, you're not going to like this much but guess where I am." I hope this explanation helps you understand the importance this has for me, personally, and why I'm making this request. Please send my "kids" home. I'll be eternally grateful.[39]

There are a number of problems with the metaphor. I will discuss two: (1) no author is an island; and (2) copyright in common law countries is an economic right in commodities, not a moral right, and is granted to facilitate trade in copyrighted works, not to ensure an ongoing parent-child relationship.

One of the most interesting rejections of intellectual property rights as an aspect of personhood comes not from a copyright claim, but from a state law claim of conversion over the use of a patient's spleen tissues to obtain a patent and reap potentially three billion dollars in royalties. John Moore had leukemia and was treated at the UCLA Medical Center. His physician was alleged to have formed the intent to benefit from treating Mr. Moore by both treating him and simultaneously conducting medically unnecessary research on him in order to support a patent claim. Mr. Moore wanted to share in the profits from the patent. The California Supreme Court rejected the conversion claim.[40]

### No Author Is an Island

The author of Kohelet (Ecclesiastes)[41] wrote around 250 B.C.E.: "That which has been is what will be, and that which has been done is that which will be done; and there is nothing new under the sun."[42] Whether the author meant this sentiment to apply to his own statement is perhaps paradoxical, but all authors not only build on the works of past authors, those works exist only in context with past and present authors and culture: readers can only understand contextually; that is, within shared communal understandings.[43] This is what Hans-Georg Gadamer meant when he wrote: "Understanding is to be thought of less as a subjective act than as participating in an event of tradition, a process of transmission in which past and present are constantly mediated."[44] T.S. Eliot made the same point more eloquently in his essay "Tradition and the Individual Talent": "The historical sense compels a man to write not merely with his own generation in his bones, but with a feeling that the whole of literature from Homer and within it the whole of the literature of his own country has a simultaneous existence and composes a simultaneous order."[45]

The Romans copied the Greeks; Shakespeare copied the works of others with wild abandon and without attribution. In music, the greatest Renaissance composers composed "parody" masses; these were not humorous works, but rather works using the melodies of other composers to create what we would call a derivative work.[46] Renaissance graphic artists engaged in open copying and alteration of contemporary artists, vying for the same customers.[47] Famous composers such Haydn, Mozart, Beethoven, and Brahms wrote variations on others' works, without permission or payment. As Professor Benjamin Kaplan wrote: "From the classical writers, as expounded by critics of the Italian and French Renaissance, the Elizabethans had received the notion that artistic excellence lay imitating the best works of the past, not in attempting free invention."[48] Even after the passage of modern copyright laws (by the Elizabethans) protection was not granted to copyright owners to stop such efforts. A translation right was not granted until 1870 in the United States; a general right to prepare derivative works not until 1909. For much of history, then, and long before appropriation art became a vogue, the scope of authors' protection was small, out of recognition that no author is an island.

Copying from other authors is not necessarily, or maybe even usually done by the talentless; quite the opposite. As Judge Posner explains with Shakespeare:

His characteristic mode of dramatic composition was to borrow the plot and most of the characters—and sometimes the actual language— from an existing work of history, biography, or drama and to embroider the plot, add some minor characters, alter the major ones, and write most or commonly all of the dialogue. For example, Shakespeare made up Antony's great funeral oration; no part of it is in his source, North's translation of Plutarch. But we shall see that for the description of Cleopatra in *Antony and Cleopatra* Shakespeare merely edited North-Plutarch's description, though he did so brilliantly and vastly improved it. Such was the extent of borrowing by the Elizabethans that some of their plays would be classified by modern copyright lawyers as "derivative" works, which infringe the original unless the author of the original has authorized them.[49]

Pablo Picasso stated, "Good artists copy, great artists steal." Igor Stravinsky said: "A good composer does not imitate, he steals." T.S. Eliot agreed: "Immature poets imitate; mature artists steal." Northrop Frye wrote: "Poetry can only be made out of other poems; novels out of other novels. All this was much clearer before the assimilation of literature to private enterprise."[50]

Harold Bloom's classic twentieth-century text, *The Anxiety of Influence*, also noted the creative result of such copying. Professor Bloom took the position that transformative influence occurs

> only with strong poets, major figures with the persistence to wrestle with their strong precursors, even to the death. Weaker talents idealize; figures of capable imagination appropriate for themselves. But nothing is got for nothing, and self-appropriation involves the immense anxieties of indebtedness, for what strong maker desires the realization that he has failed to create himself?[51]

This is what Brahms meant when he complained, "I feel the footsteps of Beethoven behind me." Notwithstanding Brahms' anxieties, we, as a public, are the richer for them.

Mr. Justice Hugh Laddie similarly remarked:

> The whole of human development is derivative. We stand on the shoulders of the scientists, artists and craftsmen who preceded us. We borrow and develop what they have done; not necessarily as parasites, but simply as the next generation. It is at the heart of what we know as progress.[52]

Dr. Martin Luther King, Jr.'s famous August 28, 1963 "I Had a Dream Speech," delivered at the Lincoln Memorial in Washington, D.C., was an amalgamation of and reworking from numerous sources, including an address by attorney Archibald Carey to the 1952 Republican National Convention from which King "borrowed virtually the whole of his [King's] conclusion, from 'My Country, 'Tis of Thee' through the incantation 'Let freedom ring."[53] Carey had himself copied from "America" composed in 1831 by Samuel F. Smith. Other sources for King's speech were the Bible, what King called Negro spirituals, "My Country, 'Tis of Thee," and "The Battle Hymn of the Republic," King in fact had "a lifelong habit of appropriating material from other sources. . . . Improvising upon familiar themes, King often took words and ideas from other preachers, from philosophers, from poets, and from essayists."[54] George Balanchine did the same thing in choreography, declaring: "if you like something of someone else's, why not take it? The important thing is that seem natural and fit in."[55] (He also took the view that only God creates *ex nihilio*: "God creates, man assembles."[56])

Thus, although children contain the DNA of both parents and genes passed on from those parents' ancestors, with authors, the DNA is from strangers. All works of authorship are to some extent communal works; it is therefore inappropriate to vest one person with rights that have the ability to impede the birth of future generations of works.[57] Thus, although many authors fervently believe in their own absolute originality or novelty, in the colloquial and legal meanings of those terms, the truth is far different. There are serious consequences to acceptance of the metaphor. Judge Posner further observed,

> [the] works of previous writers are inputs into current work, and these inputs get more expensive the more those earlier works are protected by copyright. If every author of an epic poem had to pay royalties to Homer's heirs, then Virgil, Dante, Ariosto, Milton, Pope, Goethe, and others would have had to incur an additional expense to write their epics. The expense might have deflected some of them to a different literary form or caused them to write less, resulting in a social loss.[58]

Even if authors do not write less, the current regime of copyright on steroids in which lawyers have advised biographers that they may not use one word from an unpublished manuscript[59] and in which courts have held that performing artists may not sample two seconds from another recording,[60] has resulted in less creativity, less connection to the present and the past. In their religious zeal to claim every jot and tittle of culture, copyright dwarves can see no further than their own megalomania, impoverishing all of us in the process.

### Copyright Is an Economic Commodity

A second problem with the creation-as-birth metaphor is that at least in common law countries, including the United States, copyright is an economic right, not a moral right concerned with preserving an ongoing, intimate relationship between the author and the work.[61] Acceptance of the parent-child metaphor would mean authors would not be permitted to sell or license their "children." The metaphor is not, then, to be taken as a description of the actual relationship between authors and their works. Instead, the metaphor is invoked to give authors—or more usually corporate assignees—special rights over *third parties,* rights that touch economic, not moral issues. Given the ease with which recording artists and composers now create and produce their own works without the need for expensive recording studios and other production activity, record labels are rarely creative collaborators, but are instead limited to popularizing a finished work that has been handed to them.

The lack of a touchy-feely connection between the corporation asserting the rights and the actual creators of the works in question extends to some degree even to works such as motion pictures where the work is a collaborative effort. As Andrew Currah wrote:

> [F]ilm marketing and distribution [has undergone] a process of vertical integration and globalization, as the studios were subsumed into larger international conglomerates. As a result of these changes, the studios have increasingly functioned as gatekeepers (rather than film factories), which control access to finances required to produce, market and distribute films.[62]

Frequently, motion pictures are created by independent producers who have no overall relationship with any particular studio. Even this tells only part of the story: Rights such as cable, broadcast, and home video are presold (that is sold before the movie is shot) to a wide variety of other companies. Behind them all, however, is a bank or other capital investor (e.g., Lloyds or Wall Street investors) who hold secured interests in the copyright. Those investors are the ultimate holder of title, not the studio whose name is on the copyright notice. The financiers, film makers, and studios all stand in a secondary position to the completion bond holders, who can (and do on occasion) take over pictures for their own account if, in their judgment, things are going over-budget prerelease. These highly complex financial arrangements are constructed toward ensuring that every possible aspect of the work can be monetized as often and easily as possible.[63] This reality leads to a very different basis for copyright—as a commodity, to be bought and sold—not as a personal right. As we shall see in Chapter 6, copyright as commodity reflects the actual origins of copyright in common law countries.[64]

Not surprisingly, then, the metaphor of authors as parents of their works was not first put forth by authors, but instead by London book publishers in the eighteenth century, at the dawn of modern copyright, to justify *their* assertion of perpetual commodity rights in authors' works. As commodities, those works were acquired by book publishers from authors for as little money as possible (and sometimes no money). The invocation of the metaphor was thus the beard for publishers' economic objectives. From the beginning of modern copyright, we see one of the central rhetorical features of copyright discourse—authors put forth as the basis for and beneficiaries of rights that are in truth owned by publishers and other corporations who regard authors as a negative item on balance sheets to be reduced as much as possible. It is a testament to the formidable power of the romantic emotions evoked by the metaphor that it continues to hold sway despite 300 years of empirical evidence demonstrating its complete falsity.

### Orphan Works

A more recent use of the creation-as-birth metaphor is with so-called "orphan works." "Orphan works" are described by the U.S. Copyright Office as involving "a situation where the owner of a copyrighted work cannot be identified and located by anyone who wishes to make use of the work in a manner that requires the permission of the copyright owner."[65] One could more accurately describe such works as willfully abandoned. The term "willfully abandoned" would evoke very different reactions than "orphan works." Professors George Taylor and Michael Madison have noted the power of the orphan works metaphor:

> Creators, like parents, have the presumptive right to control the experience of their "children" in the world and to shield them from exploitation and abuse, and advocates for strong authorial rights implicitly and sometimes explicitly invoke that emotional bond to justify a legislative or judicial result.[66]

The orphan works problem was created by the recent radical expansion of copyright. Before 1978, there was no orphan works problem, as the combination of formalities such as notice and renewal, and a shorter term (before 1978, a 28-year original term of protection, followed by the possibility of a 28-year renewal term), threw into the public domain the vast majority of works for which authors had gone to the trouble of claiming copyright in the first place. (As we saw at the beginning of this chapter, the number of authors who have cared about obtaining copyright protection for their works is small.) With the shift to a term of life of the author plus seventy years, and the abolition of formalities, millions of works remain under copyright that formerly would be in the public domain. The orphan works "problem" is then a problem caused by the grave mistake of abolishing formalities and extending the term of copyright to obscene levels. It is a telling indication of the impoverished policy making by national legislatures that not only can they not come up with meaningful remedial legislation to deal with the results of their own mistakes in this regard, but they appear clueless that the problem is one of their making.

Use of the term "orphan" inaccurately conjures up an emotional need to protect these works against those who would use them without the copyright owner's permission, even though the "parents" long ago dropped any interest in them. Nor should it be overlooked that corporations, which purchased rights from authors or later corporations, own many of these works. Although in some areas of law, corporations are fictionally (and metaphorically) regarded as "persons," extending emotionally freighted terms such as "orphans" in connection with companies which merely purchased works and then went bankrupt or which wrote off the copyrighted work as a worthless asset is a stretch indeed.

The public suffers mightily from the existence of millions of orphan works, as those who wish to use them in creating new works are scared off by the threat of lawsuits from heirs or other claimants coming out of the woodwork if the new use proves economically successful. The use of a false metaphor is greatly inhibiting resolution of this critical problem.

### The Agrarian Metaphor: Reaping What You Haven't Sown

One of the most common of the copyright metaphors is the agrarian metaphor: Copyright owners, as the sowers of their works, should have the exclusive right to reap the benefits of their efforts. There are many problems with this earthy metaphor, including the false assumption (detailed in the last section) that authors never reap from earlier authors. But even assuming momentarily this is the case, the metaphor ignores a host of extremely difficult questions: How long should the right last—for a set term of years, for the author's life, for a set period of years after the author's life, or perpetually? Should rights be assignable, and if so, under what conditions? How extensive should the rights be? Should quotations in a critical review be precluded? Should rights extend not just to verbatim copying, but also to abstract plots such as: boy meets girl; boy is from a rival group, boy and girl fall in love, keep their relationship secret, the boy is wrongly assumed to have died in a fight, and the girl commits suicide? Should copyright preclude others from making mash-ups from a variety of copyrighted works? Should third parties who create dual-use machines or software that can be used for non-infringing purposes and to copy authors' works be liable too, such as photocopy machine makers and computer manufacturers? Does the answer to this last question hinge on whether these third parties obtained a direct or indirect financial benefit from the unauthorized copying, whether the machines have substantial non-infringing uses or whether the machines could have been designed to block all unauthorized uses?

The appeal of the metaphor is that it ignores these and every issue of importance. The metaphor is instead stated at the level of its basest appeal: the author, through unselfish devotion and hard work, has brought forth a work of genius, which others—lazy, shiftless, immoral do-nothings—are trying to steal. Once the debate is framed this way, working out difficult questions such as those detailed above seems churlish. Instead legislatures are supposed to merely grant rights at the broadest possible level so that any unauthorized use is an infringement, a reaping where one hasn't sown. But as Professor Mark Lemley has pointed out, "Even real property doesn't give property owners the right to control social value. Various uses of property create uncompensated positive externalities, and we don't see that as a problem or reason people won't efficiently invest in their property."[67] Put in plain English, even owners of land can't stop all uses of their property by others, yet this doesn't stop people from buying or improving their houses.

For example, those whose houses are built on beaches frequently have to permit the public to have access to the beaches; yet, these properties have not lost any of their value as a result. There is every reason to believe that the same principle applies with more force to copyrighted works, given that copyright is a nonrivalrous resource, unlike real property. Professor Lemley adds: "If 'free riding' means merely obtaining a benefit from another's investment, the law does not, cannot, and should not prohibit it."[68] All parodists and satirists are in one sense free-riders, as are book reviewers. The issue is not whether third parties are using a copyrighted work without permission, but rather what is the benefit to society from the use, taking into account any legitimate potential losses to copyright owners. In this respect, we cannot do better than to follow Professor Benjamin Kaplan's rejection of the don't reap where you haven't sown metaphor, deftly turning it against those who employ it: "[I]f man has any 'natural rights,' not the least must be a right to imitate his fellow, and thus to reap what he has not sown. Education, after all, proceeds from a kind of mimicry, and 'progress,' if it is not entirely an illusion, depends on generous indulgence of copying."[69]

### Origins of the Metaphor

Mark Rose has traced some of the ancient uses of the metaphor:

> [A]s one ancient tradition likens writing to agriculture and specifically to plowing, with the writing implement or stylus being a kind of plow by which one makes furrows on the field of a wax tablet. Moreover, the conceit of a mind as a field is as old as pastoral poetry, and in the Middle Ages, under the influence of the evangelical trope of the word of God as a seed, the author was often represented as a sower of seeds.[70]

These references have nothing to do with intellectual property, which did not exist, but the ancient lineage of the metaphor illustrates why those who later sought intellectual property choose to invoke such a powerful cultural symbol. Use of the metaphor in intellectual property laws is at least 588 years old. I have traced it back to a patent privilege granted in 1421 by the commune of Florence to Filippo Brunelleschi for the design of a boat to carry heavy loads of stone on the Arno River. The stones were used for construction of the famous Duomo cathedral in that city. The grant recited Brunelleschi's apparent refusal "to make such a machine available to the public in order that the fruit of his genius and skill may not be reaped by another without his will and consent," adding, however, that "if he enjoyed some prerogative concerning this, he would open it up and disclose it to all."[71]

The metaphor was later employed in copyright, most prominently in the 1769 decision of the King's Bench in *Millar v. Taylor*.[72] That case arose out of the first Copyright Wars—the argument by London booksellers that they possessed perpetual rights over the reproduction of authors' works (even ancient authors) based on "natural rights"—rights that allegedly exist independent of any legislative enactment. The opposing view was that the 1709 English Statute of Anne, which prescribed set term limits for copyright,[73] was the sole source of rights. Copyright was, according to this view, a species of positive law; that is, legal rights which exist only if a legislature creates them, and according to the terms set out in the legislation. Under that legislation, the booksellers' rights (if any) had expired, so they had to concoct a different theory supporting their claim for continued rights; the theory of natural rights was selected.

The issue of whether there were natural copyright rights, and if so, whether they were supplanted by Parliament's passage of the Statute of Anne was fiercely debated for three-quarters of a century until it was finally decided in 1774 by the House of Lords in *Donaldson v. Beckett* that copyright rights are statutory (that is positive law), and not natural. Because the booksellers' rights had expired under the statute, they lost. The United States Supreme Court came to the same conclusion regarding federal copyright in 1834, in the case of *Wheaton v. Peters*.[74] Australia and Canada declare the same principle in their copyright acts. Despite the settled nature of the question, the power of the metaphor in the Copyright Wars continues, oblivious to law, so it is well to note its evolution in the courts, beginning with the opinion of the judges of the

King's Bench in the English case of *Millar v. Taylor*, the first real test of the booksellers' claims, and a test they won, although the victory only lasted for five years.

As is the custom in English courts, the judges in *Millar* announced their opinions orally and seriatim. Justice Wiles, the first judge to speak in the dispute, was the first to raise the metaphor: "It is certainly not agreeable to natural justice, that a stranger should reap the beneficial pecuniary produce of another man's work."[75] The next judge, Justice Aston, spoke eloquently about "every principle of reason, natural justice, morality and common law."[76] The lone dissenter, Justice Yates then spoke, expressing his discomfort with disagreeing with his colleagues. Justice Yates nevertheless enthusiastically attacked use of the metaphoric argument that those who use a copyrighted work without permission are "pirating the profits of another's labor and reaping where they have not sowed":[77]

> This argument has indeed a captivating sound; it strikes the passions with a winning address; but it will be found as fallacious as the rest, and equally begs the question. For, the injustice it suggests, depends upon the extent and duration of the author's property; as it is the violation of that property that alone must constitute the injury. . . . [I]t is insisted, "that it conscientiously belongs to the author himself . . . as being the fruits of his own labour." "That every man is intitled *[sic]* to the fruits of his own labour," I readily admit. But he can only be intitled *[sic]* to this, according to the fixed constitution of things; and subject to the general rights of mankind, and the general rules of mankind. He must not expect that his fruits be eternal that he is to monopolize them to infinity; that every vegetation and increase shall be confined to himself alone, and never revert to the common mass. In that case, the injustice would lie on the side of the monopolist, who would thus exclude all the rest of mankind from enjoying their natural and social rights.[78]

Justice Yates regarded the matter as one exclusively within the domain of the legislature, rejecting the appeal to natural rights, adding that the rights of the public were important too, and raising a number of the difficult questions the metaphor is deliberately designed to avoid. For Justice Yates, it was the legislature that determined whether there was to be a right at all, and it was, therefore, the legislature that fixed the limits of those rights. Put metaphorically, authors were entitled to reap only if Parliament said they could and only for as long as Parliament said they could.

Lord Mansfield, who had been involved in the first Copyright Wars for a considerable period of time as a private lawyer for the London booksellers, spoke last.[79] He agreed with the first two judges, and similarly remarked, in finding a source for common law copyright that, "it is just, that an author should reap the pecuniary profits of his own ingenuity and labour."[80] But it was just only because he said it was, not because there was any legal basis for the proposition.

The matter then went to the House of Lords five years later in the case of *Donaldson v. Beckett*, ironically involving the same work, Scottish poet James Thomson's, *The Seasons*, which Joseph Haydn later made into an oratorio of the same name.[81] The House of Lords came to the opposite conclusion from the majority in *Millar v. Taylor*, siding with the public against the booksellers' claims. Of the various remarks made in the upper House, the remarks of Lord Camden are the most relevant, addressing as they do the extended arguments put forth by Lord Mansfield and Justice Aston in *Millar v. Taylor*, that copyright was not positive law existing solely on an act of Parliament, but rather was based on a fundamental societal principle that one may not reap where one hasn't sown:

> But it is said that it would be contrary to the ideas of private justice, moral fitness, and public convenience, not to adopt this new system. But who has a right to decide these new cases, if there is no other rule to measure by but moral fitness and equitable right? Not the judges of the common law, I am sure. Their business is to tell the suitor how the law stands, not how it ought to be; otherwise each judge would have a distinct tribunal in his own breast, the decisions of which would be irregular and uncertain, and various, as the minds and tempers of mankind. As it is, we find they do not always agree: but what would it be, where the will of right would always be the private opinion of the judge, as to the moral fitness and convenience of the claim? Caprice, self-interest, vanity, would by turns hold the scale of justice, and the law of property be indeed most vague and arbitrary.[82]

### Rejection of the Metaphor in the United States

In 1909, in passing a new copyright act, Congress addressed the basis for copyright in the United States:

> The enactment of copyright legislation by Congress under the terms of the Constitution is not based on any natural right that the author has in his writings, for the Supreme Court [in *Wheaton v. Peters*] has held that such rights as he has are purely statutory rights, but upon the ground that the welfare of the public will be served and progress of science and useful arts will be promoted by securing to authors for limited periods the exclusive right to their writings. The Constitution does not establish copyrights, but provides that Congress shall have the power to grant such rights if it thinks best. Not primarily for the benefit of the author, but primarily for the benefit of the public such rights are given. Not that any particular class of citizens, however worthy, may benefit, but because the policy is believed to be for the benefit of the great body of people, in that it will stimulate writing and invention, to give some bonus to authors and inventors.[83]

Following these remarks, the Supreme Court authoritatively rejected the agrarian metaphor in *Feist Publications, Inc. v. Rural Telephone Service Company*.[84] Justice O'Connor, for a unanimous Court wrote:

> It may seem unfair that much of the fruit of the compiler's labor may be used by others without compensation. As Justice Brennan has correctly observed, however, this is not "some unforeseen byproduct of a statutory scheme." ... It is, rather, "the essence of copyright," ... and a constitutional requirement. The primary goal of copyright is not to reward authors, but "to promote the Progress of Science and useful Arts."[85]

*Feist* is particularly important for its rejection of the central emotional construct of the agrarian metaphor—that it is "unfair" for others to reap what they haven't sown. Whatever the merits of the metaphor as applied to stealing corn from a field, when applied to statutory privileges such as copyright enacted to benefit the public, the unfairness flows the other direction.

Despite repeated, authoritative rejections of the metaphor, its invocation continues, likely because the metaphor is all that is left to those whose legal arguments have been rejected for 235 years.[86] The purpose of the metaphor is to make the law of copyright what Lord Camden in *Donaldson v. Beckett* called "most vague and arbitrary," by replacing legislative enactments with appeals to "fairness," the dangers of which jurist John Selden noted in the seventeenth century:

> Equity is a roguish thing. For Law we have a measure, know what to trust to; Equity is according to the conscience of him that is Chancellor, and as that is larger or narrower, so is Equity. 'Tis all one as if they should make the standard for the measure we call a "foot" a Chancellor's foot; what an uncertain measure would this be! One Chancellor has a long foot, another a short foot, a third an indifferent foot. 'Tis the same thing in the Chancellor's conscience.[87]

### Forms of the Metaphor

The metaphor takes two principal forms: (1) authors should enjoy the fruits of their labors (the positive form), and (2) reaping what you haven't sown (the negative form). A recent exposition is by Lord Bingham in *Designers Guild Ltd. v. Russell Williams (Textiles) Ltd.*:[88] "The role of copyright rests on a very clear principle: that anyone who by his or her own skill and labour creates an original work of whatever character shall, for a limited period, enjoy an exclusive right to copy that work. No one else may for a season reap what the copyright owner has sown."[89] With a term of copyright set at life of the author plus seventy years, we are talking about quite a few seasons, and in any event Lord Bingham seems to have ignored the House of Lords' rejection of the "very clear principle" 227 years earlier.

The Australian Prime Minister's Science and Engineering Council took the metaphor to great extremes: "Without [intellectual property law], innovation is like a crop in an unfettered field, free to be grazed by competitors who have made no contribution to its cultivation."[90] There is, of course, no empirical evidence offered in support of the hyperbole, which in any event dodges the real issue, that is, what the scope and duration of rights should be, not whether there should be any protection at all. One should also note that the owner of the land did not create the land being tilled nor the type of crop. Both pre-existed the owner and will outlive him or her. In recognition of this and the social nature of all property, Sefer Vayikra of the Torah (the Book of Leviticus), requires that:

> When you reap the harvest of your land, you shall not reap all the way to the edges of your field, or gather the gleanings of your harvest. You shall not pick your vineyard bare, or gather the fallen fruit of your vineyard; you shall leave them for the poor and the stranger.[91]

Contrary to the view expressed in the quote from Australia, in the Torah the land is not within the unfettered right of the farmer, but rather the farmer has social responsibilities to share what he reaped. The concept that the land belongs to all generations and not just the one tilling it at the time is also seen in the Biblical requirement of "Shmita," by which every seven years the land in Israel must be left fallow: there can be no plowing, planting, or harvesting. Any produce that grows natural is considered "hefker," ownerless, and may be picked by anyone. Sefer Shmot (Exodus) declares: "Six years you shall sow your land and gather in its yield; but in the seventh year you shall let it rest and lie fallow. Let the needy among your people eat of it, and what they leave let the wild beasts eat. You shall do the same with your vineyards and olive groves."[92]

Noah Webster used the agrarian metaphor in lobbying his cousin Senator Daniel Webster for passage of a copyright bill:

> Among all modes of acquiring property or exclusive ownership, the act or operation of creating or making seems to have the first claim. If anything can justly give a man an exclusive right to the occupancy and enjoyment of a thing, it must be the fact that he has made it. The right of a farmer and mechanic to the exclusive enjoyment and right of disposal of what they make or produce is never questioned.
>
> What, then, can make a difference between the produce of muscular strength and the produce of the intellect? If it should be said that the purchaser of a bushel of wheat has obtained not only the exclusive right to the use of it for food but the right to sow it and make increase and profit by it, let it be replied, this is true; but if he sows the wheat, he must sow it on his own ground or soil.[93]

Webster omits a critical fact; that he and all authors sow a great deal they have reaped from others, often quite liberally and sometimes even without acknowledgment or payment. Webster, in creating his famous blue-back speller, copied extensively without attribution or license from the dominant speller at the time, Reverend Thomas Dilworth's.[94] As H.L. Mencken would have put it, Webster was "sufficiently convinced of its merits to imitate it, even to the extent of lifting whole passages."[95] Webster similarly copied from his former employer, Thomas Dyche.[96] Large swaths from Dyche's 1707 book, *A Guide to the English Tongue*, were reproduced by Webster, down to the typeface and layout of the title page.[97] Webster was sowing widely from others, a fact that did not in the least affect his hypocrisy on the subject.

One need not invoke Bernard of Chartres' aphorism about dwarfs standing on the shoulders of giants[98] to agree that basing a grant of rights on being the first of the giants is facetious. As Chief Judge Frank Easterbrook of the United States Court of Appeals pointed out, the metaphor of the author as prime mover is not only false but harmful to other authors:

> Intellectual (and artistic) progress is possible only if each author builds on the work of others. No one invents even a tiny fraction of the ideas that make up our cultural heritage. Once a work has been written and published, any rule requiring people to compensate the author slows progress in literature and art, making useful expressions "too expensive," forcing authors to re-invent the wheel, and so on. Every work uses scraps of thought from thousands of predecessors, far too many to compensate even if the legal system were frictionless, which it isn't. Because any new work depends on others even if unconsciously, broad protection of intellectual property also creates a distinct possibility that the cost of litigation—old authors trying to get a "piece of the action" from current successes—will prevent or penalize the production of new works, even though the claims be rebuffed.[99]

It is well past time to banish a metaphor whose roots have been rejected time and time again by legislatures and high courts, and the effects of which are harmful to authors themselves.

### Thieves and Trespassers, Pirates and Parasites[100]

Describing an opponent as a thief,[101] trespasser, pirate, or a parasite evokes powerful negative reactions,[102] but as we shall see in Chapter 5, these metaphors are of necessity the flip side of another metaphor, property. Before the law says you own something, it cannot be said that those who act contrary to your wishes are thieves, trespassers, pirates, or parasites. Describing someone as a thief or trespasser must be seen, therefore, as a metaphoric step in *gaining* property rights, and not as is usually thought, the result of *having* a property right in the first place. Thus, when Jamie Kellner, then CEO of Turner Broadcasting, alleged "Any time you skip a commercial . . . you are actually stealing the program,"[103] he was making a false statement but did so in an effort to criminalize conduct that was, in fact, completely lawful. (To say nothing of how it is possible to steal one product by *not* watching another different product, owned by a different person.)

The use of the thief metaphor has been employed in many areas outside of copyright. One example of this were efforts to describe employees who make personal calls or surf the Internet while on the clock as being engaged in theft of their employer's time: "Time theft steals money as sure as someone picking your pocket. . . . It is America's biggest crime, and until its victims—the owners and managers of American decide to do something about it, we'll continue to be stolen blind."[104]

The deliberate lies found in all such metaphoric efforts are easily identified: It is not a crime at all to make a personal phone call while working; to call it a crime, much less America's "biggest crime," is a dishonest effort to metaphorically criminalize perfectly legal behavior in an effort to cast workers as immoral. As immoral, employees must be dealt with as we do all immoral people, by punishing them, by creating new penalties that do not yet exist, by creating a new property right in employers, the property right of not having your employees make personal calls or surf the Internet. The very idea that an employee could be sentenced to jail for taking a phone call from a spouse, child, or friend well illustrates the property sickness that permeates far too much of corporate America, as well as the lack of any concept of proportionality, and a distorted view of government as a modern day Pinkerton guard force.

Canadian law professor Stephen Waddams, in a well-regarded book about how we think about law, wrote that when a dispute arises about intangibles, such as copyrighted works, information, or in the above case, time,

[T]he claimant is always eager to categorize the claim as proprietary. Thus, the conduct of the defendant is apt to be described by claimants as piracy, highway robbery, and brazen theft. This is rhetoric: the taking of a photograph, the re-broadcasting of television signals, the use of confidential information, or the copying of a design cannot, in fact or law, be piracy, robbery (on or off the highway), or theft, and if it were any of these things, the rhetoric would be unnecessary. But the choice of rhetoric is significant, showing the persuasive power of proprietary concepts.[105]

Professor Waddams' point is the same as noted above: Describing someone as a thief or trespasser is a metaphoric step in *gaining* property rights, and not the result of *having* a property right in the first place. If one already *had* a property right, the property owner would sue for violation of that right and would not have to strut around like a peacock blaring loudly about "piracy." Claims of piracy are rhetorical nonsense. They turn on its head Francis Bacon's view of the role of rhetoric as applying "reason to imagination for the better moving of the will."[106]

The English House of Commons, in debating the 1911 UK Copyright Act, provides a fascinating look at this phenomenon and lawmakers' awareness of both the inaccuracy of terms like theft and piracy and their metaphoric power. At issue was a proposal to vest copyright owners with possession of the physical, unauthorized copies made by third parties. The statutory language referred to "All pirated copies" and "all plates intended to be used for the production of pirated copies."[107] Member of Parliament Frederick Handel Booth objected,[108] and proposed that the term "unauthorized" be substituted.[109] Mr. Booth explained the reason for his amendment at length, in a speech that is worth quoting:

This Amendment to leave out the word "pirated" and to insert I hope the more acceptable word "unauthorized" is an Amendment to which I attach the utmost importance. The use of th[e] word ["pirate"] is calculated to create a large amount of prejudice. The name is apt to stick even to an innocent offender who has once been charged before the court with being a pirate, even if he disproves it. The whole idea to me is objectionable. I am glad some other features have been taken out, but I am rather surprised that a distinguished author and an able statesman in framing this Bill, should have put in a word that I cannot regard in any way other than as pure slang. I certainly think a Copyright Bill which in its drafting has had all the advantages of University men, men learned in the law, and men of superior intelligence to an humble Member like myself, should have been framed with more choice language and delicate expression than to include such a word. I have been at some trouble to look up the classical authorities for the use of this word. I have no doubt this will be stale news to some hon. Gentlemen, but the first reference I can get is in "The Perfect Pilgrim," published in 1526, and there the phrase occurs—

"Ye great pirat and olde thefe, the Devyll."

I should be obliged if any hon. Member has a reference more antiquated than that if he will acquaint the House with it, but that seems to me the first time the word appears in an authentic work. In 1640, in the "Parliament of the Bees," we find the word used, as an adjective and spelt "pyratick." The later references which I would like to take are entirely confined, where they are accurate, to water, and I object entirely to the word being used with regard to transactions on land. I think it thus against all the canons of good taste in literature. In 1802, in Sampson, there is a very peculiar use of the word "pirates," which rather astonished me. It applies there to sheep:—

"No clover is sown on account of promiscuous flocks of sheep, which are emphatically called pirates."

That is a very curious use of the term. A hundred years later, in 1902, . . . the "London Daily Chronicle" introduces the word in this way:—

"Eggs were captured by rats or other water pirates."

. . .

The word is also used in Bryon's "Corsair." They were pirates singing a song of freedom and liberty. . . . But how this description can be applied to poor people standing in the gutter and attempting to sell infringing copies of works, and looking round every moment to see if they are going to be "nabbed" by a policeman who is going to prevent them earning a penny or a halfpenny by selling literature in this way in our great streets? They cannot be said in any way to represent the noble idea of a pirate. . . . After all the term "pirate" is one surrounded by romance, and I cannot understand it being applied to these people. It is almost offensive that it should be.[1110]

The popular (and as we see from Mr. Booth's speech, romantic) view of pirates was based on the so-called Golden Age of Piracy (1680–1730), in particular the decade 1715 to 1725. Reasons for the Golden Age are of interest:

One factor was the high level of legitimacy that privateering and piracy had in England. It is interesting that an island nation like England did not have a strong professional navy for a very long time. Instead, much of England's naval power rested in its merchant fleet, which was called into service as privateers. This practice goes back to 1243 when King Henry III licensed three private merchant ships to wage war on France. English national pride and wealth both raised as a result of Sir Francis Drake's privateering career against the Spanish from 1570–1587.

Another key background issue was the expansion and competition between European empires. Ever since Christopher Columbus, the Spanish had the strongest hold on the wealth of the Caribbean, Mexico, and Central America. England, Holland and France all wanted what Spain had, and employed pirates and privateers to set up colonies in the Caribbean and take by force some of Spain's wealth.

With this backdrop of legitimacy of piracy and privateering in English society, and the competition to build national wealth and empires, there were several forces that converged in the late 17th Century that built both the myth and reality of the Golden Age. First was the book that cast the image of the swashbuckling pirate that is still with us today. The book was *The Buccaneers of America* by John Esquemeling, published in Dutch in 1678, in Spanish in 1681 and in English in 1684. Esquemeling presents this book as a first hand account of the daring deeds of French, Dutch and English pirates raiding against Spanish ships and colonies in the Caribbean. This book was very popular at the time and elevated Captain Morgan and others to hero status in England. This highly romanticized work has been used as a primary source ever since in many other historical works on pirates. Because of the very positive and heroic portrayal of the pirate captains featured in this work, it both elevated the popular image of pirates at the time and forever made it difficult to sort out the historical from the mythic pirates of this time.[111]

Piracy in this era was principally a state-sponsored activity. Richard Zacks has detailed in his book, *The Pirate Hunter: The True Story of Captain Kidd*,[112] the murky allegiances between those who made their living plying the seas, and government authorities. In the American colonies, the economy relied, to a significant extent on government officials and businessmen who bankrolled and provided official protection to Eastern seaboard captains who seized foreign ships and their bounty. A 1695 report by Peter Delanoy, a New York Assembly member stated: "We have a parcel of pirates, called the Red Sea men, in these parts, who got a great booty of Arabian gold. The Governor encourages them since they make due acknowledgment. One captain gave him a ship which he sold for £800."[113]

In our era, it is the fanciful, ill-understood nature of the term "pirate" that renders it so useful in the Copyright Wars, despite the very contemporary Somali pirates seizing ships for ransom. As David Cordingly wrote in the introduction to his book, *Under the Black Flag: The Romance and the Reality of Life Among the Pirates*:

> Pirates have always been elusive figures. They came out of the blue. They attacked, they looted, and they vanished. They left no memorials or personal belongings behind. . . . And yet the lack of physical evidence has not lessened their mysterious attraction. . . . Most of us will never meet any pirates, and yet we know, or we think we know, exactly what they looked like. We learned about them when we were children. We have seen them on stage and screen. . . . They have inspired some of the finest writers of the English language, and two pirate stories in particular, *Treasure Island* and *Peter Pan*, have become literary classics. Over the years fact has merged with fiction. Inevitably some of the stories vanish into thin air when they are examined. Most people assume that pirates made their victims walk the plank because that is the fate which Captain Hook was planning for the Lost Boys, but pirates had no time for such ceremonies.[114]

Although there is nothing childlike in the Copyright Wars, the level of discourse is childish. Metaphors such as pirate are used for the very grown-up purpose of branding one side in a debate as evil, and the other as good. In the battle between good and evil, the results are as a foreordained as the end of a Hollywood swashbuckler. Of course, good guys and bad guys shift places over time, as does conduct that once was considered sensible national policy but later is considered piracy. For example, the United States is a very recent convert to the value of international protection for intellectual property. From 1790 to 1891, no protection was available under the federal copyright laws for the works of nonresident foreign authors, causing the United States to be described as "the Barbary Coast of literature," and its citizens as "buccaneers of books."[115] The reason for this lack of protection was pragmatic. For the first century of our nation, the United States built its book industry off of massive unauthorized reproductions of foreign works, principally English books. It was not until 1989 that the United States fully joined the international copyright community by adhering to the Berne Convention for the Protection of Literary and Artistic Works. Since 1989, we have acted with the zeal of Paul after his conversion (from Saul) on the road to Damascus.

The U.S. position from 1790 to 1891 was quite consistent with the approach taken by many other countries in that same and earlier periods, when "piracy" was an official governmental policy of many European governments, pursued deliberately and ruthlessly to assist local businesses. As Peter Drahos and John Braithwaite have written:

> The French and the Dutch reprinted English editions. The Dutch and the Spanish reprinted French works. Literary piracy was in many respects a much more egalitarian enterprise than piracy on the high seas. One did not have to be a great maritime power to engage in the reproduction of foreign works. Germany and Belgium were large centers for this activity. The Irish were a constant thorn in the side of English publishers. German authors suffered at the hands of the Austrians.[116]

This history of every-nation-once-had-a-policy-of-piracy aside, the current use of the term "piracy" by copyright industries is an effort to create a false equality between nonviolent (and sometimes legal) uses of copyrighted works and crimes on the high seas that involve violence. The objective in such misuse of language is to convince policy makers in the United States and around the world to increase the penalties for infringement, and to spend public funds on protecting private business interests. Unfortunately, the content industries have achieved some success in popularizing the use of "piracy" and "theft," although such misuse has been rejected by legislatures and courts. In *Dowling v. United States*, the United States Supreme Court held that copyright infringement was not "stealing" within the meaning of the National Stolen Property Act:

> [T]he Government's theory here would make theft, conversion, or fraud equivalent to wrongful appropriation of statutorily protected rights in copyright. The copyright owner, however, holds no ordinary chattel. A copyright, like other intellectual property, comprises a series of carefully defined and carefully delimited interests to which the law affords correspondingly exact protections. . . . However, "[t]his protection has never accorded the copyright owner complete control over all possible uses of his work." ... For example, § 107 of the Copyright Act "codifies the traditional privilege of other authors to make 'fair use' of an earlier writer's work." . . . Likewise, § 115 grants compulsory licenses in nondramatic musical works. Thus, the property rights of a copyright holder have a character distinct from the possessory interest of the owner of simple "goods, wares, [or] merchandise," for the copyright holder's dominion is subjected to precisely defined limits.
>
> It follows that interference with copyright does not easily equate with theft, conversion, or fraud. . . . The infringer invades a statutorily defined province guaranteed to the copyright holder alone. But he does not assume physical control over the copyright; nor does he wholly deprive its owner of its use. While one may colloquially liken infringement with some general notion of wrongful appropriation, infringement plainly implicates a more complex set of property interests than does run-of-the-mill theft, conversion, or fraud.[117]

The appeal of the pirate/thief metaphor should not be overestimated. In *Curb v. MCA Records, Inc.* a U.S. federal judge in Tennessee was quite taken in by swashbuckling visions of the Barbary Coast.[118]

> But piracy has changed since the Barbary days. Today, the raider need not grab the bounty with his own hands; he need only transmit his go-ahead by wire or telefax to start the presses in a distant land. *Subafilms* ignores this economic reality, and the economic incentives underpinning the Copyright Clause designed to encourage creation of new works, and transforms infringement of the authorization right into a requirement of domestic presence by a primary infringer. Under this view, a phone call to Nebraska results in liability; the same phone call

to France results in riches. In a global marketplace, it is literally a distinction without a difference.[119]

Resolution of the difficult issues raised in this case (concerning the extra-territorial reach of U.S. law) was not advanced by references to the Barbary Coast, and fortunately a subsequent judge came to the opposite view, in the process also rejecting the overheated metaphors employed to achieve the wrong result.[120] Judges tempted to enlist in battles between good and evil will do well to remember Justice Benjamin Cardozo's admonition that a judge "is not a knight-errant, roaming at will in pursuit of his own ideal of beauty or goodness."[121]

Authors have also used the piracy metaphor. In the nineteenth century, Mark Twain was one of the few American authors read in Canada and England, but as a result of the lack of U.S. protection for foreign works, Twain's works weren't protected in those countries, leading publishers there to reproduce his works without payment to him. Twain hit on an idea to remedy this lack of royalties: If he were a resident of Canada at a time when his then-latest book, *The Prince and the Pauper*, was published in that country, he thought his work might be protected under Canadian law. So, in 1881, he temporarily moved to Montreal. On arrival, he is reported to have told Montrealers at a banquet that "He was there to prevent a crime—to 'fence and fortify' one's property against the literary buccaneer." [122]

The current piracy campaign is intended to create a negative association with all acts not authorized by copyright owners, including uses that are clearly fair use and therefore, lawful, such as noncommercial copying for personal use. This campaign is seen in remarks made by a representative of the record industry in response to the following question by Senator Dennis DeConcini at a Joint Senate-House of Representatives oversight hearing in 1987 on the issues raised by digital audio tape:[123]

There are two kinds of home taping. Copying copyrighted material for commercial use is clearly illegal, and I will strive as Chairman of this subcommittee to protect copyright holders from piracy. But home taping for personal use is arguably "fair use" under the copyright laws. How does the proposed DAT legislation maintain thus distinction?[124]

DAT refers to digital audio tape. Senator DeConcini asked his question in response to efforts by the recording industry to prohibit DAT tape unless the industry was given the power to control it. Jason Berman, then head of the Recording Industry Association of America (RIAA) had begun his remarks with a moral panic: "DAT poses the most significant technological threat the American music industry has ever faced."[125] (It should be noted that this claim was made almost a century earlier. In 1906, John Philip Sousa made the same claim about player-pianos.[126]) After creating such a bogey-man,[127] Mr. Berman of course offered a solution—even greater rights for his clients: "At the same time it offers a significant opportunity for Congress to craft a timely and uniquely suitable legislative response as we enter what will be the next phase of the home taping problem, a problem that has worsened over the years."[128] There is no problem so grievous facing copyright owners that amendments to the Copyright Act cannot cure, apparently. No real business people share the view that law is the ultimate answer to all economic issues; better business performance is.

In any event, Mr. Berman's answer to Senator DeConcini's question about what constitutes piracy was to reject Senator DeConcini's position, and to equate noncommercial home taping for personal use with commercial, massive counterfeiting: "Thus, there is no personal use exemption, nor any fair use immunity for home taping. Contrary to the premise of the question, there is no distinction between commercial and home personal taping."[129] Senator DeConcini then asked "Can you cite any case law for the proposition that home audio taping for noncommercial purposes violates the copyright laws?"[130] Mr. Berman answered, "There is no case law on this subject because no recording company has ever asked a court to try and solve a problem that can only be resolved by Congress." Mr. Berman then added: "Were we to bring a case for infringement against the home taper, we could prevail under existing law."[131] But there *had* been a case over home taping, three years before, involving audiovisual works. That case involved the Sony Betamax VCR, a case in which RIAA filed an amicus brief before the Supreme Court urging a finding of liability. The Supreme Court rejected RIAA's view and found home taping to be fair use.

In the summer of 2008, RIAA dusted off the piracy label in fighting a decades-old battle to get radio broadcasters to pay royalties for playing records. (Radio broadcasters do pay royalties to the composers.) Congress has steadfastly refused the labels' request, convinced by broadcasters' arguments (supported by many performers) that radio play is a valuable promotional tool. Yet, despite Congress's repeated judgment over decades that the broadcasters' conduct is socially valuable and beneficial to performers, and is 100 percent lawful, the record labels have repeatedly and falsely described radio stations as being engaged in piracy.[132] Piracy, in the eyes of some copyright owners, encompasses activity that both the Supreme Court and Congress believe to be lawful. With the advent of the World Wide Web, the piracy metaphor is once again employed, and is now the dominant metaphor for all unauthorized uses on the Internet. It is, however, the same old tired, inapt metaphor, misused for the same old tired purposes: to stop innovation and to permit copyright owners to gain economic benefits that they are not entitled to legally and should not receive as a policy matter.

# FIVE

# Property as Social Relationships

Ben Franklin's view was that "Private Property ... is a Creature of Society, and is subject to the Calls of that Society, whenever its Necessities shall require it, even to the last Farthing."[1] Another Founding Father, Thomas Jefferson, wrote in 1813: "Stable ownership is the gift of social law, and is given late in the progress of society."[2] Jeremy Bentham wrote at about the same time as Jefferson, "there is no such thing as natural property[;] [property] is entirely the work of law. . . . Property and law are born together, and die together. Before laws were made there was no property; take away laws, and property ceases."[3] Franklin's, Jefferson's, and Bentham's remarks place property in the proper context—a right created by society to further social goals. Property doesn't exist in a Hobbesian state of nature; it requires a legal system to create and allocate rights.[4] As important as many property rights are, they do not exist automatically as part of the human condition, but rather as social creations, to further social goals.

Many times the social goals in conferring property status are responsive to essential attributes such as liberty (including from the government), justice, providing for one's self and family, as well as stability of the social order and economic transactions.[5] There are also times, however, when describing something as a "property" right is a political strategy to achieve a result that denies the existence of obligations to others and that seeks to avoid all government regulation.[6] Property and regulation are, after all, usually regarded by property advocates as antithetical. Indeed—and this is the power of the property as ownership metaphor—regulation of property is regarded as unprincipled, as government denying personal liberties, as taking away what rightly belongs to you and reallocating it to those who do not own the property, and who therefore do not deserve to share in its enjoyment. It is reaping what you haven't sown, thievery, and trespass. Use of the property ownership metaphor is meant to persuade us that owners of the property are supposed to have no obligations to others, precisely because to *be* an owner[7] of something means you have an obligation only to yourself: "the baseline is freedom from government restrictions on private actions."[8]

### 🎜 The Myths of Economic Freedom and Market Fundamentalism

Doing what you want with *your* property, for good, bad, or no reason, is alleged to be the very foundation of "economic freedom"—the freedom to "live one's economic life in a sphere separated from state control, reserved to the interaction of private forces."[9] It is economic freedom that permitted the Walt Disney Company in 2006 to threaten an English stonemason with a copyright infringement suit for carving on a headstone an image of Winnie the Pooh at the request of the parents of a stillborn child. It is economic freedom that permitted ASCAP to threaten to sue the Girl Scouts with a $100,000 fine and up to a year in jail if they sang songs like Happy Birthday around the campfire unless they paid a license fee. It is economic freedom that permitted the recording artist Prince to sanctimoniously demand that a mother's home video containing 20 seconds of one of his songs being played in the background while her baby danced be taken down from YouTube.

The myth of economic freedom is supported by an ideology of what has been called free market fundamentalism. Free market fundamentalism is based on the view that free markets—meaning unregulated markets—"provide the greatest possible equity and prosperity . . . that free markets maximize individual freedom, . . . are the only means to economic growth, . . . tend naturally towards a natural equilibrium, and that the best interests in a given society are achieved by allowing its participants to pursue their own self-interest."[10] President Ronald Reagan called this the "magic of the marketplace." Others invoke Adam Smith's theory that "individuals were led in the pursuit of their own self-interest by an invisible hand to pursue the nation's interest, but also that this pursuit of self-interest was a far more reliable way to ensure that the public interest would be served than any alternative," especially government intervention.[11] Joseph Stiglitz rejoined that "the invisible hand often seemed invisible because it was not there."[12]

There is an early precedent for the view that the private pursuit of copyright rights is synonymous with the public good. In James Madison's pre-Constitutional remarks in *The Federalist Number 43*, he argued for adoption of a federal copyright right:

> The utility of this power will scarcely be questioned. The copyright of authors has been solemnly adjudged, in Great Britain, to be a right of common law. The right to useful inventions seems with equal reason to belong to the inventors. *The public good fully coincides in both cases with the claims of individuals.*[13]

Madison erred in his assertion that the "right of authors had been solemnly adjudged" to be a common law (i.e., a form of natural) right in Great Britain: the English House of Lords had *rejected* the idea of a common law copyright right in its 1774 judgment in *Donaldson v. Beckett*. Nor was there any basis for a common law right for patents, a point Madison concedes with his backhanded reliance on "equal reason."[14] But on the larger economic point, the purported symbiotic relationship between private and public good, John Maynard Keynes refuted Madison's claims:

> Let us clear from the ground the metaphysical or general principle upon which, from time to time, laissez-faire has been founded. It is not true that individuals possess a prescriptive 'natural liberty' in their economic activities. There is no 'compact' conferring perpetual rights on those who Have or those who Acquire. The world is not so governed from above that private and social interests always coincide. It is not a correct deduction from the Principles of Economics that enlightened self-interest always operates in the public interest. Nor is it true that self-interest generally is enlightened; more often individuals acting separately to promote their own ends are too ignorant or too weak to attain even these.[15]

Lest one think that the relevance of Keynes' remarks is limited to the Great Depression,[16] the deep recession of 2008 and 2009 has provided us with a reminder of the fallacy of the myth that private sector interests "fully" coincide with public interests. Secretary of the Treasury Henry Paulson's decision in the winter of 2008, at the height of the credit crisis, to simply give banks the lion's share of $350 billion of public bailout money with no strings attached, no disclosure requirements, and no requirement that banks use those public funds for public rather than private purposes, must stand as the single stupidest economic decision in an Administration infamous for letting the ideology of free market fundamentalism wreak havoc on the public.[17] Comments by John C. Hope III, chairman of the Whitney Bank in New Orleans, which received $300 million in bailout money, validate Keynes' point. When asked if the bank would, in return for having received $300 million in public money, make loans to the citizens of that devastated city, Mr. Hope scoffed: "Make more loans? We're not going to change our business model or our credit policies to accommodate the needs of the public sector as they see it to have us make more loans."[18]

The dangers to society of following ideology at the expense of ignoring human nature and empirical data are most starkly revealed in Alan Greenspan's disastrous tenure as chairman of the Federal Reserve Board. During his 18 years as Fed chairman, he imposed on the U.S. economy an ideology of economic freedom, defined as markets largely devoid of government oversight, what he oxymoronically called market self-regulation. The ideological justification for this hands-off approach was the false assumption that financial firms always act rationally and, in acting rationally, they will not take irrational, self-destructive risks. Mr. Greenspan further assumed that the markets would be able to properly price extremely risky financial vehicles such as bundles of subprime mortgages. Understanding the risks, firms would act rationally by either pricing them very low or by not investing in them. We are all now suffering from Mr. Greenspan's false assumptions and failed ideology.

In his written testimony before the United States House of Representatives, Committee on Oversight and Government Reform, on October 23, 2008, at first Mr. Greenspan attempted to blame mere data input for his profound errors: "The whole intellectual edifice . . . collapsed in the summer of last year because the data inputted into the risk management models generally covered only the past two decades, a period of euphoria. Had instead the models been fitted more appropriately to historic periods of stress, capital requirements would have been much higher and the financial world would be in far better shape today, in my judgment." Of course, the data wasn't really incomplete; it was there all along. Mr. Greenspan *chose* not to look at it; instead, he *chose* only to look at a period described as euphoric, a euphoria he himself was partly responsible for by his hands-off approach.

Under questioning from committee chairman Henry Waxman, Mr. Greenspan admitted that his errors arose not from incomplete data, but instead from dogged adherence to his ideology:

> *Mr. Waxman.* The question we have for you is, you had an ideology. This is your statement: "I do have an ideology. My judgment is that free competitive markets are by far the unrivaled way to organize economies. We tried regulation; none meaningfully worked." That was your quote. You had the authority to prevent irresponsible lending practices that led to the subprime mortgage crisis. You were advised to do so by many others. And now our whole economy is paying the price. Do you feel your ideology pushed you to make decisions that you wish you had not made?
>
> *Mr. Greenspan.* I found a flaw in the models that I perceived as the critical functioning structure that defines how the world works.[19]

The most damning part of Mr. Greenspan's testimony was his confession that companies will *not* always act in their own best interest, much less that of the public: "I made a mistake in presuming that the self-interests of organizations, specifically banks and others, were such as that they were best capable of protecting their own shareholders and their equity in the firms." Mr. Greenspan's error arose not from a paucity of data, but from the blinders of his ideology, which he followed even though there was copious evidence that companies were acting contrary to that ideology, and dangerously so. Those who did not adhere to Mr. Greenspan's ideology were able to see the calamity coming and advised Mr. Greenspan to prevent it, but he ignored them.

Copyright is suffering from the same false ideology—one that has led to an irrational exuberance that copyright owners will always act in their own best interests, and in acting in their own interests will automatically be acting in society's best interests too. What is good for GM is good for the country, as GM president Charles E. Wilson testified in his confirmation hearings to become Secretary of Defense in 1953.[20] But what is good for copyright owners is not always good for the country. As a monopoly, copyright vests copyright owners with an easy, government-created ability to act in anti-competitive and anti-innovative ways, ways that are harmful to the public interest. History tells us that copyright owners routinely act in such ways. The copyright industries will act in the public interest only when we insist that they do. Regulation in the public interest is therefore a precondition to the copyright system functioning properly; regulation for the public interest should thus not be viewed as an exception, but as the norm. This is not to suggest that the copyright industries are venal; quite the contrary, it is to argue that they are all too normal. Distorted incentives lead to distorted conduct; because our current copyright laws provide rights and remedies that are far beyond what is necessary for copyright owners to recoup their investments and make respectable profits, and instead give copyright owners powerful weapons to quash competition and control consumers, we should not be surprised that the copyright industries utilize those weapons (and then some). In this respect, the copyright industries are no different than Wall Street or any other company placed in a similar situation.

In his inaugural speech President Obama called for an era of new responsibility toward ourselves and toward others, an era in which we appeal "not to our easy instincts but to our better angels."[21] Those better angels are found in the recognition that our lives as well as our copyright laws are comprised of social relationships and not property relationships. Social relationships look to advance the public good, a good that includes protecting authors, not as privileged citizens, but as one of the many, and where the good of the many is put above the good of the few.

## 🕮 Social Relationships

The purpose of the economic freedom myth is to launder self-interest as enlightened conduct, and to thereby ensure that the government does not intervene through regulation to benefit the public good. How, after all, can the government improve on the enlightened judgment of the private sector? It can't under the myth, and so the role of government is simply to stay out of the way, much like some believe that after having created the world, God rested on a perpetual seventh day. Of course in the case of copyright, the government has to intervene in a very dramatic fashion at the outset by creating the rights themselves and by imposing penalties for their violation, but having done so, it is argued that the government should step back and let the private sector work its magic. We now know that letting the private sector operate according to its own desires, its own sense of responsibilities, and its own social conscience does not work. Free market fundamentalism is dead but not before it destroyed much of the worlds' economies. The evidence demonstrates that copyright free market fundamentalism works the same way. Because copyright is created solely by the government, the government *must* shape its contours as it sees fit to achieve copyright's social objectives; doing so is not adventitious, but is instead an obligation of governments. Copyright is not an end in itself, but instead an end to a social objective, furthering learning.

Copyright owners have attempted to avoid regulation by describing their right as "intellectual *property*." The purpose of advocating something as a property right is to take it outside of the need for any empirical, social justification. As a property right we do not ask about incentives, and we do not ask whether the property interest benefits the public. Property simply is and need not be justified. Those who own property rights are entitled to hunt down unauthorized users as free-riders, as criminals, as a threat to polite society just as surely as who break into our homes or steal our cars. Once something is deemed property, it is irrelevant that an unauthorized use does not negatively impact the copyright owner, or even that the unauthorized use may be of great societal benefit. It is enough that property is involved and that it has been "taken."

Property is, however, *never* "an extra-political institution, free of social choices. . . . Property is quintessentially and absolutely a social institution. Every conception of property reflects . . . those choices that we—as a society—have made."[22] As Professor Joseph Singer wrote in his excellent book, *Entitlement: The Paradoxes of Property*:

> Although property seems to be about power over things, it has long been understood that property rights (especially legal rights) describe not only relations between owners and things but relations among people—between owners and nonowners and among owners. Each property right involves not merely the owner of the land but also a decision, in the words of Laura Underkuffler, to "reward the claims of some people to finite and critical goods, and to deny the claims to the same goods by others." Property represents a decision to use the power of the state to allocate the thing to the owner and to prevent others from using the thing without the owner's consent.[23]
>
> [P]roperty is not just individual entitlement, but a social institution involving many owners. In practice, the interests of some owners impinge upon and may interfere with the interests of other owners.

When this happens, the legal rights of one owner must be limited to protect the legitimate interests of the other. Property rights cannot be fixed entitlements but are contingent, to some extent, on the social context in which they are exercised.[24]

John Brewer and Susan Staves have similarly written: "Although the idea of private property suggests individual autonomy, property is necessarily relational, conceivable only in the context of communities of people; property rights are rights 'against' other people, rights to exclude them from the use and enjoyment of the thing owned."[25] Property did not exist prior to the Social Contract, nor is it superior to it; property is a creature of society, created for the benefit of society. That said, scholars have long recognized the power of mythology of property as an absolute right of individuals.[26] Professor Laura Underkuffler was written:

> [The] mythical belief about the nature of the right to property protection is rooted in a deep human psychological need. Property rights in their various forms structure our daily lives, our human relationships, and our assurance of physical survival. They dictate our ability to both realize our dreams and avoid our fears. We believe that property rights are free-standing, individually protective, and socially a contextual because we want to—we need to—believe this myth.[27]

But saying something is so doesn't make it so, no matter how long or how many times the falsity is repeated.

## ⅋  Use of Metaphors in Establishing Claims to Property Rights

Professor Underkuffler was principally referring to situations where we believe we have absolute rights, only to find them regulated.[28] But what about situations where one merely asserts a property right, where the claim (or the scope of the claim) has not been recognized, and therefore does not in fact exist yet? Before the law declares you have a right, you have only hot air. *How* you get the law to declare you the victor is the real trick. There are usually two elements to pulling off the trick: (1) you argue your claim is virtuous, and (2) you simultaneously argue competing claims are not virtuous.

It is here that metaphors are impressed into the battle, forming the shock troops for establishing virtue and vice. As noted in Chapter 4, describing an opponent as a thief, trespasser, pirate, or a parasite evokes powerful negative reactions. But before the law says you own something, and much less as property, it cannot be said that those who act contrary to your wishes are scofflaws. To the contrary, they may be regarded favorably, as stalwart protectors of the rights of the public against the greedy octopus reach of evil monopolists out to strangle society (to continue metaphoric excesses).

Which label is assigned to which side is an intensely political process, the outcome of which may be codified in law. After such codification, the victor is wont to ascribe its victory to preexisting rights and the inherent justness of its claim, rather than to political muscle or sheer luck. To the victor goes the spoils, including the rewriting of history. As we shall see in the next section, when it comes to the description of something as "property," scholars have long noted that "we shall be less wrong in assuming that the pedigree was invented to account for the fact of possession than in attributing the fact of possession to the virtues of the pedigree."[29]

## Blackstone and the Nature of Property

The characterization of property as the exclusive dominion of the property owner may be traced back to the single most quoted remark about property, that of Sir William Blackstone[30] in his famous *Chronicles on the Laws of England*, published in four volumes between 1765 and 1769.[31] Blackstone wrote with seeming enthusiasm that "[t]here is nothing which so generally strikes the imagination, and engages the affections of mankind, as the right of property; or that sole and despotic dominion which one man claims and exercises over the external things of the world, in total exclusion of the right of any other individual in the universe."[32] This definition never reflected then contemporary English or U.S. law, and was in fact metaphoric.[33] Professor Robert Gordon, in a study of the actual state of property law in Blackstone's time, wrote:

What strikes the backward-looking observer as curious is simply this: that in the midst of such a lush flowering of absolute dominion talk in theoretical and political discourse, English legal doctrines should contain so very few plausible instances of absolute individual rights.

Moreover, it is curious that English and colonial social practices contained so many property relations that seem to traduce the ideal of absolute individual rights.[34]

Professor Carol Rose has helpfully explained the disconnect between Blackstone's rhetoric and reality.[35] First, however, we must give the full quote from Blackstone in which the "sole and despotic" metaphor appears, something that is very rarely done:

> There is nothing which so generally strikes the imagination, and engages the affections of mankind, as the right of property; or that sole and despotic dominion which one man claims and exercises over the external things of the world in total exclusion of the right of any other individual in the universe. And yet there are very few, that will give themselves the trouble to consider the original and foundation of this right. Pleased as we are with the possession, we seem afraid to look back to the means by which it was acquired, as if fearful of some defect in our title; or at best we rest satisfied with the decision of the laws in our favor, without examining the reason or authority upon which those laws have been built. We think it enough that our title is derived by the grant of the former proprietor, by descent from our ancestors, or by the last will and testament of the dying owner; not caring to reflect that (accurately and strictly speaking) there is no foundation in nature or in natural law, why a set of words upon parchment should convey the dominion of land; why the son should have a right to exclude his fellow-creatures from a determinate spot of ground, because his father had done so before him; or why the occupier of a particular field or of a jewel, when lying on his death-bed, and no longer able to maintain possession, should be entitled to tell the rest of the world which of them should enjoy it after him.[36]

Blackstone's remarks are similar to those of Augustine Birrell, made 134 years later (quoted below in full in Chapter 6):

> The origin of property, of exclusive ownership, is one of the subjects about which our predecessors in title loved to discourse at large after a fashion more ingenious than historical.
>
> Occupancy and Labour are the mythical parents of Property, but we shall be less wrong in assuming that the pedigree was invented to

account for the fact of possession than in attributing the fact of possession to the virtues of the pedigree.[37]

Blackstone's efforts in the Commentaries were precisely such a mythic inquiry, but as Professor Rose pointed out, it was largely unsuccessful. Blackstone, like philosophers before and after him, merely adopted and adapted whatever myth best suited his own belief system; in Blackstone's case it was a belief that no one would labor on the land or create things if someone else could "seise upon and enjoy the product of [another's] industry, art, and labor."[38] It was, as Blackstone, concluded: "Necessity [that] begat property," and not natural law. He also recognized that property had to be created by "civil society," meaning government.[39] Despite Blackstone's attempt to root his beliefs in practices of the ancients, "At the end of Blackstone's short story, the institution of property is as mysterious as it was at the beginning."[40]

Since Blackstone's "sole and despotic" language was not intended to be descriptive, why has it held such power for almost 250 years? Because the metaphor of property as necessarily entailing exclusivity is an extremely powerful idea, an idea that justifies vesting individuals (and now mostly corporations) with mastery both over themselves and over others. By describing copyright as a private property right, proponents of the description hope to get policy makers and courts to believe that only private, and not public rights are implicated.[41] Once the debate is limited to the private sphere, the analysis will be made according to tried and true binary metaphors: creators (wearing the white hats) versus pirates and thieves (wearing black hats). Copyright is, however, never a private affair; it is, as we shall now see, always a social issue.

# Why Classifying Copyright as Property Is Important in the Copyright Wars

## # Copyright as Social Relations, Not as a Property Right

In the last chapter we explored the concept of property as social relations, rather than as dominion over things. At issue is not whether social relationships are the essence of property—they clearly are—but why are the interests of one social group favored over another? What social objective is being furthered by the decision to privilege one particular group? Also not at issue is not whether to regulate, because all property constitutes regulation; the issue is "what kind of property system to create in the first place."[1] Property and regulation are not "mortal enemies. In fact, private property cannot exist without regulation."[2]

The advantage in regarding copyright as a system of social relationships is that it focuses attention where it belongs: in mediating conflicts *within* that system, and not, as the property as ownership model and the Copyright Wars erroneously do, by positing ownership as the natural state of affairs, and by regarding every effort to regulate for the public interest to be a hostile act that must be ferociously fought against as if it is an existential threat. The denial of copyright as a set of social relationships, and advocacy of copyright instead as a property right is simply an effort to switch the debate from the merits of an issue to platitudes. One of the most frequent platitudes is the call for treating copyright equivalently to real estate: copyright is property, and ergo must be treated just like real property. For example, in 1982, during hearings on home taping by consumers using VCRs, Jack Valenti, head of the Motion Picture Association of America, testified:

> No matter the lengthy arguments made, no matter the charges and the counter-charges, no matter the tumult and the shouting, reasonable men and women will keep returning to the fundamental issue,

the central theme which animates this entire debate: Creative property owners must be accorded the same rights and protection resident in all other property owners in the nation. That is the issue. That is the question. And that is the rostrum on which this entire hearing and the debates to follow must rest.[3]

Mr. Valenti was attempting to radically reframe the nature of the issue before Congress, which was far less ambitious—whether manufacturers of videocassette recorders should be prevented from marketing the recorders because those recorders could be used to copy, for time-shifting purposes, motion pictures broadcast on free over-the-air television. The Supreme Court held two years later that the manufacturers were not liable because consumers were entitled to time-shift under the fair use privilege. The trial court had held to the same effect in 1979, but the court of appeals had reversed that decision in 1981, only to later be reversed itself by the Supreme Court. The backdrop to the hearings and Mr. Valenti's remarks was an effort to legislatively codify the intervening court of appeals opinion. Mr. Valenti's purpose in seeking to equate "creative property" with "real property" was to shift the debate away from the actual legal principles governing the dispute and toward a rhetorical ground from which he thought his clients could prevail. The idea that Congress could meaningfully decide whether to permit consumers to tape over-the-air broadcasts for time shifting purposes by reference to principles governing real estate was farcical (and not at all reasonable as Mr. Valenti claimed), but was advanced with a straight face.

That Mr. Valenti was seeking to create a rhetorical advantage and not advancing a descriptive argument about law is seen in both sides of the equation Mr. Valenti was making: creative property = real property. As we saw in Chapter 4, for its entire history in the United States, copyright has never been regarded as a property right. Instead, copyright has always been a regulatory privilege granted by the grace of Congress (or in other common law countries by Parliament), as a very limited grant originally just for literary works, and conditioned on rigorous compliance with formalities. The number of authors who sought protection for their works was historically quite small. Although Congress gradually did away with formalities, at the same time it dramatically increased the number of compulsory licenses. A compulsory, or as it is also called, a statutory license, means that copyright owners do not have the ability to object to or stop uses covered by the license and are instead limited to receipt of a statutory license fee.[4] This lack of exclusivity, the lack of ability to say no and to enforce that refusal in the courts is the antithesis of a central tenet of the classical theory of property rights excludability.

Nor, for that matter has real property ever been regulation free. There are limits on use of your property for purposes that injure others, zoning laws that restrict what you can build and how, easements for the benefit of utilities or local municipalities, to say nothing of ancient rules eliminating the ability to convey your land in the future, such as the rule against perpetuities. Real property, like all property, is created by society for societal purposes. Mr. Valenti's view of both general property and copyright was a fiction, a rhetorical play at odds with reality, advanced for purely political purposes.

Professor (later Judge) Benjamin Kaplan identified the precise rhetorical fallacy argued by Mr. Valenti 15 years earlier in his book, *An Unhurried View of Copyright*:

> To say that copyright is "property," although a fundamentally unhistorical statement, would not be badly misdescriptive if one were prepared to acknowledge that there is property and property, with few if any legal consequences extending uniformly to all species and that in practice the lively questions ought to be whether certain consequences ought to attach to a given piece of property in given circumstances ... but characterizations in grand terms ... seems of little value: [W]e may as well go directly to the policies actuating or justifying the particular determinations.[5]

In other words, skip the labels and figure out instead what conduct and policies we seek to encourage or discourage. Mr. Valenti was hardly the first to make the false equation between copyright and real property, and he certainly was not the last; it is quite common today.[6] The analogy to real property is a poor one. Real property is concerned with what are in economics jargon called negative externalities—negative effects on the owner of the real property from unauthorized use by others. This concern is in turn based on the zero sum nature of real property—if you are using my land to my exclusion, I can't use it. Copyright is not excludable. If you copy and use this book without my permission, you do not deprive me or anyone else from reading it. Indeed, the very lack of excludability of copyrighted works is the reason many give for having copyright in the first place. Unless we create a government-backed right to stop those who use a copyrighted work without the author's permission, authors will be powerless to prevent economically damaging uses, and at least some authors will not write anymore. This rationale of nonexcludability is fatally inconsistent with treating copyrighted works the same as excludable real property.

## ✎ The Ahistorical Claim that Copyright Is a Natural Property Right

In Chapter 5, we discussed the positive law basis of property, property is not a natural right that exists outside of the society whose laws and practices create it. Without a society that creates and enforces rights, there is no property. Copyright is, in common law countries without question, purely a creature of statute, a regulatory privilege created by legislatures for specific goals—in the United States to promote learning.[7] Yet, it has been common for advocates of copyright owners to describe their claims as resting on natural law springing from the mere genius of the author, beginning most prominently with Sir William Blackstone. One may describe this view as the "Neo Blackstone" approach to copyright, because it is based on Blackstone's "sole and despotic" view of property, reviewed in Chapter 5.

As noted in Chapter 5, Blackstone did not apply his "sole and despotic" view of property to copyright. Blackstone's involvement in copyright issues came as a private lawyer representing the London publishers in "The Battle of the Booksellers."[8] That battle, fought out in the courts among publishers, not authors, was over whether copyright was a perpetual, common law right existing as a matter of natural justice, or instead, whether it was a creature of the Parliament, a matter of statutory grace. The House of Lords rejected Blackstone and the publisher's arguments in 1774, but during the debates much rhetoric was invoked claiming copyright was a form of property. The significance of metaphorically characterizing copyright as a property right was pointed out more than a century ago by a wonderful Victorian man of letters and member of Parliament, Augustine Birrell, in a series of lectures he gave in 1898.

Mr. Birrell reviewed the debates at the end of the eighteenth century in England in the first of the copyright wars. In pooh-poohing those claims, Mr. Birrell nevertheless recognized the power their invocation usually had:

> The reason[] th[is] question[] was asked . . . was this—Certain rights over things amounting in the aggregate to a more or less complete exclusion of others than the owner from participating, save by consent, in their enjoyment had in the Western World become recognised as property. . . . The origin of property, of exclusive ownership, is one of the subjects about which our predecessors in title loved to discourse at large after a fashion more ingenious than historical.
>
> Occupancy and Labour are the mythical parents of Property, but we shall be less wrong in assuming that the pedigree was invented to account for the fact of possession than in attributing the fact of possession to the virtues of the pedigree. But whatever its origin, the Western World has throughout its long history shown an ever increasing disposition to recognise the right of individuals to the exclusive possession of certain things, and these rights it has clustered together, recognised, venerated, worshipped, under the word property.
>
> To be allowed to enter this sacrosanct circle is a great thing. None but the oldest families need apply. . . . Once inside this circle your rights were supposed in some romantic way to be outside the chill region of positive law—they were based upon natural rights, existing previously to the social contract, and without which Society was deemed impossible.
>
> Neither were these romantic conceptions mere jeux d'esprit. Consequences flowed from them. If your right to turn your neighbor off your premises, to keep your things to yourself—was property, and therefore ex hypothesi founded on natural justice, he who sought to interfere with your complete dominion was a thief or a trespasser.[9]

The effort to describe copyright as property is intended to invoke ancient entitlement to powerful rights of exclusion, rights granted automatically as a member of the oldest families. The differences between copyright and land are, however, far greater than the similarities, if any. With land, we can chart its metes and bounds by precise measurements; we can visibly inspect it; and use by one person usually precludes use by others. With copyright, although we can examine the material embodiment of a novel in a book, we cannot chart the scope of the copyright in the novel because the copyright right itself is abstract, and its scope cannot be known until a judge or jury issues a decision.

The equation of copyright to land through the use of the property metaphor obliterates these distinctions, and it is by virtue of that obliteration that part of the danger arises. With land, there are physical realities that can serve as protection against expansion of rights; for example, we can see that if the owner of land is permitted to use his or her land in a certain manner, neighbors or the public at large will be harmed in palpable ways. With copyright, by contrast, expansion of rights occurs in an abstract world that we cannot see, cannot feel, and cannot easily calculate the resulting harm from. The metaphor of copyright as an intangible derivation of ancient tangible property is inapt and dangerously so.[10]

## 🎞 Authors and Trickle Down Economics

Blackstone's view of copyright as a natural property right vesting in the author as a result of the author's genius was of a peculiar sort. First of all, as applied to the scope of copyright, Blackstone took a very liberal view toward the ability of others to appropriate from the author's work without permission or compensation. We see this in the following report of the 1774 opinion in *Hawkesworth v. Newbery*, in which it was held that abridgments (we would call them condensations today), might not violate copyright owners' rights:

> The Lord Chancellor was of opinion that this abridgement of the work was not any violation of the author's property whereon to ground an injunction. That to constitute a true and proper abridgement of a work the whole must be preserved in its sense: And then the act of abridgement is an act of understanding, employed in a carrying a large work into a smaller corpus, and rendering it less expensive, and more convenient both to the time and use of the reader. Which made an abridgement in the nature of a new and meritorious work.
>
> That this had been done by Mr. Newbery, whose edition might be read in a fourth of the time, and all the substance preserved, and conveyed in language as good or better than the original, and in

a more agreeable and useful manner. That [the Lord Chancellor] had consulted Mr. Justice Blackstone whose knowledge and skill in the profession was universally known, and who as an author had done honour to his country.

That they had spent some hours together, and were agreed that an abridgement, where the understanding is employed in retrenching unnecessary and uninteresting circumstances, which rather deaden the narration, is not an act of plagiarism upon the original work, nor against any property of the author in it, but an allowable and meritorious work. And that this abridgement of Mr. Newberry's falls within these reasons and descriptions.[11]

Unauthorized abridgments represented an incursion into authors' potential markets (today we would call the market a derivative market), and allowing them resulted from a view of copyright as far from sole, despotic dominion as one could imagine—a third party came along, took the author's work, added no new authorship, but rather cut here and there and then sold the work to the public for a cheaper price. Such acts were deemed "meritorious" and not "plagiarism," even by Blackstone, a unflagging partisan for authors.

The sense in which Blackstone regarded authors' property rights was as a commodity, not as an aspect of the author's personhood, even though, like Cyrano de Bergerac, it was the author as a person who was advanced as the justification for the rights. To Blackstone's clients (book publishers, and *not* the vaunted authors over which he poetically weeped), copyrights were commodities, bought and sold as such typically by "congers." Even among the relatively small number of London booksellers, a small subset benefited the most from the 1710 Statute of Anne, a subset that had seen the handwriting on the wall before passage and figured out how to best not only authors (a given), but also their fellow publishers (not a given). As Russell Sanjek explains:

When it became evident that the House of Commons was at long last of a mood to pass [the Statute of Anne], the publishers were almost solely motivated by their concern for the continued use of the recently devised scheme known as a "conger." This was a pool of fewer than twenty booksellers, combined to participate in profits from mutual ownership of valuable publications. The name came from the eel that swallowed up all small underwater life within its reach, usually far beyond its seven- or eight-foot length. Like that marine creature, such combines fattened and grew off their neighbors, picking up copyrights for very little at trade sales and auctions from which nonmembers were barred. Production costs were then prorated among the members, each participant taking his quota of the finished edition of printed sheets and binding them himself. Such a partnership had its own peculiar trade benefits. Benjamin Tooke, one of three stationers who had petitioned the crown for a copyright law in 1707, was the warehouse keeper of the company's supplies and was several times found guilty of buying paper and paying for it out of guild money, but withholding parts of the shipment for a conger's use. Members of a conger got finished sheets at a special rate, well below that charged others, and as a result the book trade had fallen into conger control. In 1704 alone, one such group distributed 47,000 books, considerably in excess of the Stationers' Company's own English Stock monopoly of almanacs and psalters.[12]

This power persisted into the nineteenth century. Aside from the clear monopolistic objective, another of the purposes of the congers was to share both risk and expense by dividing copyrights, no differently than traders divided shipments of rum. Copyrights were sold only at trade sales, and admittance to these was strictly controlled to those in the club. It was the exclusion of the Scottish bookseller, Alexander Donaldson,[13] from the sale of the rights of James Thomson's bucolic poem, *The Seasons*,[14] that led to the first copyright wars and to the book publishers' loss in the 1774 House of Lords' decision in *Donaldson v. Beckett*, which ultimately weakened the conger system. But the congers would have been impossible without a prevailing legal attitude that works of authorship were commodities, produced by author-laborers who should be free to sell their goods for next to nothing just as industrial workers sold their labor for producing widgets for impoverished wages. We forget, in an age of royalties, that such royalties are a relatively recent development. For most of the history of copyright, authors were paid a small, one-time fee.

The reality of authors as little different from a cow whom once purchased can be milked every morning was too stark to be publicly stated, and thus had to be disguised by a far different and loftier political theory that asserted free alienability would benefit society as a whole: Free trade, it was said, would increase the number of available goods. To be effective, the theory had to be adopted as law, in the period in question by English common law judges. Blackstone himself emphasized the importance of free alienability: "It is an object indeed of utmost importance in this free and commercial country, to lay as few restraints as possible upon the transfer of possessions from hand to hand."[15] These sunny expressions of the value of free trade omit the efforts of London book publishers to squash not only competitors but to also (successfully) prevent authors from directly selling their works to the public. As Russell Sanjek has written: "An author attempting to publish a work would find that the bookseller invariably took the copyright. Authors who kept their copyrights would find that their works were unaccountably unsaleable."[16] The first copyright war was fought entirely among publishers; authors were nowhere to be seen, and not only because the early suits involved authors long dead—authors were simply not a consideration, having sold their rights for a one time fee, they were out of the picture entirely.[17]

The current situation for authors is worse now in a number of respects than it was in Blackstone's day, because of our use of the work for hire doctrine to strip creators of their very status as author. Section 201(b) of the U.S. Copyright Act reads: "In the case of a work made for hire, the employer or other person for whom the work was prepared is considered the author for purposes of this title, and, unless the parties have expressly agreed otherwise in a written instrument signed by them, owns all of the rights comprised in the copyright." The concept of work for hire extends well beyond works created by 9-to-5 employees and sweeps in works by many independent contractors. In 1999, in the middle of the night, with no hearings or notice, the Recording Industry Association of America (RIAA) through the chief counsel of the House intellectual property subcommittee (and who was very shortly thereafter hired by RIAA) snuck in an amendment to this definition to treat recording artists as work for hire employees of their labels. The bill passed and was signed into law. When recording artists found out what happened, they went ballistic, and a shame-faced Congress was forced to repeal the law the following year.[18] The purpose for the amendment was to deprive recording artists of their right to terminate assignments they had previously made. In 1978, Congress, concerned about corporations forcing authors to give away all rights for the entire duration of the life of the author plus a fifty-year term, gave authors a second bite at the apple. After a set period of time (the period depends on when the work was created), authors can terminate their assignment of rights and get their copyright back free and clear.

There is, however, an exception for works created for hire: Creators for hire do not enjoy a termination right. RIAA's effort was an after-the-fact effort to treat recording artists, including very famous ones, as mere employees of their labels and therefore to strip them, retroactively, of their statutory right to get their copyright back through terminating their transfer.[19] Efforts to treat nonemployees as employees for copyright purposes—but not as employees for benefits such as insurance, health benefits, and vacations—is not limited to the recording industry, and are in fact, quite common. If copyright is a natural right, corporations' view of authors as employees is most unnatural: authors must content themselves with the trickles from the trickle down of rights their contracts permit. At the very same time, when the introduction of compact discs resulted in resuscitation of the record industry and a large infusion of money, the labels contractually reduced performing artists' royalty rates, and added on substantial "new technology" and other costs. As a result, artists' share of the CD bonanza was marginalized, while the labels rolled in the dough. This disparity between the amount artists and the labels received was, as Sony executive Mickey Schulhof observed, a not "insignificant reason for the overall improvement in the record industry,"[20] with the record industry being defined narrowly as the labels, not the actual creators.

Nor are performing artists faring better in the digital age. With compact discs, performing artists receive approximately 9 percent of the sales revenue: the labels receive 46 percent, and retailers 45 percent. With digital downloads, performing artists' share is reduced to 8 percent, record labels share is increased 22 percent to 68 percent, digital service providers receive 15 percent and credit card companies receive 9 percent, one percent more than the performing artists whose creativity after all is the reason all the money is made in the first place.[21]

These figures are from a report by Andrew Gowers to the then Exchequer of the Her Majesty's Treasury, Gordon Brown, now the Prime Minister of the United Kingdom. Mr. Gowers noted that even for those performing artists who do receive royalties, the "distribution of income [is] highly skewed, with most income going to the relatively small number of highly successful artists whose work is still commercially available after 50 years."[22] He also observed: "Evidence suggests that most sound recordings sell in the ten years after release, and only a very small percentage continue to generate income, both from sales and royalty payments, for the entire duration of copyright do not sell for 50 years."[23] Based on the inability of a longer term to help the vast majority of performing artists at all, and the harm to the public, Mr. Gowers recommended against lengthening the term of copyright for sound recordings. Mr. Brown accepted the recommendation. Upon becoming Prime Minister, however, and after intensive lobbying from celebrity musicians, Mr. Brown changed course 180 degrees, led by his star-struck Secretary of State for Culture, Media and Sport, Andy Burnham, who rather than dispute any of the empirical data in the Gowers report, referred to a previously unknown "moral case at the heart of copyright law."[24]

President Barack Obama in his campaign cogently noted that "For eight years, we've been told that the way to a stronger economy was to give huge tax breaks to corporations and the wealthiest Americans, and somehow prosperity would trickle down. We now know the truth. It didn't work. Instead of trickling down, pain has trickled up."[25] So too an extra twenty years of copyright royalties paid by the public: Mr. Burnham cannot disguise the fact that the benefits he seeks will go exclusively to the wealthiest, with credit card companies receiving more than those performing artists his heart swells for. Where's the morality in that?

### ℳ Copyright Now as Then: *Plus ça Change, Plus C'est la Même Chose*

We are now in another era when the "property talk" about copyright is strong, but why? The answer must, of course, be found in current conditions, not those of Blackstone's eighteenth-century London publishers. But the reasons are the same then as now: A concentration of ownership of copyright in a (relatively) small number of companies, who in turn are part of larger conglomerates. Congers have been replaced by conglomerates.

There are only four major record labels in the world: Sony/BMG, Universal Music Group, Warner Music Group, and EMI. Of these four, only EMI and Warner are not part of larger conglomerates, and Warner was itself only sold off from TimeWarner in 2003 to an investment group.

These four labels control more than 80 percent of the U.S. market and approximately 75 percent of the world market. The same figures hold for music publishing. There are only six major U.S. motion picture studios: Paramount Pictures, Sony Pictures Entertainment, Inc., Universal City Studios, LLLP, Walt Disney Studios Motion Pictures, Twentieth Century Fox Film Corporation, and Warner Bros. Entertainment Inc. All six are part of a larger conglomerate: Paramount is part of Viacom, Inc.; Fox is a part of News Corporation; Universal is part of General Electric; Sony Pictures is part of Sony Corporation; Walt Disney is part of ABC, and Warner is part of TimeWarner. Owning and exploiting assets is what these large conglomerates do, and the greater the control over the assets that can be obtained, it is believed the greater the profit margins will be. Yet, the belief that control equals profits has been refuted in the only arena that counts—the marketplace. Consumers want choice, not control. In the past, in the world of physical hard copies, consumers lacked the ability to break through the controls put in place by corporate copyright owners, nor did they have much incentive to do so. Why bother duplicating a videocassette if you could rent it for $3? Why copy an album if you could buy a cassette tape for $4? With the Internet, the public now has the ability to break through those controls, and with a dearth of lawful selections, an incentive to do so.

Efforts to regain this lost control are couched in terms of "respecting property rights," but the goal is no different from the early eighteenth-century congers—copyright is a commodity, bought and sold like all others, with little or no thought to authors or to consumers. The effect is as bad on the twenty-first century public as it was on the eighteenth-century public—artificially high prices, tight control over what can be read, heard, or seen, and a dramatic shrinking of the public domain and the ability to engage in unauthorized uses even in the creation of new works of benefit to the public. As Professor Mark Lemley has written:

> [W]hat is going on here is not the product of some eighteenth-century vision of authorship with unfortunate consequences. Rather, it is a wholesale attack on the public domain in intellectual property law. The attack does not simply consist of multiple efforts to whittle away the scope of that domain for the benefit of those who get to own pieces of it, though that is certainly part of it. Rather, the attack is more fundamental—a challenge to the very idea of the public domain as an intrinsic part of intellectual property law.[26]

Lest one think Professor Lemley is exaggerating, consider only three laws that Congress has recently passed: (1) the extension of copyright term in 1998 for another twenty years for existing and new works, resulting in twenty years of works from around the world not falling into the public domain; (2) the retroactive protection for foreign works that *had* fallen into the public domain in 1994, a grant that went back to 1919; and, (3) the abolition of the renewal requirement in 1992 for works first published between 1964 and 1977. This change had the effect of saving from the public domain approximately 90 percent of the works that would not have been renewed and therefore would have been in the public domain. In a mere six years, then, as a result of only these three amendments, millions of works were either prevented from falling into the public domain or were actually "pulled out" of the public domain and given protection again. The 1998 Digital Millennium Copyright Act completes the picture by giving copyright owners control over the design of consumer goods and digital forms of distribution. Copyright has become the mechanism to eliminate consumer choice, innovation, and the creation of culture. Copyright is now a serious impediment to technological and social progress.

## Copyright as a Statutory Tort

Courts in the United States have uniformly held copyright infringement to be a statutory tort, and not a violation of a property right; that is, copyright provides remedies for the injury caused for violating conduct protected by the statute.[27] Torts are directed to conduct, not things. Torts can be based on negligent behavior, or, in the case of copyright, strict liability, meaning copyright owners need not prove an infringer deliberately set out to cause injury. Tort law is premised on a duty of care, usually determined after the fact through case law. Property, by contrast, starts from the premise that someone already owns something (either a "tangible thing," or in more modern times an "intangible thing"), and that something has been wrongly taken away. In the case of real estate, one can measure the metes and bounds of the land. In the case of a car, one can take pictures of it, describe the make and model, and trace the vehicle identification number (VIN). Not true with intangibles such as copyright, which cannot be seen or measured. Instead, the scope of copyright is always determined after the fact, by court decision: Are two movies substantially similar to each other? Is a parody a privileged parody or an infringing parody? There is no way of knowing until a judge or jury tells us. It is an odd form of property that does not exist (to the extent claimed) until after litigation.

The difference between property and torts has never been water tight,[28] however, and indeed for some purposes, such as the ability to assign an interest in a copyright or patent, or to bequeath them, such interests are categorized as "personal property."[29] A famous article, published in 1972 by Guido Calabresi and Douglas Melamed, *Property Rules, Liability Rules, and Inalienability: One View of the Cathedral*,[30] offered a theory for creating a unified theory of entitlements merging tort and property, but although the article has been enormously influential within academia,[31] it has not led to any legislative reforms.

## ∭ Property Rights Involve Burdens, Not Just Benefits

Copyright owners' efforts to describe their statutory tort as a property moreover involves considerable cherry-picking of only those aspects of property that favor their agenda, while ignoring those aspects that don't. Professor Stephen Munzer has written:

> The idea of *property rights* is narrower than that of property. Property rights involve only advantageous incidents. Property involves disadvantageous incidents as well. Meant here is advantage or disadvantage to the right-holder or owner. Although property obviously involves disadvantages to persons other than the right-holder, it is important to see that there can be disadvantages to the right-holder as well. Suppose that someone owns a single-family home in a suburban area. Then she has a duty not to use it in ways prohibited by the law of nuisance or by zoning regulations.[32]

> . . . .

> For [property] owners, property imposes burdens as well as confers benefits. Burdens such as liability to taxation and responsibility for management and proper use.[33]

In the example given of the single family home, it should be pointed out that nuisance is a tort, the violation of which will trump the home owner's property interest. In the case of copyright, the equivalent duty to not using your land in a way that harms your neighbors' would be not interfering with uses that promote the progress of science, for example, those uses that encourage learning or further other socially beneficial purposes, such as criticism, comment, research, and the creation of new works. The Constitution is quite clear that Congress can only grant copyright to promote the progress of science, and thus this "burden" exists from the inception of the rights, and follows those rights for the duration of the copyright.

Copyright owners, however, only speak in terms of the *advantage* of property rights, and never the *burdens* that necessarily go with property ownership. Such cherry-picking of only those things that you like isn't the way our legal system works: If copyright owners insist on describing their statutory tort as property, they must be willing to accept the burdens as well as the benefits, something they have yet to even remotely consider, much less do. Although copyright owners routinely invoke property as "one of the basic tenets of a free society," they ignore the more fundamental tenet—the obligation of all citizens, including copyright owners, to society: "Owners do not live alone and when their exercise of property affects others, the interests of those others need to be taken into account. . . ."[34] Obligation is not inimical to property; indeed, as the Supreme Court has long affirmed, obligation is inherent in property."[35]

Copyright owners also ignore that what they regard as a right is instead a government grant specifically for the benefit of society, *not* authors. Our Supreme Court has repeatedly held: "The *sole interest* of the United States and the primary object in conferring the monopoly lie in the general benefits derived by the public from the labors of authors."[36] The benefits to the public are, therefore, of greater importance than the benefits to authors. One of the basic tenets of a free society is to be able to do things without the government telling you can't. The fundamental freedom at stake in copyright, therefore, is the freedom of the public to enjoy new innovations, to access and use information, freedoms that can be curtailed if and only to the extent that such curtailment is necessary to ultimately benefit the public by giving limited incentives to authors. Freedom in the field of copyright is not the freedom of copyright owners to be free of government regulation, but rather the freedom of consumers to be free from excessive copyright. The business of copyright is not businesses who own copyright, but the public.

### Why Do Copyright Owners Continue to Refer to Copyright as a Property Right?

When we regard copyright as a system for furthering social relationships, the inquiry shifts away from *whether* we should regulate—because the entire enterprise is regulatory—and toward what kind of relationships we want to create. The answer is clear, based on the constitutional text: We want to (and constitutionally can only) create relationships that further learning. Regarding copyright this way does not prejudge the outcome in any particular dispute; it does not mandate a lack of concern for the needs of copyright owners to have adequate incentives, nor does it treat those who use copyrighted works without permission as inherent infringers. That is the greatest benefit of the approach—no side has its thumb on the policy scale; instead all sides must make their cases on the merits.

Why then do copyright owners insist on referring to the limited regulatory privilege as their "property?" There are at least two reasons. First, description of copyright as a property right is a rhetorical device, intended to shift the burden to others in any debate about the proper scope of copyright. Second, despite rejection of copyright owners' claims from the inception of copyright, they have a psychological block in accepting reality, perhaps as a result of what behavioral economists call the endowment and attachment effects. We shall now examine both of these reasons.

### Property Rights as a Burden-Shifting Tool

The assertion of copyright as property is a political strategy, intended to advance copyright owners' political objectives. Those objectives consist of two goals: (1) to continually expand the scope of copyright; (2) to fight off any attempt to enact amendments or obtain court decisions that are in the public interest or that permit any unlicensed uses. As Joseph Singer wrote, even when ownership rights are limited (as copyright is):

> [W]e imagine those limits to be exceptions to the general rule that owners can do whatever they want with their property. The burden is always on others (meaning nonowners or the state) to explain why the

owner's rights should be limited, and in today's political climate that burden is heavy.[37]

If ownership means presumptive control by an owner, and if the existence of ownership rights is a good thing then limitations on the rights of the owner must be justified by sufficiently strong presumptions of legitimacy.[38]

One way to test the importance of classifying something as property is to classify it as something other than property, for example, as a privilege. Professor Susan Sell has written: "The language of rights weighs in favor of the person claiming the right. The language of privilege weighs in favor of the person granting the privilege."[39]

One sees heavy emphasis on such burden shifting in copyright owners' strong positions taken in current international debates about "limitations and exceptions."[40] The phrase "limitations and exceptions" captures nicely the point being made. The phrase assumes that the natural order is Blackstonian absolute rights, and that every effort to permit behavior not authorized by the copyright owner is a limitation on those absolute rights, an untoward exception from the natural state of affairs. But because copyright is *not* a natural right, the natural state of affairs is the public being able to use works of authorship without permission and without payment, and for good reason in a capitalist economy: Competition and innovation are the engine of capitalism. It is competition and innovation, and not monopoly power that leads to market efficiency and the creation of the best products and services. That it is necessary to create limited monopolies to take into account problems of nonexcludability of some resources, such as works of authorship, does not in any way change the fact that such monopolies *are* exceptions, nor does it excuse the need to ensure the monopoly rights are themselves limited to the bare minimum to achieve their purpose. As Lord Thomas Macaulay put the matter in the 1841 British House of Commons debates on term extension: "It is good that authors should be remunerated; and the least exceptionable way of remunerating them is by a monopoly. Yet monopoly is an evil. For the sake of the good we must submit to the evil; but the evil ought not to last a day longer than is necessary for the purpose of securing the good."[41]

The term "limitations and exceptions" is thus inaccurate. The term is a semantic device intended to hide the fact that it is copyright that is the exception to the natural state affairs. This semantic overturning of the natural state affairs takes the form of casting in a negative light those seeking amendments to copyright laws in the public interest. This is common tactic in many areas—you draw attention away from your own lack of merit by focusing attention on the alleged threat caused by someone else. In concrete terms, one sees the use of the limitations and exceptions dodge in statements that limitations and exceptions will be allowed *if* "there is a public interest . . . that justifies overriding the private rights of authors in their works in . . . particular circumstances."[42] There are a number of debatable assertions here, principally the assertion that private rights are presumed to trump the public interest, and that private rights should not be "overridden" unless a heavy burden is met.

This framing of the issue must be rejected, at least in common law countries such as the United States:[43] There is no such thing as copyright rights privately created and privately enforced. Copyright is created by public officials in the government for public reasons and is enforced by public laws and by public judges. Copyright laws are created as an entire fabric consisting of certain entitlements given to copyright owners, and certain entitlements given to the public. There is no support for treating any one entitlement as more privileged or important than another. In the case of the current limitations and exceptions debate, the uses in questions are at the core of the public's interest: educational uses; copying for archival purposes; criticism and comments; copying for personal use such as uploading a lawfully purchased CD or DVD to iTunes or other services; parody and satire; news reporting; copying for the visually or hearing impaired; and transient copying that is technically required by the operation of the Internet. To describe such uses as "exceptions" to the societal goals of copyright, and which require a heavy burden to be justified is merely a political position, and not an appealing one. Should advocates for the visually and hearing impaired really be required to meet a heavy burden to establish that copyright laws should be revised to permit the visually or hearing impaired access to eBooks? If copyright owners of literary works had their own access restricted to those works that have been licensed for eBooks for the visually or hearing impaired, there would be no talk of burdens at all, much less a heavy burden. The assertion of copyright as a property right, then, is a tactical move by copyright owners to frame debates by putting others on the defensive, including those who are the most vulnerable in our society. It is a position that is fatally at odds with the nature of copyright as a creature of society created for society's benefit.

One example will show how the limitations and exceptions issue plays out in practice, that of fair use. Judge Pierre Leval, of the United States Court of Appeals for the Second Circuit in Manhattan, one of the two leading judicial authorities on the fair use doctrine (the other being Seventh Circuit Judge Richard Posner), has rejected the view of fair use as an exception. In his widely cited 1990 article in the *Harvard Law Review*, called "Toward a Fair Use Standard," Judge Leval wrote: "Fair use should not be considered a bizarre, occasionally tolerated departure from the grand conception of the copyright monopoly. To the contrary, it is a necessary part of the overall design."[44] In Canada, the Supreme Court took a very similar position but holding that fair dealing is a "user's right." In CCH *Canadian Ltd. v. Law Society of Upper Canada*, the Chief Justice wrote:

> Before reviewing the scope of the fair dealing exception under the Copyright Act, it is important to clarify some general considerations about exceptions to copyright infringement. Procedurally, a defendant is required to prove that his or her dealing with a work has been fair; however, the fair dealing exception is perhaps more properly understood as an integral part of the Copyright Act than simply a defence. Any act falling within the fair dealing exception will not be an infringement of copyright. The fair dealing exception, like other exceptions in the Copyright Act, is a user's right. In order to maintain the proper balance between the rights of a copyright owner and users' interests, it must not be interpreted restrictively. As Professor Vaver, *supra*, has explained, at p. 171: "User rights are not just loopholes. Both owner rights and user rights should therefore be given the fair and balanced reading that befits remedial legislation."[45]

Here is another example, from the United States, which demonstrates that it is not only copyright owners who are infected with an erroneous approach to the issue. Compulsory licenses, the U.S. Copyright Office insists, are a derogation of copyright owners' rights and as such must be narrowly construed:

> The Copyright Office has long been a critic of compulsory licensing for broadcast retransmissions. A compulsory license is not only a derogation of a copyright owner's exclusive rights, but it also prevents the marketplace from deciding the fair value of copyrighted works through government-set price controls.[46]

Such a view regards unfettered rights as the natural state of affairs, and any exception, even those created by the legislature, as hostile to the natural state of affairs. The legislature however created both the right and the compulsory license in the same document, *within* the same system, and for the same purpose, to encourage learning and the distribution of copyrighted works. Regarding compulsory licenses as exceptions from otherwise unfettered rights is to place those licenses and exceptions outside the very system that created them, and which they are designed to foster. They are *not* exceptions: They exist *within* the system and are every bit as important to that system as the grant of rights is. They must accordingly be given the same dignity and liberal interpretation according to their statutory language and purpose, as is the grant of rights in Section 106. The Office's views are based on the same failed free market fundamentalism that led Alan Greenspan to give Wall Street, mortgage lenders, and the real estate industry free rein: the magic of the marketplace is always the best solution, while government intervention is always the worst solution.[47] We know all too painfully now that the captains of industry can be wrong, and terribly so. In the case of copyright, there can never be a free market where price is set at what a willing buyer and a willing seller would agree on, because the very existence of the copyright monopoly permits copyright owners to restrict supply and to prohibit competition.

Contrary to the Copyright Office's views, the U.S. Supreme Court has repeatedly taken a balanced, non-property-oriented approach. In *Bonito Boats, Inc. v. Thunder Craft Boats, Inc.*,[48] a unanimous Court, in an opinion by Justice O'Connor, held that "[f]rom their inception, the federal patent laws have embodied a careful balance between the need to promote innovation and the recognition that imitation and refinement through imitation are both necessary to invention itself and the very lifeblood of a competitive economy."[49] Two years later, in *Feist Publications, Inc. v. Rural Telephone Service Co.*,[50] Justice O'Connor, again writing for a unanimous Court (this time in a copyright case), wrote:

> It may seem unfair that much of the fruit of the compiler's labor may be used by others without compensation. As Justice Brennan has correctly observed, however, this is not "some unforeseen byproduct of a statutory scheme." ... It is, rather, "the essence of copyright," ... and a constitutional requirement. The primary goal of copyright is not to reward authors, but "to promote the Progress of Science and useful Arts."[51]

Three years later, in *Fogerty v. Fantasy, Inc.*,[52] Chief Justice Rehnquist, also for a unanimous Court, soundly rejected the dual standard applied by the lower courts of awarding attorney's fees to prevailing plaintiffs in copyright cases as a matter of course, but awarding attorney's fees to a prevailing defendant only when it was shown that the suit was frivolous or brought in bad faith:

> While it is true that one of the goals of the Copyright Act is to discourage infringement, it is by no means the only goal of that Act. In the first place, it is by no means always the case that the plaintiff in a copyright infringement action is the only holder of a copyright; often times, defendants hold copyrights too, as exemplified in the case at hand. . . .
>
> More importantly, the policies served by the Copyright Act are more complex, more measured, than simply maximizing the number of meritorious suits for copyright infringement. . . . We have often recognized the monopoly privileges that Congress has authorized, while "intended to motivate the creative activity of authors and inventors by the provision of a special reward," are limited in nature and must ultimately serve the public good. . . .
>
> Because copyright law ultimately serves the purpose of enriching the general public through access to creative works, it is peculiarly important that the boundaries of copyright law be demarcated as clearly as possible. To that end, defendants who seek to advance a variety of meritorious copyright defenses should be encouraged to litigate them to the same extent that plaintiffs are encouraged to litigate meritorious claims of infringement. . . . [A] successful defense of a copyright infringement action may further the policies of the Copyright Act every bit as much as a successful prosecution of an infringement claim by the holder of a copyright.[53]

One might have hoped that three unanimous Supreme Court opinions would have killed the metaphoric property maneuver, but alas, like recurring bad dreams, it keeps coming back.

### The Endowment and Attachment Effects

A second reason copyright owners insist on referring to copyright as property is that some of them believe it notwithstanding that the proposition is demonstrably false.[54] Indeed, use of the metaphor would ring false in the mouth of someone who either did not believe it or who was not a good enough actor to convince people he or she did. Conservative Republican pollster Frank Luntz wrote in *Words That Work*: "Messengers who are their own best message are always true to themselves."[55] This is why Jack Valenti was such a magnificent messenger: His personal passion and his extreme comfort around politicians gave him credibility that others in the same position, saying the same things would lack. Mr. Valenti personified the old maxim that "the greatest art is the art that concerns its own art." Those who were privileged to see Mr. Valenti offstage—talking openly with his clients about what could or could not be achieved, and what artifice would or would not work—are aware that Mr. Valenti's clients frequently disagreed with his advice and directed him to deliver a different message through a different artifice. Mr. Valenti was a consummate salesman, who like all great salesmen (and oral advocates) worked himself up into believing the truth of his clients' message. Mr. Valenti was a great actor working on the stage of Washington, D.C., (and sometimes globally) on behalf of an industry that appreciated his craft, but that never let him forget that the message was theirs and not his.

### The Endowment Effect

The term "endowment effect" was coined by Professor Richard Thaler in his 1980 article "Toward a Positive Theory of Consumer Choice."[56] The endowment effect is a hypothesis about behavior, a hypothesis which, through hundreds of tests, has demonstrated that we value far more highly things we already possess over equivalent goods we could acquire at a lesser cost.[57] The endowment effect conflicts with neoclassic economics, which asserts that the differences in valuation between selling the same item or acquiring it should be either nonexistent or small (assuming no transaction costs). The endowment effect explains why neoclassic economists get this wrong,[58] at least in those areas where the endowment effect operates.[59]

Professor Dan Ariely gives a number of examples of the endowment effect in his book, *Predictably Irrational*.[60] One example is the value that students at Duke University place on tickets to national-title basketball games. For these games, because of the small size of the stadium, the number of seats is quite limited. Duke has, accordingly, devised a complicated lottery system to allocate tickets: Students must camp out in tents for weeks, and then only for a chance to participate in a lottery. Even if you are in the first tent, you have no greater chance of obtaining one of the coveted tickets than the students in the last tent because being in a tent only means your name will be placed in the container from which the winning tickets will later be drawn. During the weeks leading up to the lottery, students must respond to air horn alerts and reaffirm their desire to participate in the lottery. After the lottery concluded, Professor Ariely interviewed students who had won tickets and students who had not. Both groups had invested the same amount of effort in camping out. He found that those who had won the tickets would, on average, not take less than $2,400 for the sale of their tickets, whereas those who had not won would not pay more than $175 to buy the tickets.[61] Many other experiments have been done with all sorts of different objects or rewards, toward the same point—if we possess something, we value it far more than we rationally should. In the case of copyright, this leads to wildly inflated views about the worth of one's copyrighted work, which in turns leads to substantial problems in licensing uses.

### The Attachment Effect

Professor Russell Korobkin has written that "there is evidence that [the endowment effect] is stronger when the good is obtained as a result of skill or performance rather than as a result of chance,"[62] and where, as is often the case with copyrighted works, for goods where there is no close market substitute.[63] In short, we become very attached to things we have created, even ideas, as anyone who has been in a meeting with someone who simply will not give up a bad idea can attest to.

One of the most pernicious effects of the attachment effect is the belief that once we have an ownership interest in something, we think we have that ownership because of our own merit; using that thing without our permission is then seen as a personal attack on us, as immoral. What we forget in the case of copyright is that Congress created rights for the purpose of benefiting the public not us. All this is forgotten, however, even by those who did not create the work, such as heirs and corporate assignees. This psychological failure to recognize that the (limited) copyright rights exist as a matter of Congressional grace and not because of individual merit, may be forgiven at the emotional level, but such beliefs are nevertheless deeply wrong. As Professor Ariely would say, the mistaken beliefs are predictably irrational.

Long before behavioral economics, Justice Holmes noted the attachment effect:

> It is in the nature of a man's mind. A thing which you enjoyed and used as your own for a long time, whether property or opinion, takes root in your being and cannot be torn away without your resenting the act and trying to defend yourself, however you came by it. The law can ask for no better justification than the deepest instincts of man.[64]

We may not be able to extinguish such instincts, but policy makers and judges should be aware of their presence and reject them when asserted.

# Moral Panics, Folk Devils, and
## as a Tactical Weapon

The power of the concepts "thief" and "trespasser" is traceable to the fundamental negative associations they invoke. Thieves and trespassers are usually metaphoric, fictive creations (outside of course, people, who actually do
steal your wallet or enter your land without your permission and refuse to
leave).[1] They are also examples of moral panics. Moral panics in copyright
are the flip side of the initial classification of copyright as property. The
appellation thief or trespasser is meaningless without an owner of property
from whom one can steal or commit trespass. In Daniel Defoe's famous
novel, did the cannibals care a hoot about Robinson Crusoe's fencedin
habitation and cave? Hardly; to them, he was food, and if they had eaten
him, they would not have taken over his created space; nor would it have
prevented Crusoe from becoming an entrée if he had claimed a fee simple
absolute over his living quarters and refused entry to the cannibals as trespassers. What good, then, is it to say you own property if there are no thieves
or trespassers to do battle with? Copyright owners claiming status as property owners *need* to create conflict with others to create their status; the
classical way in which such conflict is created is through moral panics.

## 𝒲 Moral Panics

The concept of *moral panics* was most famously expounded by British
sociologist Stanley Cohen in his 1972 book, *Folk Devils and Moral Panics*.[2]
Professor Cohen was curious about what was called the "mods and
rocker" phenomenon: "rampaging teenage gangs confronting each other
at seaside resorts during English Bank Holidays."[3] Although part of this
era was covered in the Austin Powers movies, many will not be familiar
with it, so I quote this brief, droll description from Wikipedia:

> Gangs of mods and rockers fighting in 1964 sparked a moral panic
> about British youths, and the two groups were seen as folk devils.

> The rockers adopted a macho biker gang image, wearing clothes such as black leather jackets. The mods adopted a pose of scooter-driving sophistication, wearing suits and other clean-cut outfits. Rockers poured scorn on the mods. . . . The rockers considered mods to be weedy, effeminate snobs. Mods saw rockers as . . . oafish and grubby.[4]

Both groups were regarded as a threat to "proper" society. This phenomenon of regarding those who are young and different as a threat to the moral fabric was hardly limited to the United Kingdom. Elvis Presley was believed to pose such a threat to society that when he made his second appearance on TV's *Toast of the Town* hosted by Ed Sullivan on October 28, 1956, singing "Hound Dog," the television cameras were forbidden to show him from the waist down.

An amusing example of alleged danger posed to society by rock and roll was the FBI investigation into the lyrics of the song "Louie Louie," as recorded in 1963, by the Kingsmen, a short-lived rock band from Washington State.[5] The song was written in 1955 by Richard Berry, a Los Angeles musician who wrote a first-person song in which a Jamaican sailor tells Louie, a bartender, that he's leaving to meet his girl ("Louie, Louie/Me gotta go"). The band broke up shortly after the recording, with lead singer/rhythm guitarist Jack Ely never to return. Ely's voice on the recording could not be replicated by those who came after because of its uniqueness—Ely wore braces at the time of the recording and had strained his voice the night before in a ninety-minute jam session; as a result the lyrics were slurred and indecipherable, which oddly enough led to the moral panic.

The moral panic was launched by the FBI at J. Edgar Hoover's personal insistence, although it was Hoover's obsession that gave the song its seemingly enduring popularity. Hoover was convinced that the lyrics were obscene and launched an extensive two-year investigation. There was also an FCC hearing at which the FCC attempted to discern the actual lyrics.[6] (It was an urban legend that the "true" lyrics could be discovered by playing the 45 rpm single at 33-1/3 rpm). The Post Office conducted an investigation too. The song was banned on many radio stations and in Indiana by fiat of the governor. Nothing came of the government's more than two-year investigation, because the lyrics were not in fact even "dirty."

Because this is a book about copyright, I want to point out that for 30 years, the Kingsmen were not paid any royalties; it was only after suit in 1998 that they were awarded ownership of all their early recordings, including "Louie Louie."[7] Richard Berry, who wrote the song and recorded it in April 1965 with the Pharaohs, was paid a one-time, flat amount of $750 for all publication rights, and thus didn't benefit from the sale of the 2,000 covers of his song.[8]

Moral panics have been described as "a reaction by a group of people based on the false or exaggerated perception that some cultural behavior or group, frequently a minority group or a subculture, is dangerously deviant and poses a menace to society." It has also been more broadly defined as an "episode, condition, person or group of persons" that has in recent times been "defined as a threat to societal values and interests."[9] Moral panics have occurred in many cultures and times, including the well-known examples of the Salem witch hunts, comic books,[10] and McCarthyism. They play on deep fears, and are greatly aided by the media's eagerness to sell papers or gain viewers. Youth are a particular target for moral panics:

> The problematization of youth can be seen to partake of a longstand-ing popular association of youth with 'crime' and 'delinquency.' Historically, youth have been the subject of successive waves of social anxiety or moral panics, which focus on the threat that young people supposedly represent to morality, body, and property.[11]

It is not coincidental that the vast majority of the Recording Industry Association of America's (RIAA) 35,000 lawsuits have been filed against young people.

John Springhall wrote in his engaging book, *Youth, Popular Culture and Moral Panics: Penny Gaffs to Gangsta-Rap, 1830–1996*,[12] that "[e]ach new panic develops as if it were the first time such issues have been debated in public and yet the debates are strikingly similar."[13] The formal working out of a moral panic can be described this way:

1. Signs appear indicating that imminent danger is threatening.
2. The danger occurs, followed by an immediate unorganized response.
3. Those affected by the danger form a preliminary picture of what has happened and of their own condition.

4. A number of different responses are developed to help those affected by the danger to return the community to its former equilibrium, either by suppressing the danger or controlling it so that it no longer poses any danger. This typically occurs through legislation or police action.[14]

It is important to keep in mind that the term "panic" in "moral panic" is not intended to "evoke the image of a frenzied crowd or mob: atavistic, driven by contagion and delirium, susceptible to control by demagogues and, in turn, controlling others by 'mob rule.'"[15] Nor does it imply that the subject of the moral panic "does not exist or happened at all and that reaction is based on fantasy, hysteria, delusion or being duped by the powerful."[16] Moral panics are not always based on "The Big Lie."[17] Instead, moral panics can take an existing problem of little or no consequence and turn it into an existential one to further a political agenda.[18] Moral panics are not irrational acts by those who construct them, but rather are the result of deliberate political opportunism. Chas Critcher has written, "The problem is . . . distorted and exaggerated . . . hyped up by the media and other interest groups[;] unspeakable monsters are . . . manufactured [with] the end result . . . the adoption of measures all out of proportion to the actual threat."[19]

In copyright, the Digital Millennium Copyright Act of 1998, which vested copyright owners with control over the design of consumer goods through new rights against anticircumvention devices and a right to require the inclusion of industry-mandated digital rights management information is a perfect example of the use of a moral panic that resulted in the adoption of measures all out of proportion to the original threat. Testifying in favor of the legislation, here is the moral panic, courtesy of Jack Valenti:

Like Emerson's doctrine that "for every gain there is a loss and for every loss there is a gain," within the glittering potential of the Internet lies the darker forms of thieves, who armed with magical new technology, are capable of breaking-and-entering conventional barriers to steal copyrighted material borne by the Internet by just about anybody with a working computer.[20]

Later, in reaction to the advent of peer-to-peer networks, Mr. sought to tie such networks to the dissemination of child porn asserting that peer-to-peer file sharing made available "the mos choking child porn" "on a scale so squalid it will shake the very core of your being."[21] Two years after the events of September 11, 2001, Mr. Valenti linked copyright infringement to terrorists, testifying before Congress that trafficking in counterfeit and pirated goods "accounts for much of the money the international terror network depends on to feed its operations."[22] This moral panic was so enticing that in February 2008, a member of Congress used it in testifying in favor of a bill proposing protection for high-end fashion designs.[23] The Congressman was quoting not directly from the source, but rather from a retelling contained in an op-ed piece published in the *New York Times* by *Newsweek* contributor Dana Thomas on August 30, 2007:

> Most people think that buying an imitation handbag or wallet is harm-less, a victimless crime. But the counterfeiting rackets are run by crime syndicates that also deal in narcotics, weapons, child prostitution, human trafficking and terrorism. Ronald K. Noble, the secretary gen-eral of Interpol, told the House of Representatives Committee on International Relations that profits from the sale of counterfeit goods have gone to groups associated with Hezbollah, the Shiite terrorist group, paramilitary organizations in Northern Ireland and FARC, the Revolutionary Armed Forces of Colombia.[24]

Note here the media's role in perpetuating a moral panic and in a context far removed from its subsequent invocation, fashion designs. Note too that Mr. Thomas doesn't say that the listed terrorist groups or paramilitary organizations themselves are involved in the condemned behavior, but rather "groups associated with" them, a description of deliberate vagueness. He didn't do his own research into the issue but instead quoted from someone else, and without doing any investigation into the truth of the assertions. Indeed the same asser-tion was made by an Administration official before the House of Representatives intellectual property subcommittee. That witness was unable to point to a single criminal organized crime group connected to file sharing.[25]

## ⅏ Folk Devils

The alleged source of the problems leading to a moral panic stampede are "folk devils":

> A folk devil is a person or group of people who are portrayed in folklore or the media as outsiders and deviant, and who are blamed for crimes or other sorts of social problems.
>
> The pursuit of folk devils frequently intensifies into a mass movement that is called a moral panic. When a moral panic is in full swing, the folk devils are the subject of loosely organized but pervasive campaigns of hostility through gossip and the spreading of urban legends. The mass media sometimes get in on the act or attempt to create new folk devils to create controversies. Sometimes the campaign against the folk devil influences a nation's politics and legislation.[26]

Folk devils are portrayed as deviants, but as Stanley Cohen noted, this description leads to questions such as: "'deviant to whom?' or 'deviant from what?'; when told that something is a social problem, [one] asks 'problematic to whom?'"[27] The answer is of course the status quo, the existing social, political, or in the case of copyright, business order. But because the "existing" social, political, and business orders are constantly changing, new folks devils have to be invented to meet the occasion. Folk devils are a tool to accomplish social, political, or commercial objectives, and there is no better way to gain society's acceptance of such control than through the manufacture of fear, which explains the copyright industries' regular use of it.

# EIGHT

# Copyright Owners and Moral Panics

The transparent obviousness in the use of moral panics and folk devils is so simple to document that one might ask why they continue to be employed. The answer is because they are successful in achieving the goals of those who use them. Much like negative political advertising continues to be used despite polls showing the public disproves of it, moral panics and folk devils are used because they effectively appeal to our "easy instincts, not our better angels."[1] Moral panics "reveal a lot about the workings of power, specifically who has the capacity to define a social problem and prescribe appropriate action."[2] Moral panics thus reveal disturbing truths about our political and legal process, in which a false public perception is created "by emphasizing emotional threats . . . in order to increase support for risky policies."[3]

Moral panics are essential to proponents of ever-expanding copyright rights[4] and for the most pragmatic of reasons: It is hard to enact controversial legislation granting powerful new rights to those who already have excessively powerful rights unless you can convince legislators that folk devils pose an existential threat. In the United States, the most colorful expositor of moral panics and folk devils was Jack Valenti.

## ✐ Jack Valenti: Master of Moral Panics

Throughout his career as the Motion Picture Association of America's (MPAA) chief lobbyist, Mr. Valenti skillfully and successfully employed moral panics and folk devils before Congress in an effort to gain increased copyright protection. As metaphors, Mr. Valenti's moral panics provided the means by which busy and sympathetic members of Congress could appear to be engaged in sober reasoning. Moral panics in copyright involve the construction of a political strategy for obtaining political benefits. They are not hyperbole; they are the core of a careful strategic plan to alter the copyright landscape. And it is a landscape that was and remains conducive to Hollywood. In a December 13, 1974, interview on National Public Radio, Mr. Valenti candidly explained the affinity between members of Congress and Hollywood:

> I think politicians and movie actors and movie executives are similar in more ways than they're different. There is an egocentric quality about both; there is a very sensitive awareness of the public attitude, because you live or die on public favor or disfavor. There is the desire for publicity and for acclaim, because, again, that's part of your life. . . . And in a strange and bizarre way, when movie actors come to Washington, they're absolutely fascinated by the politicians. And when the politicians go to Hollywood, they're absolutely fascinated by the movie stars. It's a kind of reciprocity of affection by people who both recognize in a sense they're in the same racket.[5]

It is not coincidental that Mr. Valenti's background was in the advertising and political consulting worlds. In 1952, he cofounded Weekley & Valenti, a Texas advertising and political consulting agency. For 13 years, until November 22, 1963, he perfected the type of messaging that is common to both worlds. On the day of President Kennedy's assassination, Mr. Valenti and his agency were handling press for the trip. After the assassination, Valenti, a friend of fellow Texan Lyndon Johnson, was present at the swearing in of Johnson onboard Air Force One, and can be seen in the left-hand corner of the famous picture of the swearing in.[6] He rode with Johnson on the plane to Washington, and became a "special assistant" to him in the White House. In 1966, at the request of Lew Wasserman, head of Universal Studios (and the force behind the Betamax suit against Sony), he left the White House and became the president of the Motion Picture Association of America, where he remained for 38 years. He died on April 26, 2007. In my seven years working in the federal legislative branch, he was the best lobbyist I knew. I always felt happy to be in his presence, even though he was lobbying on behalf of clients who did not always deserve what he sought. Unlike most advocates, he knew the audience he was playing to—in his case, Congress (and its staff), and he was a master of what rhetoricians call *comprobatio* ("complimenting one's judges or hearers to win their confidence"[7]). As Mr. Valenti wrote in his book, *Speak Up With Confidence*:

> The ultimate ambition of a good speaker is to create a rapport with the audience. What a decisive piece of language is that French word, *rapport*. Rapport is an embrace, an affectionate warmth, a mutual reaching out, a harmonious friendliness that is the warranty of affinity and concord among people.[8]

In my thirteen years working in Washington, D.C., including seven in the legislative branch, I saw no other witness who thought of testifying before Congress as involving an "embrace, an affectionate warmth, a mutual reaching out, a harmonious friendliness that is the warranty of affinity and concord among people," but Mr. Valenti did, and his audience felt that he did. This "concord among people" was also a shrewd device for the transference of his metaphoric assertions through feelings. Scientists have long studied how facial gestures and feelings play an important role in the way we form meaning. Dr. Arnold Modell, in an article called "Emotional Memory, Metaphor, and Meaning," explained: "[N]umerous studies . . . document the reciprocal tracking of the facial expressions that are exchanged . . . . [suggesting] that we are born with the capacity to construct intersubjective meanings in reaction to the interchange of feelings."[9] Mr. Valenti also knew that mutual affection leads to better believability; again from his book: "Believability is the largest asset a speaker can project. Your own words, words that flow from your heart, and your brain, fall on more receptive ears."[10] No one who heard Mr. Valenti's flowery, metaphorically charged testimony had any doubt Mr. Valenti followed his own advice.

Mr. Valenti was also a voracious reader, especially of history and the classics, including the Greek and Roman rhetoricians. He was quite familiar with the ancient Greek concept of *decorum*, which had a very different meaning than its current usage, polite behavior. In ancient times, it referred to the rhetorical concept, developed by Aristotle in his *Rhetoric*, and worked out further by Cicero and Quintilian that the style of speaking should be tailored to the subject, the audience and the occasion. As Richard Lanham observed: "No idea was more carefully worked out in rhetorical theory nor more universally acclaimed; everyone writing about rhetoric touches on it one way or another."[11] Professor Lanham also makes another point; that is, that the style in which one addressed one's chosen audience was part of a careful construction of an alternate reality:

> Decorum . . . amounts to . . . the "social trick" par excellence. We create, with maximum self-consciousness and according to precise rules, an intricate structure of stylistic forces balanced carefully as to perceiver and perceived, and then agree to forget that we have created it and to pretend that it is nature itself we are engaging with. Rhetorical theory has spent endless time discussing how to adjust utterance to this preexistent social reality without reflecting on how that reality has been constituted by the idea of decorum. Like the human visual system, rhetorical decorum is a bag of tricks which constitutes for us a world that it then presents as "just out there" awaiting our passive acceptance.[12]

Professor Lanham could just as easily have been referring to Hollywood motion pictures and the "suspension of disbelief" that is the essence of the art of movies and other forms of art.[13] A critical part of this process was persuading members of Congress that a dire threat existed to the motion pictures industry, copyright law, and the public at large. In trying to persuade his Congressional audience, Mr. Valenti used moral panics with a deftness that would have astounded Stanley Cohen.

## ⚌ Moral Panics, Home Video, and the Boston Strangler: The Real Story

### The Home Video Market and Thomas Edison

The question of whether people prefer to view motion pictures in private or in public has existed from the inception of the art form. On May 20, 1891, Thomas Edison unveiled both a motion picture camera, called the "kinetograph," and a viewer for movies, called the "kinetoscope." The kinetoscope was contained in a wooden cabinet; customers would insert coins and look ("peep" in the parlance of the day) through an individual kinetoscope at a continuous loop of a twenty-second 35-millimeter black-and-white film. Kinetoscope parlors grew up showing multiple shorts for a single admission. Other exhibitors, especially the Latham brothers, thought there was more money to be made in showing longer films, on a larger screen, to a mass audience. Edison disagreed because such an approach would cut into his market of selling the kinetoscope machines: money from viewing went to the exhibitors. Edison is reported to have scoffed that his company was

> making these peep show machines and selling a lot of them at a good profit. If we put out a screen machine there will be a use for maybe ten of them in the whole United States. With that many screen machines you would show the pictures to everyone in the country—and then it would be done. Let's not kill the goose that lays the golden egg.[14]

As an historian of the motion industry observed in language that could be applied to all the copyright industries, regardless of the era:

> At the time, Edison was not just an inventor, but also a manufacturer selling kinetoscopes, and a studio head, producing movies for them. Like studio chiefs who'd succeed him decades later, Edison seemed to be hoping that technological progress would hold off, so it didn't pinch his profits. And he was assuming that no new technology would ever vault past the existing technology's revenue generating abilities.[15]

Once it became apparent that mass theatrical exhibition was the future, Edison decided to use his patents to eliminate his competitors for the movie projection market. After Edison lost a patent infringement case against the sole remaining serious competitor, Biograph, Edison created a trust among a number of companies in the movie industry and the Eastman Kodak company, which supplied the film. Called the Motion Picture Trust, the new enterprise pooled patents, drove out middlemen, prohibited the sale of movie prints to theaters, all toward extracting monopolistic prices and eliminating competitors. The Trust even created its own enforcement arm, the General Film Company, to engage in heavy-handed, coercive conduct toward those who resisted, conduct that included seizing and destroying unlicensed machines and refusing to supply movies to the so-called "independent" exhibitors. A number of these independent exhibitors moved to Hollywood, helping to establish the West Coast film industry. The independents attacked the trust in the courts as an unlawful restraint of trade, as it indeed was. On October 1, 1915, a federal trial court held that the trust had violated anti-trust laws. In language that may be applied to the conduct of so many copyright owners in the various copyright wars, the court wrote: "There is deep-grained in human nature the impulse to influence, and, so far as it can be done, control the actions of others. It is too much to expect that this control, when secured, will always be exerted for altruistic ends."[16]

### Cartrivision and the First Home Rental Market

In 1972, about three years before the introduction in the United States of the Sony Betamax videocassette recorder, Cartridge Television Inc. of Palo Alto, California, introduced the Cartrivision system. The system was contained in a combination 25-inch color TV/VCR console that sold at the equivalent of $6,800 in 2008 dollars. The Cartrivision system had both playback and off-the-air taping capabilities. In addition to shows they had taped off-the-air, playback capabilities included pre-recorded 8-inch square cassettes, but because there were no video rental or sale stores, consumers had to order the cassettes by mail from a catalogue provided by a retailer like Sears or Montgomery Ward. The rental tapes had red colored cassettes (to distinguish them from the tapes sold to copy off-the-air), and could not be rewound by the consumer. If a consumer wished to view the movie again, he or she had to take it to a retailer who had a special rewinding machine, and a new rental fee had to be paid. Thirteen months after introduction, manufacture of the Cartrivision system stopped. There were many reasons for the system's failure, not all of which were attributable to the restrictions placed by copyright owners, but efforts to control marketing and pricing of the home video market would repeat itself a mere three years later with the filing of the infamous Betamax lawsuit.

### The Betamax Case and the Fight for the Home Video Market

On April 12, 1982, Jack Valenti testified before Congress as the lead witness about the alleged dangers posed to the motion picture industry by videocassette recorders:

> We are facing a very new and a very troubling assault . . . and we are facing it from a thing called the video cassette recorder and its necessary companion called the blank tape.

We are going to bleed and bleed and hemorrhage, unless this Congress at least protects one industry . . . whose total future depends on its protection from the savagery and the ravages of this machine.

[Some say] that the VCR is the greatest friend that the American film producer ever had. I say to you that the VCR is to the American film producer and the American public as the Boston Strangler is to the woman home alone.[17]

Note here that Mr. Valenti spoke of the VCR as a threat not only to the large corporations he represented, but also and much more broadly to the American public. It is the essence of moral panics that folk devils be demonized as a threat to society itself. Mr. Valenti knew keenly that it was not enough to appear before Congress as a special pleader for his clients; instead, he had to appear as the savior of society itself, which could only be saved, of course, by Congress giving powerful rights to his clients. Canadian criminologist Laureen Snider noted the phenomenon of turning formerly acceptable behavior into criminal behavior—something that is de rigueur in copyright and which Mr. Valenti regularly lobbied for:

[C]alling something "criminal" is an ideological and moral claim. It categorizes a particular behaviour as an act that causes social harm, one that injures everyone in a geographically defined area. The act is [no] longer a private matter, nor a dispute to be settled by the parties directly involved. Furthermore, calling an act a crime is a claim for public resources, a summons that obligates the state to monitor and enforce.[18]

Majid Yar has noted that calling something a crime in the context of the Copyright Wars is not meant to be descriptive of acts that violate statutes but is instead a political strategy to redefine social norms in a way that will lead the state to intervene and criminalize behavior that is not, in fact, criminal:

[C]rime and criminality need to be understood as constructions that emerge from processes taking place beyond the sphere of legislation and judicial judgment. The identification of conduct with crime depends crucially upon a wider consensus that the behaviour in question constitutes a breach of acceptable social norms, that it partakes of some moral wrongdoing or injury that offends certain very strong collective sentiments. . . . [R]ecent attempts to construct rhetorically intellectual property offences (specifically breaches of copyright, dubbed "piracy") as beyond the bounds of morally acceptable behavior. These efforts can be viewed as forms of . . . . "moral entrepreneurship," a concerted enterprise on the part of empowered social actors to redefine the boundaries and limits of transgressions.[19]

There is no corporate industry better able to develop, shape, and market such a social and political campaign than Hollywood. Who, in Mr. Valenti's opinion, did American society have to be saved from in the case of VCRs? Mr. Valenti selected one of the crudest tactics in the book of moral panics: jingoism, in the form of Japan-bashing. In this one piece of testimony alone, I have excerpted only a few of Mr. Valenti's attacks on the Japanese:

Now, my first card, Mr. Chairman, deals with what I consider to be one of the essential elements that you cannot ignore and, indeed, you must nourish. The U.S. film—and I will read this—"The U.S. film and television production industry is a huge and valuable American asset." In 1981, it returned to this country almost $1 billion in surplus balance of trade. And I might add, Mr. Chairman, it is the single one American-made product that the Japanese, skilled beyond all comparison in their conquest of world trade, are unable to duplicate or to displace or to compete with or to clone. And I might add that this important asset today is in jeopardy.

. . . .

It is a piece of sardonic irony that this asset, which unlike steel or silicon chips or motor cars or electronics of all kinds—a piece of sardonic irony that while the Japanese are unable to duplicate the American films by a flank assault, they can destroy it by this video cassette recorder.

. . . .

Now, again, citing the fact that 100 percent of these machines are made in Japan and 85 percent of all of the blank tapes are made in Japan, and I say that, Mr. Chairman, because I have to keep coming back to this trade asset because if the Congress doesn't act, then what we are going to be doing is exporting our jobs out of this country to another country, beyond the real of our own shore.

. . .

There is going to be a VCR avalanche. Exports of VCR's [sic] from Japan totaled 2.57 million units in 1981. No. 2, the United States is the biggest market. No. 3, February 1982, which is the latest data, shows the imports to the United States are up 57 percent over 1981. This is more than a tidal wave. It is more than an avalanche. It is here.

. . . .

Here is the weekly *Variety*, Wednesday, March 10[,] [h]eadline, "Sony Sees $400 Billion Global Electronics Business by the Decade's End," $400 billion by the decade's end. In 1981, Mr. Chairman, this United States had a $5.3 billion trade deficit with Japan on electronic equipment alone.

. . .

Now, the question comes, well, all right, what is wrong with the VCR[?] One of the Japanese lobbyists, Mr. Ferris, has said that the VCR—well, if I am saying something wrong, forgive me. I don't know. He certainly is not MGM's lobbyist.

. . .

I am one who has a belief that before the next few years the Japanese will have built into their machines an automatic situation that kills the commercial.

. . .

Mr. Ferris has said that the opposition is saying that the American producers are greedy and it is terrible that they want to extract more money and they are triple and double and quadruple dipping in all these markets and they are saying why in the devil should we go and make all this money. Why don't we stop? Haven't we got enough? Aren't we rich enough off of television and everybody?

Well, this charge is so riddled with absurdities that I hardly know where to begin, but, by jingoes, I will begin. Now, I think it is quite intemperate—I hope they don't make this argument tomorrow because of the answer I am about to give you—to charge the Americans with greed when the Japanese companies are swollen with profits.

. . .

Now, I have here the profits of Japanese companies, if you want to talk about greed. Here, Hitachi, Matsushita, Sanyo, Sony, TDK, Toshiba, Victor, all of whom make these VCR's [sic]. Do you know what their net profits were last year? $2.8 billion net profit. Indeed, Matsushita, one company alone, makes more net profits than the entire American film and television industry combined. He wants to talk about greed.[20]

The nature of Mr. Valenti's remarks were so exaggerated that in concluding that day's hearings, the committee chairman, Congressman Robert Kastenmeier joked, "our witnesses tomorrow, as Mr. Valenti would call them, [are] the Japanese witnesses," although none of the witnesses were Japanese, but instead all Americans, representing American companies and groups.

Mr. Valenti's VCR remarks are oft-repeated for their "Boston Strangler" reference but are usually censored to exclude his Japan-bashing. The context of his remarks has not, to the best of my research, ever been spelled out. His remarks were not off the cuff, or reflective of an isolated event; instead, they were part of sustained, well-financed effort to ban VCRs by the motion picture studios that began in 1976, six years before his remarks; an effort that was fought in the courts all the way to the U.S. Supreme Court, which heard oral argument in the case an unusual two times and then split 5-4 after an earlier 6-3 vote the opposite way. The battle was fought as well as in Congress, which held three years of hearings on the issue, including on video rental, another area Mr. Valenti and his clients attempted to control.

The story of the motion picture studio's war against the videocassette machine is told in an excellent 1987 book by James Lardner called *Fast Forward: Hollywood, the Japanese, and the VCR Wars*—note the use of "wars" here. Mr. Lardner traced his interest in the intersection of copyright and technology (specifically VCRs) to a spring 1982 legal panel discussion on the issue. At the discussion, Mr. Valenti, in the days when vulgar xenophobia against the Japanese was both common and acceptable in polite society, railed against the Japanese and their machines, which would, he predicted, turn the United States into an "entertainment desert,"[21] by which he presumably did not mean Palm Springs. (The record industry earlier had xenophobic fears about the introduction of the compact disc; the head of consumer electronics manufacturer Dennon observed, "in [19]82, most folks in the American record business had figured that the CD was some kind of foreign trick."[22]) Mr. Lardner also heard the opposite view, from Charles Ferris, representing the electronics industry, who described the VCR as "the best friend Hollywood ever had."[23] Mr. Ferris' remark is what led to Mr. Valenti's later "Boston Strangler" metaphor.

The VCR wars had a far more prosaic beginning, in 1976, in a lawsuit brought by MCA/Universal Pictures against the Sony Corporation over the latter's Betamax VTR (video tape recorder, as it was then known). The first Betamax VCR[24] was part of a combined video and 19-inch TV console set. The VCR was placed side by side with the TV, to the right (facing the TV), on a pedestal base.[25] In Japan it was called a Sony LV-1801, and the VCR was called an SL-6300. In the United States, the machine was called an LV-1901, and the VCR was called an SL-6200 and sold for $2,295 ($9,202 in 2008 dollars). Importantly, although it had audio/video inputs/outputs, it had no tuner, and thus could not tape off-air.

On April 16, 1975, Sony introduced the first freestanding Betamax, the SL-7300 (called the 7200 in the United States and not marketed until February 1976). The SL-7300 was the SL-6200 without the console but (importantly) with a built-in tuner and audio/video outputs, and was the machine MCA representatives saw. The recording time was short, which became an issue with the introduction of VHS VCRs, which offered from two to four hours of recording time. In 1977, the second generation Betamax, the SL-8300 (the SL-8200 in the United States) was the response to the JVC HR-3300 VHS, introduced in 1976.[26] The SL-8300 was the first Betamax to have two recording speeds and used the new L-500 Beta videocassette.

The machines were, it goes without saying, expensive. The SL-7300 had a price of $1,295 ($5,192 in 2008 dollars; and it should be noted that at the time there was no market at all for prerecorded videocassettes because the SL-7300 was the first machine on the market, and it caught the motion picture studios by surprise). As we shall now discuss, the studios and others were developing the video laser disc as a possible home format, but not videocassettes.

In the summer of 1976, Sony's advertising agency sent MCA a mock-up of an ad for the Betamax, touting its ability to permit viewers to tape for later viewing shows that were being simultaneously broadcast, what became known as time-shifting.[27] The news of such a machine on the market drew a quizzical, and then highly negative reaction. The mock-up had been sent to MCA's legal department, which in turn sent it to MCA's president, Sidney Sheinberg.[28] The following week, Sheinberg and his boss, Lew Wasserman, chairman of MCA's board, had a dinner meeting with Akio Morita, the chairman of Sony and Harvey Schein, president of Sony's American affiliate. MCA had been developing a video laser disc called DiscoVision for which it had been trying to find a partner for manufacture, and Sony was deemed such a possibility.[29] Laser discs weren't recordable, a distinct advantage from the studios' perspective. Much to Sony's shock, at the dinner, MCA threatened Sony with an infringement action if it did not withdraw the SL-7300.

MCA then made good on its threat, after speaking to other studios to get them on board. Disney agreed to be a co-plaintiff, and Warner would assist with legal costs. The studios' trade association, the Motion Picture Association of America (MPAA) would participate as an amicus.[30] In addition to suing Sony and its American subsidiary (for contributory infringement), other defendants were the advertising agency (Doyle Dane Bernbach), retail stores at which the Betamax were sold, and a straw consumer—a client of MCA's law firm. Although Sony quickly tried to settle the case by proposing a compulsory licensing scheme, according to James Lardner, the head of Sony of America, Harvey Schein, felt that

> The real obstacle … was MCA's commitment to the videodisc. "Because why buy a videodisc machine when you buy a videocassette machine that does everything it does plus it records off the air and makes home movies? I don't think it was accidental that the company that took the lead in fighting the videocassette was the company that had all the patents on the videodisc."[31]

MCA quickly employed a full range of metaphors. Mr. Sheinberg, debated with Mr. Schein on Walter Cronkite's show; as recounted by Mr. Schein: "He called me a 'highway man.' He equated Sony with the highwaymen of old who stole other people's property."[32]

At this time, there was no home video market (the Cartrivision system having failed), and thus no harm to such a nonexistent market. Nor, as the suit was only about taping off-air, free, over-the-air broadcast works, would there be any possible harm to that market—people were merely taping works they had already been invited to watch for free and at a more convenient time. The lawsuit was not, therefore, concerned with infringement of copyright: The studios did not care about consumers copying. Rather, the suit was intended to eliminate a competing format and loss of advertising revenue.[33]

Litigation was simply a means to gain control over the technology in order to perpetuate existing business models. Sidney Sheinberg was quite candid about this, at least after he lost in the Supreme Court: "The case was really about leverage. If we won, we would have the leverage to get a royalty on the sale of the machines and blank tapes."[34] The royalties on the machines were simply a naked grab to profit off a competitor's superior technology. The royalty on blank tapes were not designed to compensate for lost sales, but rather for perceived lost advertising revenue: Laser discs could not record, and thus the motion picture industry could retain its existing business model, that is, movies would be released exclusively in theaters, and then well after the theatrical run was over, they would appear on television. The TV networks would pay Hollywood for airing the movies, supported by advertisements. Laser discs would fit into this scheme by being released after the TV run. Videocassettes upset this scheme because people could tape the TV airing and, in doing so, "zap" or fast-forward (hence the title of the Lardner book) through the commercials. The Nielsen company started tracking this phenomenon, and by 1984 estimated that 60 percent of VCR owners "frequently" or "usually" fast-forwarded through commercials.[35] Fewer viewers of commercials meant less revenue for the TV networks as the advertisers would pay the networks less, and if the networks got paid less, Hollywood believed it would get a lower price for their goods. James Lardner relates the reaction of the advertisers:

> Fear of "zapping" became an obsession. Burger King produced a series of "speedproof" ads designed, it was said, to get the message across even when viewed at an accelerated pace by an impatient VCR user. NBC went this trick one better with its broadcast of the World Cup soccer matches: it made the program and the commercial inseparable,

by parking ads in a corner of the screen while the game continued around them. Other sponsors turned their commercials into epic productions lush with special effects and exotic locations in the style of Steven Spielberg and George Lucas.[36]

This effort continues today, it should be noted, from direct product placement in movies, to making products an integral part of TV plots.

We can now put Mr. Valenti's "Boston Strangler" comment in better context, beginning with the xenophobic introduction. The hearing was a rare one outside of Washington, in Los Angeles:

> Now, the question comes, well, all right, what is wrong with the VCR. One of the Japanese lobbyists, Mr. Ferris, has said that the VCR—well, if I am saying something wrong, forgive me. I don't know. He certainly is not MGM's lobbyist. That is for sure. He has said that the VCR is the greatest friend that the American film producer ever had.
>
> I say to you that the VCR is to the American film producer and the American public as the Boston Strangler is to the woman home alone.
>
> The VCR avalanche, I told you about that. Now, what about the VCR owners. Now, from here on out, Mr. Chairman, I am going to be speaking about a survey done by the Media Statistics Inc., which is a prestigious firm out of Silver Spring, [Maryland]. We, meaning the MPAA, did not commission this survey. We bought it after it was done when we heard about it. So, this was not a case—we have commissioned a lot of things, but this is not one of them.
>
> Now, I want to tell you about it because I think it is absolutely fascinating. This survey was taken in October 1981. It is the newest and freshest data available. Here is what it says. Median income of a VCR owner is between $35,000 and $50,000 a year. Not a lot of what we call today the truly needy are buying these machines. One-third of all the owners have incomes of more than $50,000. Now, here is the next one: 87 percent, 86.8 percent of all these owners erase or skip commercials. I have here, Mr. Chairman, if you are not aware of how this works—this is Panasonic. This is a little remote control device that you use on machines. It has on here channel, rewind, stop, fast forward, pause, fast advance, slow, up, down, and visual search, either going left or right.
>
> Now, let me tell you what Sony says about this thing. These are not my words. They are right straight from McCann Erickson, whom you

will hear from tomorrow, who is the advertising agency for Sony and here is what they say. They advertise a variable beta scan feature that lets you adjust the speed at which you can view the tape from 5 times up to 20 times the normal speed.

Now, what does that mean, Mr. Chairman? It means that when you are playing back a recording, which you made 2 days or whenever— you are playing it back. You are sitting in your home in your easy chair and here comes the commercial and it is right in the middle of a Clint Eastwood film and you don't want to be interrupted. So, what do you do? You pop this beta scan and a 1-minute commercial disappears in 2 seconds.

Mr. RAILSBACK. Is that all bad?

Mr. VALENTI. If you are watching a Clint Eastwood film it is the most cheerful thing you can do. However, if you are an advertiser who has paid $280,000 a minute to advertise, he feels a very large pain in his stomach as well as in his checkbook because it destroys the reason for free television, the erasure, the blotting out, the fast forwarding, the visual searching, the variable beta scans. The technology is there and I am one who has a belief that before the next few years the Japanese will have built into their machines an automatic situation that kills the commercial.

Being advertised today in all the video magazines, and if any of you take video magazines, here is a marvelous little device called the Killer. It eliminates those black and white commercials. You put the Killer onto your Sony and it automatically takes out the commercial. You don't like the Killer, try the editor. The editor will do the same thing. It will wipe out commercials.

The technology is there in my judgment, in the next several years, where an integral part of the machine will be automatic Killer. But you don't need that now as long as you have this. Indeed, when my son is taping for his permanent collection, he sits there and pauses his machine and when he is finished with it, he has a marvelous Clint Eastwood movie and there is no sign of a commercial. It is a brand new movie and he can put three of those on one 6-hour tape.

Now, the average—

Mr. KASTENMEIER. May I interrupt, Jack, on that point?

Mr. VALENTI. Yes.

Mr. KASTENMEIER. And it is a point that just occurs to me. Actually, the advertiser doesn't pay for a taped replay of any program of that sort. He pays only for a live telecast, where his commercial appears and no matter how it is deferred, he doesn't pay for the deferral because that person wasn't there watching it the first time, presumably it is missed for commercial—

Mr. VALENTI. Mr. Chairman, I am going to defer that question because I have at this table Mr. Eliasberg, for 34 years a practitioner and a student of research in what Nielson and Arbitron present to networks and advisers, what they pay for and what they don't pay for. And rather than me, race over, take time, may I defer the question to Mr. Eliasberg.[37]

Once Mr. Valenti had exhausted his store of metaphors, he was unable to answer the real economic question at the heart of the dispute.

The other necessary context to Mr. Valenti's testimony was that it took place six months after the Ninth Circuit Court of Appeals in California had issued its opinion in the suit brought by MCA against Sony, and finding Sony liable for infringement.[38] The circuit court had reversed a 1979 ruling in Sony's favor by the trial judge,[39] meaning that the court of appeals had ruled in the studios' favor. Congress' reaction to the court of appeals was swift and negative; multiple bills were introduced to permit sale of VCRs and home-taping; it was reaction to those bills that Mr. Valenti testified as the lead witness. His purpose was to raise a moral panic that would defeat the legislation. In addition to his metaphors and folk devils, there was an array of experts hired to provide the statistical support for the moral panic. Indeed, Mr. Valenti was well aware (and rightly so) of the skepticism of such experts, and adverted to this in his testimony. The other side of course had its witnesses and experts too, but Congress was spared the trouble of enacting legislation when, on January 17, 1984, the Supreme Court, by a 5-4 vote reversed the Ninth Circuit, ruling for Sony. [40]

### Hollywood and Video Rental

The motion picture industry was not done with the VCR however. Between the first oral argument in the Supreme Court and the second, the Senate intellectual property subcommittee held a hearing on a bill introduced by Senator Charles McC. Mathias of Maryland.[41] The bill would have amended Section 109 of the Copyright Act to ban the unauthorized rental or lending of motion pictures. Section 109 codifies what is called in the United States the "first sale" doctrine and in other countries the "exhaustion doctrine."[42] When a copyright owner voluntarily sells or gives away a copy of his or her work, the purchaser or possessor of that copy is free to do what he or she wants with it. The first sale doctrine is what permits secondhand bookstores to operate, and it is what permitted video rental stores to operate. Those stores purchased lawfully made copies of videocassettes, and although the studios had no objection to the sale of those copies to consumers, they did object to their rental. The reason for the objection was easy to discern. If a video store bought 10 copies of a movie for sale, the studios would get a cut of all 10 sales. If a video store bought one copy and rented it 10 times, the studio would get a cut of only one copy, while the video store would earn money from 10 rentals (after deducting the cost of the cassette and overhead).

The studios' approach to video rental was the same as it is to every issue: If someone else is making money off of one of our products, that money should be ours, even if that someone else had paid the full price the studios had asked for at the time. Indeed, although the bill gave the studios the right to stop all rentals, in a wink-wink-nudge-nudge, Congress was assured that the studios wouldn't exercise that right[43] but would instead use the right to extract monopolist prices from store owners. In typical Orwellian fashion, this would lead to, in the studios' words, "negotiat[ing] and establish[ing] correct business practices so that the retail method of lending motion pictures will continue."[44] The best way to ensure that video rental stores would continue was to leave them alone, and although this is ultimately what happened, the studios attempted, from 1983 to 1986, to change the business practices through a radical revision to Section 109. The studios' strategy had been clear since at least 1981, as this quote from a video rental store executive reveals: "The studios want total control of the cassette from the manufacturer. The odds of that total control are fairly low, but in an attempt to do that we'll see constant revisions of rental schemes . . ."[45] In 1985, Blockbuster Video was founded, and in 1986, there were over 2,500 video rental stores. The stores would buy pre-recorded videos from the studios for about $50 and then repeatedly rent the same tape to consumers. For top movies, this was a profitable practice, and one the studios wanted a share of. An alternative response by the studios would have been to significantly drop the retail sale price of videocassettes in order to spur sales, an approach a few studios like Paramount and Disney took, but not Universal/MCA.

All the studios sought legislation that would have given them the ability to strangle the home video market, a point made by Senator Dennis DeConcini in his questioning of Register of Copyrights David Ladd:

> Given the early unsuccessful efforts by [the studios] to develop the market for video cassette and rentals, why should we assume here in the committee that a handful of producers, all from California or other far distant places from the marketplace, will make better decisions about pricing and marketing than the thousands of retailers who, after all, are closer to the consumer, and are currently free to make those decisions under the First Sale Doctrine, and have worked hard and successfully in developing those markets?[46]

Senator DeConcini here identifies the central trope of the Copyright Wars: Copyright industries fail to innovate but are saved by others who do. Resenting the success of the innovator, copyright owners then claim that the innovator's success is caused solely by the value provided by the copyright owner. The innovator is described metaphorically as a parasite, fattening itself off of copyright owners. The solution put forth is for the innovator to disgorge a healthy share of its profits to copyright owners (who, left to their own devices, would have starved to death decades ago). After such economic castration, innovations are no longer regarded as a threat but rather as one more dependable source of income feeding the beast.

Following Register Ladd in testifying was Jack Valenti. Mr. Valenti, this time testifying in *favor* of the legislation, was again careful to couch his special pleading on behalf of his clients in terms of the public interest:

> The bill you have before you is going to be of lasting benefit to the public, because it is aimed directly at the folks who want to buy or rent prerecorded video cassettes and video discs. Today, that market is fenced off. It is entangled in an ancient barrier that baffles competition, flexibility of action and flexibility of pricing, which is the ready companion of any marketplace.[47]

The market Mr. Valenti was describing was the free market, the very market that had allowed the studios to set a punishing $20 surcharge on the sale price for the cassettes that were rented by stores. What Mr. Valenti was miffed about was his clients' inability to *legislatively interfere* with the free market, seen in this comment: "a [studio that] makes [its] product available to VCR owners can deal *only* in the sale market, because [it] has no control [over] the videocassettes [it] has sold to distributors/ retailers once they leave [its] hands."[48] What the studios sought was for Congress to interfere with the free market by giving the studios full down-stream control.

The alleged threat to the free market came from the first sale doctrine, which had been a part of copyright law from the nineteenth century and is based on ancient abhorrence of restrictions on trade, the sort of restrictions Mr. Valenti, with an Orwellian twist, was attempting to impose in the name of free trade. In short, Mr. Valenti was attempting to overturn centuries of common (and later statutory) law that *protected* the free market. The studios of course were trying to have things both ways. They could have refused to release any movies on videocassette and killed the rental market. But because others had developed that market at no expense to the studios, the studios didn't want to kill the rental goose that laid the golden egg; they wanted the gold for themselves and were unconcerned with the health of the geese—rental stores that developed the market off of which copyright owners were fattening themselves. The studios believed the foie gras belonged to them. This attempt to have things both ways—to have others develop the distribution market and to then come in and monopolize it—has been followed by copyright owners from the inception of copyright and demonstrates that copyright is not an engine of free expression, but a yoke around innovation put on to retard progress by preserving existing and failed business models.

The original market for VCRs was time-shifting, thanks to the *Sony* decision. A nascent videocassette sale and rental market began in the late 1970s, but the studios priced the cassettes at a price from $55 to $75—from $225 to $300 in 2008 dollars. It was the studios that had retarded the sale market by pricing them far too high. This mistake is born out in the statistics. In 1979, rentals outnumbered sales by a four-to-one margin. By 1982, when the bills were introduced, the spread was 22 to 1 with sale prices reaching $100 per videocassette. It is this spread, caused by the studios' own greed that led them to attempt to alter the first sale doctrine so that they could control the rental market.

The studios failed, however, and it was in the public's and their best interest that they did. As Sumner Redstone, chairman of Viacom, later remarked, home video was "the bonanza that saved Hollywood from bankruptcy."[49] Alas, Hollywood did not learn from the VCR experience, and what they didn't learn was that home copying leads to greater viewing and therefore more money, and they didn't learn that the courts are not about to interfere with home copying.

### ℳ The Redbox Suit

The most recent episode in the studios' long-running efforts to control the home video market to the detriment of consumers is revealed in a dispute between Universal Studios and Redbox, a company that sells and rents DVDs through kiosks. As explained in a declaratory judgment action filed by Redbox against Universal[50] in October 2008, in the Delaware Federal District Court:

> 22. Kiosks typically hold up to 700 DVDs comprising 70–200 individual titles. The kiosks are updated weekly with a supply of new release DVDs. A single kiosk may hold up to as many as forty-five (45) copies of a popular release.
>
> . . . .
>
> 24. . . . Much of Redbox's success depends on maintaining a business model that satisfies the expectations of the retail outlets and consumers.
> 25. Consumers can rent DVDs from Redbox kiosks for $1 per night—a lower cost than alternative brick-and-mortar outlets or alternative sources for DVD rental. In comparison, some 175 million DVDs were rented in the United States last month, at an average cost of approximately $3.25.
> 26. Consumers can also purchase previously-viewed DVDs from Redbox, beginning 12 days after their release, for only $7. In comparison, 50 million newly-released DVD movies were sold last month at an average price of approximately $18.50 from other sources.
> 27. Consumer preference for Redbox rentals can largely be attributed to its ability to conveniently provide consumers with lowcost rentals on the same day that a DVD is released by a studio and made available

for home viewing. This date is known as the "street date." Over 60% of the rental demand for a particular title offered by Redbox occurs within 45 days of the 60% of the rental demand for a particular title offered by Redbox occurs within 45 days of the street date.

As we shall see, consumer choice and availability of DVDs for rental on the "street date" are alleged by Redbox to be an anathema to Universal. In August 2008, the problems began. As asserted in Redbox's court papers:

37. On Tuesday, August 26, 2008, USHE representatives visited Redbox's headquarters in Oakbrook Terrace, Illinois. . . .

39. During the meeting USHE presented the Revenue Sharing Agreement to Redbox and stated that Redbox had until the close of business the following day (i.e., August 27, 2008) by which to sign the Revenue Sharing Agreement. Redbox had no prior notice as to the nature of this proposal, which would materially and adversely alter the conditions under which consumers are able to rent and buy DVDs from kiosk outlets.

40. During the meeting USHE said that if Redbox refused to sign the Revenue Sharing Agreement and the distributors continued to supply Universal DVDs to Redbox, USHE would stop selling any Universal DVDs to VPD and Ingram.

41. . . . USHE has threatened to cut off sales to VPD and Ingram if they continue to provide these services without a signed Revenue Sharing Agreement from Redbox.[51]

In other words, the papers allege that unless Redbox agreed to Universal's terms, Universal would demand that Redbox's suppliers cut Redbox off, and that if those suppliers refused, they too would be cut off. The proposed deal, by contrast, would have had Universal cut out the suppliers by selling directly to Redbox. The proposed revenue-sharing agreement is attached to Redbox's complaint, but the relevant provisions of it for our purposes are detailed in Redbox's papers:

45. The Revenue Sharing Agreement is a naked restriction on output that directly reduces the supply of goods to consumers, and will increase the prices consumers must pay.

a. The Revenue Sharing Agreement artificially constrains output by prohibiting Redbox from renting to consumers any DVD until "forty-five (45) days following [the] DVD sell-through street date established by USHE with respect to a Title";

b. The Revenue Sharing Agreement also limits the number of DVDs of a single copyrighted work that any particular kiosk may carry based upon a formula that correlates to the gross box office revenue of the movie. Although Redbox would offer as many as forty-five copies of a popular DVD in one kiosk to meet consumer demand, the maximum number of copies per kiosk authorized under the Revenue Sharing Agreement is eight.

c. The Revenue Sharing Agreement also seeks to require Redbox to "destroy 100% of the units removed from an active rental machine" and certify that it has done so. This directly reduces the supply of previously-rented disks available in the market place, artificially restricting supply and increasing prices.

46. The provisions of the Revenue Sharing Agreement will substantially limit consumer access to copyrighted works and simultaneously damage Redbox's ability to meet consumer demand.

47. Not only is Redbox's distribution system more efficient than other existing methods of providing DVDs to consumers ($1 per night vs. $3.25 for the average rental; $7 sale price for a 12-day old DVD vs. $18.50 for a new one), but it is also less expensive than other methods that USHE seeks to develop including internet download services (the typical price of a new full-length purchased on iTunes, for example is $14.99 and the so-called "rental" price for time-limited access to the downloaded copy is $3.99, USHE's affiliates have said) and Video-on- Demand (the average price of watching a video-on-demand movie is $4.00).

48. The Revenue Sharing Agreement will have the effect of restricting output, eliminating competition in the rental and sales markets and raising prices to consumers.[52]

The Redbox litigation is unique only because one company refused to comply and chose to reveal the terms a studio sought to impose. The studios can say publicly whatever they want about their concern for consumers and their efforts to satisfy consumer desires, but the Redbox agreement stands as irrefutable evidence to the contrary.

The studios' perpetual insistence on controlling consumer behavior in Redbox is small potatoes compared to what they achieved in the Digital Millennium Copyright Act.[53]

## ✍ The Digital Millennium Copyright Act

### Access Controls

In 1998, the MPAA and the RIAA successfully lobbied Congress for powerful new rights in the Digital Millennium Copyright Act (DMCA), making it a civil and criminal violation

- to circumvent a technological measure that effectively controls access to a work protected under this title;[54]
- to manufacture, import, offer to the public, provide, or otherwise traffic in any technology, product, service, device, component, or part thereof, that—

  (A) is primarily designed or produced for the purpose of circumventing a technological measure that effectively controls access to a work protected under this title;

  (B) has only limited commercially significant purpose or use other than to circumvent a technological measure that effectively controls access to a work protected under this title; or

  (C) is marketed by that person or another acting in concert with that person with that person's knowledge for use in circumventing a technological measure that effectively controls access to a work protected under this title;[55]

These provisions mark the Rubicon in copyright as they vested for the first time in the then 208-year history of copyright: (1) a right to control access to works; (2) a right to control the design of consumer electronics created by third parties; and, (3) a right to prohibit acts designed to circumvent (1) and (2). Taken together, these three rights vest in copyright owners the right to impose their preferences on the market and to ignore consumers' preferences. Prior to these provisions, the copyright laws were technology neutral: They did not regulate technologies, but rather uses of copyrighted material, regardless of the technology employed. Use of copyrighted works was the essence of copyright, not technology. With the access provisions of the DMCA, the entire history of copyright was thrown out the window. Now it is technology that is regulated—technology developed by third parties, and legitimate technologies at that. The DMCA is the twenty-first century equivalent of letting copyright owners put a chastity belt on someone else's wife.

The access provisions of the DMCA are not concerned with preventing copying of works, but instead with control over business models. Circumventing access controls placed on by the copyright industries, even for otherwise lawful purposes such as fair use criticism, comment, or educational purposes, is a violation of the DMCA—a violation that the copyright industries point out at every opportunity might also be a crime. The DMCA is the reason, for example, you cannot load a lawfully purchased DVD onto your iPod. In November 2006, the motion picture studios sued a service, Load 'N Go Video:

> According to the suit, Load 'N Go sells both DVDs and iPods and loads the former onto the latter for customers who purchase both. The company then sends the iPod and the original DVDs to the customer. So the customer has purchased every DVD, and Load 'N Go just saves them the trouble of ripping the DVD. The movie studios' suit claims that this is illegal, because ripping a DVD (i.e., decrypting it and making a copy) is illegal under the DMCA. The suit also claims that this constitutes copyright infringement.
>
> Although this lawsuit happens to be aimed at Load 'N Go, the DMCA theory in the complaint makes it crystal clear that the MPAA believes it is just as illegal for you to do the same thing for yourself at home. Apparently, Hollywood believes that you should have to re-purchase all your DVD movies a second time if you want to watch them on your iPod.[56]

The truth of this statement was born out by a later deal the motion picture studios entered into with Wal-Mart, where even though you buy a DVD at Wal-Mart at full price, to copy that DVD to other devices—activity that is fair use—you nevertheless have to pay an additional $1.97 to copy the DVD onto a portable device, and $2.97 to a personal computer, or both for $3.97.[57] The DMCA is the reason you cannot play a legitimate DVD bought in the United Kingdom on your DVD player in the United States. Rather than take a global product and make it globally available, the studios use the DMCA to ensure that ill-fitting territorial and distribution partnerships and licenses developed during the hard copy era are preserved into the twenty-first century for digital works.[58] The DMCA is the reason that Linux, an open-source operating system cannot be run on certain devices (such as DVD players), although there is no question of copying a single work of authorship. The DMCA is the reason in the very near future you may be permitted to only rent but never to buy particular works. Nor is misuse of the DMCA limited to the traditional copyright industries: despite a January 2009 announcement from Apple that music downloaded from its iTunes store will no longer carry digital rights management restrictions (DRM), the Electronic Frontier Foundation has pointed out that for its own products, Apple is quite fond of digital locks:

- Apple uses DRM to lock iPhones to AT&T and Apple's iTunes App Store;
- Apple uses DRM to prevent recent iPods from syncing with software other than iTunes (Apple claims it violates the DMCA to reverse engineer the hashing mechanism);
- Apple claims that it uses DRM to prevent OS X from loading on generic Intel machines;
- Apple's new Macbooks feature DRM-laden video ports that only output certain content to "approved" displays;
- Apple requires iPod accessory vendors to use a licensed "authentication chip" in order to make accessories to access certain features on newer iPods and iPhones;
- The iTunes Store will still lock down movies and TV programs with FairPlay DRM;
- Audiobook files purchased through the iTunes Store will still be crippled by Audible's DRM restrictions.[59]

Amazon.com's Kindle ebook reader has more digital locks than CIA headquarters, designed to ensure that Amazon's customers will have to use the Kindle even if a superior, cheaper alterative is developed. To obtain passage of the DMCA, copyright owners, aided by a few gullible, partisan academics,[60] told Congress there would be a proliferation of works on the Internet but only if they were given control over consumers and consumer electronics. Without that control, copyright owners testified they would withhold their works resulting in the Internet not living up to its potential—or so went the argument Congress bought. The copyright industries had no intention of "putting their cars on the Information Superhighway,"[61] as revealed in the 11 years since passage of the DMCA. Rather, the copyright industries regarded the Internet then and largely do now still, as an enemy to be killed off, or at least wounded badly enough to be unappealing to consumers as a distribution resource.

Thanks to the DMCA, the copyright market has now come to resemble the planned Soviet economies of the early twentieth century, but with the market planning is done by corporations exercising government-created monopoly power. The government's role in this scheme is limited to setting up the laws that make it an unlawful to circumvent whatever rules corporations establish *for us*. What results is a form of "corporatism." "Corporatism" involves actions by unelected bodies (not necessarily corporations) whose purpose is to exert control over the social and economic life of their respective areas through agreements that are reached internally but that find support in elected, political bodies.[62] Such special interests reach agreement among themselves and privately, but after agreement is reached, the agreement is touted as being for the public's benefit, not that of the corporatists. Corporatism only works if the government uses *its* coercive power to demand compliance with what the corporatists have agreed to, and that is the precise role played by the DMCA. Corporatism was previously thought to have reached its zenith during Mussolini's Fascist Italy, but with the DMCA it is enjoying a healthy resurgence.

The cultural implications of the DMCA and digital rights management (DRM) have been spelled out by Professor Tarleton Gillespie:

> While it poses challenge for copyright in a new medium, DRM is also an intervention in a very old struggle: the relentless commodification of culture by its powerful commercial providers. Marketing strategies not only shape the production and distribution of culture in ways suited more to the corporations' economic self-interest than to democratize society; they also shape our experience of culture in similar ways. The manner in which cultural goods are served up as commodities choreographs how users are likely to engage with them, and how they envision their subject position vis-á-vis culture. . . . The concern, broadly, is that we are moving inexorably toward a "pay-per-use"

society, in which every instance in which we interact with culture will be commodified.[63]

Business practices are forever outpacing the law's consideration of them, and it is time once again to ask whether this is the case with copyright. DRM is, primarily if not wholly, a way to regulate the sale of cultural expression, and it does so in ways that profoundly reshape what users can do with culture once they have it.[64]

The supreme irony of the access provisions of the DMCA is that they impose control over a technology—the Internet—which presents the most greatest opportunity in history for consumers to make their preferences known, the greatest opportunity for there to be perfect information, enabling both buyers and sellers to possess complete knowledge about each other (and all other buyers and sellers), instantaneously updated as new information arises. Under these conditions, consumers can choose the best products; the market will reward, with higher sales, those copyright owners who make the best products.

One of the new rights in the DMCA granted the motion picture studios the power to dictate the functional design of consumer electronic devices. The DVD was the perfect vehicle for the studios' new rights. As a studio lawyer wrote, "There was no existing installed base of DVD players or DVD drives for personal computers; copy protection could therefore be designed and built into these machines at the outset."[65] Crippling new technologies before they are commercially released has enormous advantages for the copyright industries: consumers can't miss what they never had; there is also no installed base of users to complain that something is being taken away from them. In any event, translating the studio lawyer's comments, they mean DVD players and DVDs were crippled from the outset. Here's how the crippling occurs: Motion picture studios insert a few short pieces of encrypted software code into DVD versions of their movies. The code prohibits access to the movie unless the DVD player has a built-in key to de-encrypt the access code. In the case of motion pictures, the key is the Content Scramble System (CSS), which is a

forty-bit encryption algorithm that scatters the digital data of the film around the surface of the DVD. Playing the disc requires the algorithm decryption key, which is built into the authorized DVD players, to match the two keys on the disc itself. When this match is assured, the player can access the encrypted disc, recover the scattered data bit by bit, and display the film.[66]

Obtaining the CSS de-encryption key requires entering into a CSS license from the motion picture studio-controlled DVD Copy Control Association.[67] The license agreement goes beyond technical specifications and fees to be paid, banning consumer behavior permitted under the Copyright Act, such as copying for personal use. For example, to get the key to de-encrypt CSS, DVD manufacturers agreed not to offer DVD machines with a record button.[68] VCRs have record buttons, of course; indeed, the function was an important selling point for them. In the late 1970s, the motion picture studios sued Sony Corporation over the VCR record function, but in 1984 the U.S. Supreme Court approved their use for home taping of free over-the-air broadcasts in the famous "Betamax" case.[69] However, because of the CSS license, consumers did not have the chance to engage in the same activity with their DVD players, even though DVD manufacturers would have loved to offer consumers a DVD player record button. The crippling effects of our current copyright laws have extended far beyond DVD players. As Bennett Lincoff wrote:

> [C]onsumer electronics makers, fearing liability, have been slow to offer greater interoperability between the many recording, playback, and communication devices that are available. They have also been reluctant to offer new products with next generation capabilities, such as web-based home entertainment systems or embedded device recording capabilities. In addition technology firms and their investors, also fearing liability, have withdrawn support for certain of their operations off-shore. One can only speculate as to the magnitude of the revenue opportunities lost by consumer electronics makers and technology firms because of the continued irresolution of the crisis in digital music licensing.[70]

Although CSS and other efforts to block the development of new technologies of the sort referred to by Mr. Lincoff are mistakenly regarded by many to be anti-piracy tools, that is not their principal intended function. The CSS encryption key is a lock, not a blocking device, and does not stop copying of DVDs:

> Encryption is not itself a copy protection, at least directly; CSS does not render the data uncopyable. If someone wanted to duplicate

Hollywood DVDs on a massive scale and sell them cheaply, CSS would not stop them; they could merely reproduce the DVD verbatim and press it onto a new disc, using the same equipment the studios use to make them in the first place. The pirated copy would still be encrypted, exactly as the original is; anyone who bought this black market disc could watch it on their licensed DVD player. What CSS does is to prevent consumers from watching the DVD using the wrong device— that is, one that hasn't been certified by the movie studios.[71]

Building mousetraps has always instilled a desire in others to defeat them. CSS was quickly and successfully hacked by, among others,[72] a 19-year-old Norwegian, Jon Leech Johannes, who on October 6, 1999, released computer code called DeCSS. DeCSS can be written in as few as 434 characters and printed on a T-shirt; indeed, I have a T-shirt with DeCSS printed on it (so prosecute me!). Johansen was criminally prosecuted in Norway for creating and disseminating DeCSS but was acquitted because there was no provision of Norwegian law that banned his activity.

In the United States, the DMCA makes it illegal (under both civil and criminal law) to circumvent CSS and other such codes or devices. The coercive power of the DMCA explains why manufacturers of DVD players agreed to the onerous CSS license. If DVD manufacturers were not subject under the DMCA to heavy monetary fines, injunctions, or prison terms, they would have done what teenagers were able to quickly do, defeat the motion picture studios' encryption. They would have then offered DVD players with the functionalities consumers want, including a record button. The DMCA therefore operates to distort the market, forcing manufacturers to build machines that are crippled, not innovative, and do not offer consumers what they want.

Why would Congress intervene so dramatically in the market and thwart innovation, consumers' desires, and render a Supreme Court opinion irrelevant in the digital world? The short answer in the specific case of the DMCA is that Congress was told by the copyright industries that the Internet was an existential threat to them, and that unless they were given the power to control it, they would not make their works available on it. The public would thereby lose by not having access to popular movies and music.[73] But if copyright owners were given the power to lock up the Internet and digital playback machines, then a golden age would ensue, one in which copyrighted works would be available in abundance. Congress genuinely believed that making works available on the Internet in exchange for the new unprecedented rights granted in the DMCA was also in the public's interest.

Eleven years later, copyright owners as a group have miserably failed to keep their part of the bargain. In 2003, some members of Congress, upset at copyright owners' failure, proposed amending the DMCA. This effort met with the following response, made without a hint of irony:

> [H]ow companies satisfy consumer expectations is a business decision that should be driven by the dynamics of the marketplace, and should not be regulated. . . . The role of government, if needed at all, should be limited to enforcing compliance with voluntarily developed functional specifications reflecting consensus among affected interests. If the government pursues the imposition of technical mandates, . . . record companies may act to ensure such rules neither prejudice not ignore their interests.[74]

These remarks are striking. Not only is all of copyright government intervention, but the DMCA was invention by the government in the marketplace on a massive scale at the request of the very copyright industry groups that made the above statement. Congress not only imposed compliance technical mandates in the DMCA but delegated to the copyright industries the power to dictate the future terms of those mandates, resulting in a substantial and reckless abdication of governmental responsibility to set public policy. The Congressional recommendation to dial back on that abdication by amending the DMCA was thus a proposed amendment to earlier government intervention. The copyright industries' description of those recommendations as interference with companies' efforts to satisfy consumer demand (by implication in an unregulated market) was hypocritical.

Viviane Reding, European Commissioner for Information Society and Media, summed up the effect of such conduct: "Anti-competitive actions often dress themselves up as arguments in favour of protecting us from harm. But the greater harm would come from the foreclosure by vested interests and incumbents of the future of the Internet as a force for innovation and change."[75]

### Take-Down Notices Under the DMCA: Suppression
### of Free Speech and Creativity

Another provision of the DMCA is found in Section 512 of the Copyright Act. Section 512 provides what are called "safe harbors" to Internet "service providers,"[76] for engaging in certain activity such as transitory digital network communications, system caching, for information residing on systems or networks placed there at the direction of users, and for information location tools. For the third and fourth of these activities, the safe harbor is conditioned on the service provider taking a number of steps. One of these steps is taking down allegedly infringing material in response to a takedown notice of claimed infringement sent by a copyright owner. Once such a notice has been received, the person whose material was taken down (disabled is perhaps a better term), may send a counter notice asserting he or she is legally entitled to post it. In this case, the material will be restored unless the complaining copyright owner files suit.

The original intent of the takedown provision—to give copyright owners a way to expeditiously have infringing material taken down without the need to bring a lawsuit—was a good one, but that intent has now been seriously abused. Hundreds of thousands of takedown notices are sent that have nothing to do with copyright by people who aren't copyright owners, whose purposes are to suppress criticism or to punish Internet service providers (ISPs). One company sent more than 100,000 takedown notices in one day to YouTube. Record and motion picture companies have outsourced take-down notices to third-party firms, who rely on automated processes, indirect evidence of infringement, but who have a direct financial incentive to send out as many notices as possible. Some of these companies send out over a million take-down notices a year. Such outsourcing flouts copyright owners' statutory responsibility to ensure that all notices represent a good faith belief that "use of the material in the manner complained of is not authorized by the copyright owner, its agent, or the law," and that the information in the notification is accurate.

Individuals have had their own videos taken down when corporate content owners have falsely claimed that they owned it;[77] the voting machine company Diebold was fined for using DMCA notices to suppress speech;[78] a satire of the satirical *Stephen Colbert Report* was taken down by a take-down notice;[79] a 29-second home video shot by a woman showing her toddler bouncing to a scratchy version of Prince's song "Let's Go Crazy" playing in the background was taken down.[80] In the 2008 Presidential campaign, Senator John McCain had a number of political videos taken down by overzealous news organizations, usually because he included short snippets from Senator Barack Obama's campaign speeches.[81] There is an entire clearinghouse devoted to tracking and displaying abusive and false take-down notices, the Chilling Effects Clearinghouse, which is a joint project of the Electronic Frontier Foundation and legal clinics at Harvard Law School, Stanford Law School, Berkeley Law, University of San Francisco School of Law, Maine Law Institute, George Washington University School of Law, and Santa Clara University School of Law, *available at:* http://www.chillingeffects.org/. Taked-down notices have become a formidable weapon in the Copyright Wars.

# NINE

# How Innovation Occurs
## Creative Destruction and Disruptive Technologies

American economist Robert Solow,[1] who won the Nobel Prize in 1987 for his work on growth models,[2] calculated that approximately four-fifths of the growth in output per worker in the United States is attributable to technological progress. The figure is higher now as much of Solow's work covered decades before his award.[3] Viviane Reding, European Commissioner for Information Society and Media stated in a November 2008 speech that information and communication technology (ICT) is

> the enabling technology of our age. It underpins the entire economy. According to a recent authoritative macroeconomic analysis, ICT was responsible for 50% of overall productivity growth in the economy for the ten years up to 2004. The industry itself, which represents only about 6% of the economy, drove fully 20% of the total productivity increase across the economy.[4]

A March 2007 study by the Information Technology and Innovation Foundation think tank concluded that information technologies have been "the key factor responsible for reversing the 20-year productivity slowdown from the mid-1970s to the mid-1990s, and in driving today's robust productivity growth."[5] An April 2008 study by the Brookings Institute of productivity growth from 2001 to 2005 in the 100 largest metropolitan areas in the United States showed that the highest annual productivity growth rate was for the computer and electronic products sector, 22.8 percent; the motion picture and sound recording industries were in twenty-fifth place at a mere 3.7 percent.[6] (Lawyers were in fifty-first place with a *decline* of 0.9 percent.) These percentages are important because "every 0.1 percentage point increase in annual productivity growth adds $50 billion annually to the federal budget after 10 years have passed."[7] It is not only greater productivity per worker that matters but, more importantly, the fact that the Internet industries create jobs, and those jobs pay almost twice as much as the average wage for all jobs: $70,000 per year versus $38,000 per year.[8]

The same study noted that there has been a shift away from the belief that capital accumulation is the key to growth, in favor of innovation being the key to improving standards of living. Economist Paul Romer has written that "[n]o amount of savings and investment, no policy of macroeconomic fine-tuning, no set of tax and spending incentives can generate sustained economic growth unless it is accompanied by the countless large and small discoveries that are required to create more value from a fixed set of natural resources."[9]

But if innovation and technological progress are the overwhelming drivers of the U.S. economy and contribute vastly more than the entertainment industries,[10] one would never know it from our copyright policies, which are dominated by a blinkered, one-dimensional ideology, in which copyright is inherently good, and ever more extensive rights and control over consumers and technology is even better. In this endless expansion, the contributions of the consumer electronics and Internet sectors are ignored, despite data demonstrating their critical importance to the economy; not even lip service is paid to the negative impact of this false ideology on the public. Led astray by the copyright industries' false data and framing, policy makers have treated the consumer electronics and Internet industries much like a vampire regards garlic.[11] The haphazard, inadequate, and shortsighted nature of our federal policies in genuinely encouraging innovative industries is perhaps best seen in an example given by the Brookings Institute:

> The Defense Advances Research Program (DARPA) has funded some innovation programs. The Internet grew out of a DARPA initiative. In recent years, however, DARPA has shifted toward a more short-term, mission-oriented development. Indeed, it is not an exaggeration to state that if DARPA were making the kinds of investments it makes today 30 years ago, the Internet never would have been developed.[12]

The failure of vision by the federal government is even worse than the Brookings Institute stated, because by default we are now reliant on the private sector to develop, fund, and commercialize our next Internet-like inventions (and many of a lesser order). It is national economic suicide to crush, through our copyright laws, those entrepreneurs willing to take the risks. Professor Jan Fagerberg has explained why: "The function of innovation is to induce novelty ... into the economic sphere. Should the state of ... innovation dry up, the economy will settle into a 'stationary state' with little or no growth. Hence, innovation is crucial for long-term economic growth."[13]

Far from being innovative, the copyright industries have been stagnating for some time, although this hasn't stopped them from having taxpayers all over the United States subsidize their inevitable decline. In the October 3, 2008, federal "Emergency Economic Stabilization Act," legislation that provided a bail-out of Wall Street's bad debt, Congress provided, at the MPAA's request, $478 million in tax credits to motion picture studios to simply film movies in the United States. Motion picture companies have also been hitting up states and cities around the country for generous subsidies. As described in an October 12, 2008, article in the *New York Times*:

> Already on the hook for billions to bail out Wall Street, taxpayers are also finding themselves stuck with a tab for state programs intended to increase local film productions. One of the most shocking bills has come due in Louisiana, where residents are financing a hefty share of Brad Pitt's next movie—$27,117,737 to be exact, which producers will receive by cashing or selling off valuable tax credits.
>
> . . . .
>
> Michigan its own budget sagging, is in the middle of a hot political fight over a generous 40 per cent rebate on expenditures to filmmakers ... which some have estimated could quickly hit $200 million a year. In Rhode Island ... producers of a straight-to-DVD picture called "Hard Luck," which starred Wesley Snipes and Cybill Sheperd, had picked up $2.65 million in tax state credits on a budget of $11 million, even though it had reported paying only $1.9 million of the total to Rhode Islanders.[14]

The studios are deft at playing states against each other, threatening to move production out of state if their demands aren't met. The result of this tax credit arms race is not more works—the amount stays the same—but rather reduced state revenues. Yet, when the motion picture studios seek greater copyright protection, the pitch is always that they are a significant driver of the economy, rather than what they apparently are, corporate welfare recipients. Indeed, the analogy to welfare may be more apt than one would think. In a 2003 article, Professor Thomas Bell made a case for regarding the entirety of copyright as form of welfare for authors.[15] How else, for example, to describe the 1998 extension of copyright term by twenty years even though that extension will not and cannot conceivably lead to the creation of a single work of authorship beyond what would have been created under the then-existing term of copyright—life of the author plus fifty years? The term extension also covered works that had already been created, so there was no *ex ante* incentive for those works, as well as covering works of dead authors, who are unable to be incentivized. Because term extension had nothing to do with providing incentives, the only way to regard this largesse than as corporate welfare.

We will never be a productive country unless we focus on those who are innovative rather than on large entertainment corporations whose defining characteristics are quixotic battles against technologies, their own customers, and the very nature of capitalism as a dynamic, competitive force. According to Austrian economist Joseph Schumpeter, the process by which innovations challenge and then replace existing products, services, and business models "is the essential fact about capitalism. It is what capitalism consists in and what every capitalist concern has got to live in."[16] Capitalism is, according to Schumpeter, "by nature . . . a method of economic change and not only never is but can never be stationary."[17] Far from being a threat to capitalism, Schumpeter's great insight was that creative destruction "incessantly revolutionizes the economic structure *from within*, incessantly destroying the old one, incessantly creative a new one." "Stabilized capitalism is a contradiction in terms."[18] Capitalism is inherently dynamic, but with the centralization of ownership in a very few large, vertically integrated corporations, copyright has unfortunately become a captive of backwards-looking, anti-innovative business models.

Innovation—the generative force of creative destruction—is the way capitalism survives its own tendency toward monopolization and stagnation, even as innovation gives rise to opposition from the established businesses. In Schumpeter's words, "a new firm's intrusion into an existing industry always entails 'warring' with an 'old sphere,' which tries to prohibit, discredit, or otherwise restrict every advantage afforded to the new form by its innovation."[19] To ensure the continued vitality of innovation and capitalism itself, we must embrace innovation rather than, as illustrated by the copyright industries' conduct in the Copyright Wars, try to kill it off. As Schumpeter observed, markets in capitalist societies are not intended to optimize profits for existing businesses but rather are "institutions to facilitate change, to permit entrepreneurship, to encourage challenges to the existing order."[20]

Established businesses *can* meet new challenges. They need not "go gentle into that good night," nor set their faces against the future. As Professor Theodore Levitt wrote, "early decline and certain death are the fate of companies whose policies are geared totally and obsessively to their own convenience at the total expense of the customer."[21] But "maturity, decline, and senescence are not inevitable, and stasis is avoidable."[22]

One example of this is the S.L. Christie company, which in 1929 began to make movie projectors for the film industry in Los Angeles. In 1999, its seventieth anniversary, the firm was highly profitable making 35-millimeter projectors. The company's executives had dismissed digital video projectors as inferior, but nevertheless kept an eye on digital developments. In November 1999, one of the company's engineers snuck into a demonstration of digital projectors hosted for theater owners. The engineer reported back that digital projectors were going to be the future much sooner than they had thought. At that point, Christie's was in no position to move toward manufacturing digital projectors; a presentation was made to the board of directors, during which the board was told that in two years, the company would be out of business if it don't get into digital projection. Christie's quickly acquired a Canadian company that already manufactured digital projectors. It also became the first company to license a different technology from Texas Instruments.[23] By 2005, Christie had more digital projectors in theatres worldwide than any other company, and its technology is used by all the major studios.

Creative destruction is a positive force that can spur existing firms into being innovative, and therefore remaining productive and profitable. Although innovation frequently arises from small start-up companies, as the Christie example shows, where there is a will to be innovative, companies will find a way. There is no reason larger, established businesses cannot learn from the newcomers, other than a lack of will. Silicon Valley is innovative and productive because of its climate of creativity and bottom-up structure; even established Silicon Valley businesses are constantly acquiring start-ups and thereby injecting new ideas, products, and business models. The approach of the larger entertainment conglomerates is the opposite: top-down, hierarchical structures,[24] and a business model of litigating start-ups out of existence. Circling the wagons is a dead end, but it is a path too many in the copyright industries take.

A common, but erroneous assumption, is that all innovations involve new technologies or scientific discoveries. Muhammad Yunus won the Nobel Prize for Economics in 2006 for developing "micro credit," the loan of very small amounts to poor women in rural Bangladesh villages who either had no access to capital or were offered usurious rates that made it impossible to ever pay the loan off. Professor Yunus' innovation was his belief that widely distributed amounts of small loans could transform rural economies. He set up a bank, Graeme,[25] to put his innovation into practice.[26] By 2006, his bank had loaned more than $6 billion to seven million individuals. In addition to his Nobel Prize, *Newsweek* hailed him as one of the greatest entrepreneurs of all time.[27]

Innovation is thus not the same as invention. The Brookings Institute has properly defined innovation as "putting new ideas into commercial use."[28] Without a successful commercial application, an invention cannot realize its potential. John Seely Brown, director emeritus of the famed Xerox Palo Alto Research Center (PARC) pointed out, "innovation often demands an innovative business model at least as much as it requires an innovative product offering."[29] Mr. Brown came to this knowledge the hard way: Many important inventions, including graphical user interfaces, occurred at PARC, but were commercialized by other companies when Xerox either declined interest in them or failed to back them in a significant way.[30] In 1996, Steven Jobs stated: "'Xerox could have owned the entire computer industry today." Mr. Jobs' comment was based on Xerox's introduction in 1981 of the Star workstation, which used Ethernet technology (also developed at PARC) to link word processors, e-mail, and printers. Using the exact business model it had employed for sale of its printers, Xerox restricted sale of this innovation to its existing customer base of large corporations and government agencies,[31] pricing the system at $16,959 and prohibiting use of third-party equipment or software.

By contrast, IBM took a very different approach to selling its new personal computers. IBM priced its machines at $2,995 and sold them through retail chain stores, aided by a Charlie Chaplin-like ad campaign, which although I found it deeply annoying, was intended to appeal to ordinary consumers lacking a technical background. IBM deliberately departed from its existing business model for mainframes and used an open systems architecture that permitted third parties to develop peripheral hardware and software. Although Xerox's Star was a superior technology, Xerox lost out to the "vastly superior business model of the IBM PC."[32] Henry Chesbrough noted: "The value of an idea or technology depends on its business model. There is no inherent value in technology per se. The value is determined instead by the business model used to bring it to market."[33] In the Copyright Wars, it is innovative business models that represent the real threat to the status quo, not technology.

By definition, innovation requires creative and significant change from the past. Creativity involves a recasting of prior relationships and prior strategies; creativity is inconsistent with embalming existing relationships and existing business models. Creativity is change, not the status quo. Creativity is bottom-up, not top-down. Schumpeterian creativity exists in abundance in Silicon Valley (witness Apple and the iPod/iTunes), but rarely in Hollywood. Innovation is the lifeblood of Northern California but is regarded as a fast-moving cancer in Southern California. There are of course some (almost all younger) brave souls employed by the copyright industries who do want to be innovative, but as Schumpeter realized, "in the breast of one who wishes to do something new, the forces of habit rise up and bear witness against the embryonic project."[34] The structure and environment in the large, multinational entertainment companies is a very strong repellant to those few innovative souls:

> [T]here are limited economic or cultural incentives for senior executives to risk their careers and reputation . . . on an unproven market, and worse, being held accountable for any potential failure. . . . [T]he Internet clashes with the social world in which studio executives happily live and go about their daily business. The technology demands new approaches to the strategic management of space and time in the form of changes to the pattern of release windows. However, executives in large firms such as studios are generally unable to pioneer the creative destruction of revenue streams and the economic landscape more broadly. . . . [T]hey attempt to remake the world in their image.[35]

The result is that although existing markets are obviously in serious decline and new markets are opening up, those who control the copyright industries choose to focus on protecting existing markets at all costs, and at great cost to the future. This error is so commonplace that Schumpeter pointed it out 81 years ago: "Mere husbanding of already existing resources, no matter how painstaking, is always characteristic of a declining position."[36] Mere husbanding is also reflective of monopoly rights, as Nobel Prize winner in Economics Kenneth Arrow detailed in his classic 1959 article, "Economic Welfare and the Allocation of Resources for Invention."[37] Once one obtains monopoly rights, say in copyrighted works, there is far less incentive to be inventive than in a competitive environment without such rights. This phenomenon even has a name, the Entrenched Player's Dilemma. As explained by Don Tapscott and Anthony Williams:

> The problem with mature companies is that the very commercial success of their products increases their dependency on them. Making radical changes in the product's capabilities, underlying architecture or associated business models could cannibalize sales or lead to costly realignments of strategy and business infrastructure. It's as though popular and widely adopted products become ossified, hardened by the inherent incentives to build on their own success. The result is that entrenched industry players are generally not motivated to develop and or deploy disruptive technologies.[38]

In a free-market economy, entrenched players either adapt or fail, although the financial bail-outs in 2008 and 2009 are an important exception. One of the many downsides of monopolies is that they can stave off for an unnatural period of time such inevitable results, and in the meantime wreak havoc on the market and the public. Copyright has become a tool to construct the barricades against the inherent creative destruction of capitalism, a tool by which creativity and innovation are stifled. To use a Hollywood movie, copyright infringement claims have become a "Wag the Dog,"[39] the diversion used to cover up the lack of leadership in the entertainment industries in their decision to fight against rather than harness new markets.

### ✼ The Design of the Internet and the World Wide Web

Back in the days before the Internet, before the federal government broke up AT&T, AT&T had complete control over the services that were transmitted on its telephone network. AT&T was therefore the gatekeeper of innovation. If the Internet had expanded beyond its initial DARPA incarnation into the popular application it now is while AT&T was still the gatekeeper, AT&T would have throttled it, at least that's what AT&T said at the time. As recounted by James Naughton, when RAND researcher Paul Baran showed an early design idea for the Internet in the 1960s to AT&T's Jack Osterman, Osterman replied: "First, it can't possibly work, and if it did, damned if we are going to allow the creation of a competitor to ourselves."[40] Gatekeepers, not surprisingly, act anti-competitively.

The design of the Internet is the antithesis of AT&T's views[41] and of gatekeepers generally. The Internet[42] and the World Wide Web are social, and not technological creations. As Tim Berners-Lee[43] wrote in his history of the Web: "I designed it for a social effect—to help people work together—and not as technical toy. The ultimate goal of the Web is to support and improve our weblike existence in the world."[44] That goal is achieved through a decentralized, open system rather than a closed, controlled system—through a nonproprietary approach and not one locked down by ownership claims.

Vint Cerf, often called the Father of the earlier designed Internet agreed:[45]

The Internet's open, neutral architecture has proven to be an enormous engine for market innovation, economic growth, social discourse, and the free flow of ideas. The remarkable success of the Internet can be traced to a few simple network principles—end-to-end design, layered architecture, and open standards—which together give consumers choice and control over their online activities. This "neutral" network has supported an explosion of innovation at the edges of the network, and the growth of companies like Google, Yahoo, eBay, Amazon, and many others. Because the network is neutral, the creators of new Internet content and services need not seek permission from carriers or pay special fees to be seen online. As a result, we have seen an array of unpredictable new offerings—from Voice-over-IP to wireless home networks to blogging—that might never have evolved had central control of the network been required by design.[46]

In designing the World Wide Web, Tim Berners-Lee followed Dr. Cerf's philosophy, with a goal of linking all the information that existed on computers so that it would be available to people around the world.[47] According to Mr. Berners-Lee:

> The art was to define the few, basic, common rules of "protocol" that would allow one computer to talk to another, in such a way that when all computers everywhere did it, the system would thrive, not break down. For the Web, those elements were, in decreasing order of importance, universal resource identifiers URIs [later called URLs], the Hypertext Transfer Protocol (HTTP), and the Hypertext Markup Language (HTML). What was often difficult for people to understand about the design was that there was nothing else beyond URIs, HTTP, and HTML. There was no central computer "controlling" the Web, no single network on which these protocols worked, not even an organization anywhere that "ran" the Web. The Web was not a physical "thing" that existed in a certain "place." It was a "space" in which information could exist.[48]

As important was the decision not to claim intellectual property rights in any of the design elements of the Web. At the same time Mr. Berners-Lee was creating the Web, the University of Minnesota was developing a gopher information system that similarly allowed people to share documents over the Internet. In the spring of 1993, the University announced that it would require a license to use the server software and would charge commercial entities a fee for that use. This claim of proprietary rights sent shock waves around the world, and effectively ended use of the gopher system.[49] The University's announcement also had a direct impact on the Web. Mr. Berners-Lee had previously suggested to his employer, CERN, that they release the intellectual property rights to the Web under the GPL (General Public License) developed by Richard Stallman and the Free Software Foundation, but the experience with the University of Minnesota and gopher convinced him that abandonment was the only acceptable route. CERN agreed, and so it is that the design of the Web is in public domain.[50]

In his history of the Web, Mr. Berners-Lee took the trouble to debunk three myths that "have crept into the 'common wisdom' about the Web. . . ."[51] The third myth involved privacy concerns, but the first two concern copyright:

> Myth One: "A normal link is an incitement to copy the linked document in a way that infringes copyright." The ability to refer to a

document (or a person or anything else) is a fundamental right of free speech. Making the reference with a hypertext link is efficient, but changes nothing else. . . .

Myth Two: "Making a link to an external document makes the first document more valuable, and therefore is something that should be paid for." It is true that a document is made more valuable by links to other relevant, high-quality documents, but this doesn't mean anything is owed to the people who created those documents. If anything, they should be glad that more people are being referred to them. If someone at a meeting recommends me as a good contact, does that person expect me to pay him for making the reference? Hardly.[52]

As we shall now see, Mr. Berners-Lee vastly underestimated the copyright industries' desire to remake the Web to conform to their pre-Net business model of centralization, closed systems, and tight control over access and over consumers.

## ※ The Barbarian as the Gatekeeper

Given the dire state of the newspaper industry, one would think newspapers would be the most likely to employ innovative business models, if only out of desperation. And, many have. In May 2008, the Reuters wire service made its news content available to the developer community through the use of a noncommercial application programming interface (API). Through the API, bloggers and other noncommercial Web sites can copy Reuters news content, create applications around it, or incorporate it into blogs and Web sites. By doing this, Reuters will extend its distribution, and increase its consumer base. An article about Reuters' release of the API makes the connection between the release and innovation.

Further proof that innovation breeds more innovation, Reuters has announced that it's making news content available to the developer community through the use of a non-commercial API. The service will be offered via Reuters Lab, a test site where Reuters can showcase some of their latest product innovations and developments and where users can discover, use and comment on products and services still in progress.[53]

The *London Guardian* newspaper has its own developer platform and hired a former Yahoo engineer in March 2008 to assist it. The *Guardian* even has a helpful online beginner's guide to APIs.[54] Another example is the *New York Times*, which has ten times the number of online readers as it does hardcopy readers, approximately one million hardcopy subscribers versus ten million consumers who go to the *Times'* Web site. The *Times* also released an API that will make the *Times'* Web site programmable. This will permit outside developers to mash up different data on the site—think of the overlays on Google maps. Derek Gottfrid, an API programmer for the *New York Times*, explained the *Times'* decision:

> We're geared to whoever is going to find the content interesting. Anyone that's interested in it, we're interested in making it accessible and having them use it. This isn't something that's driven off of market research or anything like that. This is fulfilling a basic gut-level instinct that this is how the Internet works. This is really going from being "on the [I]nternet" to being "part of the [I]nternet"—intermingling our stuff with the full experience of things around the Internet.[55]

National Public Radio (NPR) had earlier opened up its APIs, and explained the advantage of doing so for consumers:

> If you go to NPR.org, you're getting NPR's presentation of our data. It's our compilations and our topic structures. Through the API, users can come and slice the content however they want it, create their own custom feeds and we'll leave it up to them to build exactly what they want. Things we couldn't even envision.[56]

The innovative responses of Reuters, the *New York Times*, NPR, and other news organizations should be contrasted with that of the Associated Press.

### ✼ The Associated Press

The Associated Press (AP) is a cooperative owned by contributing member domestic newspapers,[57] radio and television stations.[58] With the collapse of the United Press International in the early 1990s, the AP has had the field of English-language national news service to itself in the United States. The Associated Press was founded in 1846 as the Harbor News Association, by five New York newspapers, the *New York Sun*, the *Journal of Commerce*, the *Courier and Enquirer*, the *Herald*, and the *Express*. The theory behind the association was to have a single source for information sent via telegraph. As Professor Douglas Baird detailed in his article, "The Story of *INS v. AP*: Property, Natural Monopoly, and the Uneasy Legacy of a Concocted Controversy":[59]

> In the first part of the twentieth century, a wire service consisted primarily of a large network of leased telegraph lines. The expense of creating and maintaining such a network dwarfed the cost of actually gathering the information. These fixed costs created a natural monopoly.[60]

Indeed, the actual telegraph cable contained the barest of data, and in a format that had no expressive elements. Professor Baird gives this example of a typical AP cable at the time:

> t sectus tdy dodd 5 pw f potus dz n xtd to t pips, ogt all pst cgsl xgn q sj is uxl[61]

The telegraph operator then translated this as:

> The Supreme Court of the United States today decided that the power of the President of the United States does not extend to the Philippines, on the ground that all past Congressional legislation on the subject is unconstitutional.[62]

So translated, individual editors at newspapers took the information and made it into an actual news story with their own language and additional information, without an AP attribution. Professor Baird rightly concludes: "The value of the information lay entirely in its transmission across great distances."[63] AP's practices in this period were contradictory—copying with wild abandon from foreign sources but claiming a property right in the news itself—while doing all it could to ensure that it had a monopoly on the transmission of the news, and a monopoly, through its members, on the news stories themselves. AP's practices led Upton Sinclair to condemn the organization in his 1919 book on journalism, *The Brass Check*.[64]

AP's early efforts to claim proprietary rights in the news also extends to how news stories are written, although copyright law excludes claims in writing style,[65] and even though AP did not create the style in question, known as the "inverted pyramid." The inverted pyramid refers to putting the most important facts first and then information of decreased importance. There are many myths about the "invention" of the inverted pyramid, including its birth from telegraph wire bulletins during the Civil War. The most complete study of the history of the summary news lead form (a study that involved extensive research into contemporary newspapers) concludes that neither the telegraph nor AP were responsible for its adoption. Rather, the adoption was a reaction by the public against the prevailing ornamental style of writing and a desire by the public for more fact-based reporting.[66] Despite the lack of any legitimate claim to inventing such a non-copyrightable style, AP's current CEO, Tom Curley, stated in a November 29, 2007, speech:

> As early as 1883, AP agents were instructed to put the vital news first and add the story detail later, if at all. This policy was codified in an instruction sent to correspondents in 1903: "When the news is of extraordinary character or very sensational, file at once a bulletin of 100 words and await instructions before sending the details. . . . The news should be given in the first paragraph."
>
> [Walter] Mears explains that the "lead first, details later" writing style is taught as the inverted pyramid, and emphasizes the five Ws of news: who, what, when, where and why.
>
> You can see why AP would complain about the free-riders who claim to be only taking the five Ws of news in real time, at no cost to themselves and with no revenue to AP.[67]

No person outside of AP should see why AP would complain about the use of a style of writing that AP neither created nor owns. How would such a right be defined and enforced? Would it give AP the ability to enjoin all news stories that begin with the most important facts, regardless of the actual content of the story?[68] Mr. Curley thinks so, but no court in the United States would accept his claims. Mr. Curley, who cut his own journalist teeth at *USA Today*, is fond of the term "free-riders" as seen in the same speech, in which he condemned search engines for providing links to news stories that newspapers permit search engines to crawl and thus provide links to:

> A lot of this aggregation and syndication of AP content in new business models occurs without our permission.
>
> Basically, these new models free ride on the investment and efforts of AP. In addition, they dilute the value of content licensed by AP's thousands of licensees.[69]

These remarks treat new opportunities as threats, threats caused by "free-riders," a metaphor used because the law rejects any actual claim of free-riding. The free-riders referred to are search engines like Google and Yahoo. Search engines, however, neither aggregate nor syndicate information—the use of those terms was deliberately misleading. Instead, search engines *index* whatever appears on Web sites, whether it is a news Web site, a video site, a toy store's Web site, or a blog. In response to a consumer's search query, the search engine returns relevant responses to the query, along with a bibliographic-like snippet providing consumers with enough information —but no more—to enable consumers to decide whether to link onto the Web site where the information index resides.[70] If the consumer clicks onto the link, the consumer is taken to the originating Web site, for example the *New York Times* online. Search engines are *not*, therefore, collecting and storing news stories that consumers then retrieve from the search engines' own servers. To the contrary, once the consumer clicks onto the link returned by the search engine, the consumer is sent to the *New York Times* Web site, where the requested story resides on the *New York Times'* computers, surrounded by ads served up by the *New York Times*. Such conduct is entirely legal, requiring no payment to AP or any news organization. In his rebuttal to the copyright myths of the Web quoted above, Tim Berners-Lee rejected the precise claims made by Mr. Curley.

Nor is the indexing by search engines done without permission. To the contrary, by putting their content up on the Web, all of AP's members know their sites will be crawled and indexed by search engines. They not only know this, they very much *want* search engines to crawl their sites because, as with a bibliography, unless consumers not only know the material exists but where to find it, having a Web site does no good: No one will be able to find it, and if they cannot find it, AP's members cannot monetize those sites. If anyone is free-riding, it is AP members who are free-riding on the investments made by search engines to drive traffic to AP members' sites. Those investments dwarf the entire investment that AP has made from its founding in 1846. Curiously, no copyright owner has ever stated an obligation, moral or otherwise to make a contribution to those who make their monetization on the Internet possible.

Mr. Curley's use of free-riding also extends to extracting fees for the quotation of uncopyrightable words and small phrases, all of which are legally permissible and thus require no payment. Mr. Curley does not concern himself with such niceties, however: "What the free-riders overlook is that taking a little of something does not lessen the free-riding."[71] But if the law states, as it does,[72] that the little taken is not subject to ownership, there can be no free-riding.[73] How little is little? Here are two of AP's guidelines for *nonprofit* Web site usage of AP stories:

| Number of Words Quoted | Fees |
| --- | --- |
| 5–25 | $12.50 |
| 26–50 | $17.50[74] |

The argument that five or more words from a new story is copyrightable is, from every perspective, ridiculous. Courts have, from the inception of copyright, followed the adage *de minimis non curat lex*: The law doesn't bother itself with trifles.[75]

## ✽ ACAP

In falsely asserting that free-riders are engaged in unauthorized conduct, Mr. Curley was well aware there exists, and has since 1994, a simple and effective computer protocol (software code) that AP's members can use to either prevent search engines from crawling their site, or to control which parts should not be searchable or remain visible during search results. For example, an online newspaper can direct any search engine to display results in Web search but not image search, can exclude robots access to individual directories or pages of a particular type. This protocol is called a "robots.txt" extension.[76] The robots.txt protocol was created by consensus by members of the robots mailing list.[77] It has been widely adopted by search engines and has worked well for 15 years. It has evolved in response to feedback from the general Web publishing community and is dynamic, meaning that it incorporates new tools, in particular metatags.

"Robots.txt" is easily understood and applied, and for that reason is the standard crawling protocol on the Web. For those who, for whatever reason have difficulty applying the robots.txt extension, Google and others have developed simple lines of code that can be cut and pasted and will permit Web site owners to preclude Web crawlers from indexing a site, from following internal and external links in the document, from archiving a site, from displaying snippets, from blocking the images on a page from being crawled separately, or that permit Web site owners to specify that a content item be removed after a certain date.[78]

To describe search engines' crawling and indexing of AP members' sites as unauthorized is false. A federal judge rejected the same argument by a lawyer/Web site owner who set the issue up as a test case:

> Field concedes he was aware of these industry standard mechanisms, and knew that the presence of a "no archive" meta-tag on the pages of his Web site would have informed Google not to display "Cached" links to his pages. Despite this knowledge, Field chose not to include the no-archive meta-tag on the pages of his site. He did so, knowing that Google would interpret the absence of the meta-tag as permission to allow access to the pages via "Cached" links. Thus, with knowledge of how Google would use the copyrighted works he placed on those pages, and with knowledge that he could prevent such use, Field instead made a conscious decision to permit it. His conduct is reasonably interpreted as the grant of a license to Google for that use.[79]

It is no coincidence that Mr. Curley's remarks were made at the first International ACAP Conference. (ACAP stands for Automated Content Access Protocol.[80]) Unlike robots.txt, ACAP was not developed by independent Internet experts, but instead by private consultants paid by publishers. ACAP is also not a product developed by consensus—it is a product developed and paid for by publishers solely to further their own commercial agenda of controlling access to the news. The organization that administers ACAP speaks for approximately 0.5 percent of all Web sites. Robots.txt covers more than 100 million content producers. Any standard must work for all Web sites, not just a tiny fraction of them, and must be consistent with the decentralized nature of the Internet: ACAP isn't.

The first version of ACAP was released at the conference Mr. Curley spoke at, and it has been the subject of withering criticism ever since its launch by independent computer experts and even by some newspapers,[81] such as the UK Telegraph, that are members of Associated Press. The Telegraph's digital production head, Ian Douglas wrote in that paper:

> The [ACAP] website claims that ACAP aims to refine business models between online partners, "create opportunities for the development of collaborative new premium products" and give "confidence to publishers that they can retain a direct influence over what is displayed to users and other access conditions," thus emboldening them to publish online.
>
> Throughout ACAP documents I found no examples of clear benefits for readers of the web sites or increased flexibility of uses for the content or help with making web searches more relevant.
>
> The new protocol focuses entirely on the desires of publishers, and only those publishers who fear what web users will do with the content if they don't retain control over it at every point.[82]
>
> It's ill-conceived, poorly implemented, overly controlling and concerned only with the nervousness of some publishers, not the needs of the readers.[83]

An independent commenter remarked: "In the interests of fairness I tried to find a positive article about ACAP, but there's absolutely nothing."[84]

Aside from obtaining complete control over consumers' access to news, another principal objective of ACAP is to require search engines to pay newspapers for the very act of indexing content, an objective that is akin to requiring libraries to pay for creating bibliographic card catalog entries, or requiring Amazon.com to pay to deliver search results for a book. Not only would such an approach be prohibitively expensive (it would lead many other types of sites to also demand payment) and be difficult to apply, it makes no sense as a business matter as it inhibits those who bring awareness of creators' goods to the consuming public. Finally, ACAP will result in Web sites being able to dictate search results, destroying in the process the core function of modern search engines to provide the most relevant, unbiased results.

The control sought by ACAP ultimately comes at the expense of consumers, whose access to and use of news reports would be severely restricted.

ACAP is the wrong business model and even the wrong technical implementation for that wrong model. ACAP fails in every respect, but is illustrative because it represents the archetypal response of copyright owners to innovation—kill it off under the guise of making it safe for copyright owners to exploit. There is no reason to deny that this is, in fact, what is going on. The Associated Press' campaign to fight the Internet is a reaction to rapidly diminishing revenues in the newspaper industry, and a sea change in how people access news. In December 2008, the Pew Research Center for the People & the Press released a study showing that the Internet has, for the first time, overtaken print newspapers as the principal source for national and international news: 40 percent of respondents listed the Internet versus 34 percent for newspaper. The figures were even higher for those Americans under 30 years of age, 59 percent of whom preferred the Internet over print.[85] This trend will only continue. The Associated Press' reaction to this dramatic trend has not been to deliver to consumers (or even to its own members) what they want and then figure out how to monetize, but to instead start from the premise that they have a God-given right to an income stream, and to then shake others down to obtain that revenue, oblivious or unconcerned with the realities of monetization on the Internet.

There is no reason to pretend that the metaphors of the Copyright Wars are descriptive of actual challenges faced by the copyright industries. There is no reason to keep pretending that the Copyright Wars involve matters of morality or principle—they don't and never have. The Copyright Wars and their predecessors have always been about one thing and one thing only—a fruitless effort to resist, to the end, the very nature of capitalism, which is its dynamic, creative force by which new innovations and business models replace old ones.

There is also every reason to reject those efforts and to change course, to encourage those who are innovative, those who do promote the progress of science and the social good, those whose technologies and business models are tailored to the Internet and not against it. This effort will involve substantially reforming our copyright laws, not just at the margins. Failure to undertake such reforms will result in the United States slipping from its current status as a second-world digital country into third-world status. We shall now review a country with first-world digital status, Korea, to see what is possible if we do change course.

## ⅏ South Korea and Japan: The Future Is Here

### South Korea

Ninety-three percent of South Korean households have broadband access,[86] compared to 57 percent of households in the United States.[87] But beyond this figure, the average median download speed in Korea is 49.5 Mbps.[88] Only Japan has a faster median rate, 63.6 Mbps, but only 55 percent of Japanese households have broadband access compared to 93 percent of South Korean households. South Korea is currently developing the infrastructure to increase the rate to 100 Mbps by 2010 (a speed that already exists in Japan for subscribers of NTT East at a cost of approximately $27 a month). When that occurs, the United States, with its abysmal 2.3 Mbps rate,[89] will sink further into the digital dark ages. In 2007, the United States fell from fifteenth to seventeenth place in broadband growth worldwide. Even among the G-7 countries, the United States is in fifth place. A 2008 study by the Communications Workers of America found little improvement in the U.S. on this score from 2007 to 2008 (4/10s of a megabit per second), and concluded: "At this rate, it will take the United States more than 100 years to catch up with current Internet speeds in Japan."[90]

As the report notes, even this is a "rosier picture than reality" because those consumers with a dial-up connection did not participate in the survey's speed test due to their slow connection speed, thereby skewering the numbers higher. The report noted that Japanese consumers can download an entire feature length movie in two minutes, while it takes two hours or more in the United States, even though Japanese consumers pay no more for their Internet connection than U.S. consumers do. Speed matters because

> speed defines what is possible on the Internet. It determines whether we will have the 21st century networks we need to create jobs of the future, develop our economy, and support innovations in telemedicine, education, public safety, and public services to improve our lives and communities. Most U.S. Internet connections today are not fast enough to permit interactive home-based medical monitoring, multi-media distance learning, or to send and receive data to run a home-based conflict.[91]

By all criteria, South Korea trounces the United States in this area. The lowest monthly price per Mbps in South Korea is 37 cents compared to $2.83 in the United States. South Korea has almost 45 million mobile phone subscribers, representing a 91 percent market penetration. In South Korea, young people use cell phones rather than credit cards to make most of their payments. In South Korea, "the biggest bank in Korea says that their competition is not from American Express and Visa and MasterCard, or other traditional banks. They say their competition comes from money on cell phones."[92] For young people, who are the biggest users of cell phones, they may not be old enough to get a credit card or qualify for one, but they can make cell phone payments, including for copyrighted works. Forty-six percent of South Koreans use cell phone mobile payments systems. In 2005, four years ago, the value of payments made by credit cards in South Korea, a country with one-sixth the population of the United States, was more than a billion dollars.[93]

The availability of such inexpensive, super-fast broadband as well as the communal nature of digital connectedness has led to phenomena that exist on a scale in South Korea unimaginable in the United States. Here are two examples: The first is massively multiplayer online games (MMOG). One game alone, *Kart Rider* has been played by 25 percent of all Koreans.[94] In 2006, the value of virtual property sold in MMOGs for real cash was $830 million.[95] Forty-three percent of all Koreans maintain personal profiles in Cyworld, a Web community site operated by SK Communications, a subsidiary of SK Telecom. Cyworld is a combination of social networking sites like MySpace, an online dating service (its original purpose), a virtual world like *Second Life*, a blog-hosting site, and a shopping mall where, among other things, legal downloads of music are sold. As explained by Wikipedia:

> Cyworld has had a big effect on Korea's Internet culture, which differs from the blog culture of the United States. This item-based business model has bolstered Internet community sites that had previously struggled as free services. Many renowned Korean socialites and celebrities have been known to possess a [C]yworld account in which details of their upcoming tours and works are posted. . . . In South Korea young people, when meeting for the first time, ask for the other person's "cyaddress" instead of their phone number.

The corporate world has also used Cyworld . . . to accompany product launches.

. . . .

Also in 2006, Cyworld received the Wharton Infosys Business Transformation Award for its society-wide transformation of interpersonal interaction.[96]

Although Cyworld only sells music in South Korea, in 2006 it became the world's second largest music store, behind iTunes.[97] As a result of the far higher broadband rate in Korea, the average amount of daily consumption of DMB digital television (developed in South Korea)[98] *on their cell phones* is 129 minutes a day.[99] This is possible because of the high resolution TV screens on South Korean cell phones, high speed of the connections, and the reliability of the connections, all of which are lacking in the United States. Where I live in Connecticut, I cannot a get T-Mobile signal at all, thereby rendering useless a Blackberry I have through work. You cannot even get a continuous signal on the main New Haven Metro-North train line from Grand Central Terminal, regardless of your service provider.

In short, South Korea has all of the elements to satisfy the preferences of young (and many older) consumers; those elements have, not surprisingly, led to an environment for a vibrant digital economy. The success story in South Korea is attributable to the initiative of the Korean government, as described in this 2004 story from CNet:

The Seoul government's clearly articulated vision for modernizing the country's infrastructure stands in stark contrast to the regulatory morass that has stunted development in U.S. telecommunications for several decades. South Korea's policy—the cornerstone of a national technology initiative to help revive a devastated economy—has created true broadband competition, which in turn has helped prices fall and speeds rise.

. . . .

The country's achievements are even more impressive considering its starting point in technology. In 1995, fewer than 1 percent of South

Korean residents used the Internet.... By 2004, more than 71 percent of South Korean households subscribed to broadband Net services, according to local estimates.

The decision to focus on broadband began in the mid-1990s and intensified after South Korea's economy was crippled by the collapse of the Asian financial markets in 1997, when policy makers targeted technology as a key sector for restoring the country's economic health.

Korean regulators set out a clear path for the network industry with well-publicized national goals. All big office and apartment buildings would be given a fiber connection by 1997. By 2000, 30 percent of households would have broadband access through DSL or cable lines. By 2005, more than 80 percent of households would have access to fast connections of 20 mbps [sic] or more—about the rate needed for high-definition television.

....

The government also spent $24 billion building a national high-speed backbone network linking government facilities and public institutions.

Even skeptics in the United States say that the South Korean government's advocacy role and intense focus can serve as a model for other countries looking to modernize their infrastructure. . . . The daily pervasiveness of broadband in South Korea is one of the primary reasons that Intel created a new lab dedicated to the digital home in Seoul. The company is studying how Koreans use the Internet, from shopping to gaming, to understand how the technology can be developed for other countries. . . .

In many ways, the most important question answered in the country's grand broadband experiment has been one of demand. Broadband progress has long been delayed in the United States and other countries as a result of uncertainty about how much interest consumers would have in paying for the expensive infrastructure needed for high-bandwidth services.

As a result, entire industries have been paralyzed for years by a classic Catch-22, as content companies and network carriers waited for one another to make the first move before investing in broadband products.[100]

No such Catch-22 exists in South Korea, where people can watch music concerts on their cell phones and can access huge libraries of karaoke songs and instructional dance videos. The fast video speeds can be a double-edged sword, however, because in the absence of lawful alternatives, unauthorized downloads or streaming of movies will occur, and did in South Korea, at significant rates. Here, one motion picture studio, TimeWarner stepped up and broke with the past business model of staggered release: theatrical, then DVD, and maybe some remote time in the future, digital delivery. In October 2008, TimeWarner began releasing its films online in South Korea *before* they are released in the country on DVD. In addition to curbing unauthorized uses, profit margins on digital rentals and sales are higher than with DVDs. Hopefully, other studios will follow TimeWarner's lead.

The response of the music industry, alas, has been typical: Others are to blame, and those others should clean up their act; record labels apparently have no need to satisfy consumer desires. One sees this response in January 24, 2008, comments by John Kennedy, head of IFPI, the international arm of the record industry:

> The whole music sector, governments and even some ISPs themselves are beginning to accept that the carriers of digital content must play a responsible role in curbing the systemic piracy that is threatening the future of all digital commerce. After years of discussing and debating, I am convinced it is no longer a question of whether the ISPs act—the question is when and how.[101]

Mr. Kennedy got way ahead of himself, however, as nine months later the European Parliament decisively rejected a proposal put forth by the French at Mr. Kennedy's request, instead adopting an opposing amendment to a Telecom package. The amendment reads, "no restriction may be imposed on the rights and freedoms of end users in accordance with Article 11 of the Charter of Fundamental Rights of the European Union on freedom of expression and information, without a prior ruling by the judicial authorities, except where dictated by force majeure or by the requirements of preserving network integrity and security, and subject to national provisions of criminal law imposed for reasons of public policy, public security or public morality."

Commenting on the rejection in October 2008, European Information Society Commissioner Viviane Reding remarked: "Too often when we talk about stakeholders in the world of the [I]nternet, we think of the telcos and the rights holders as the only stakeholders. But our citizens are stakeholders too."[102] The consequence of the music industry's failure to innovate is seen in the raw statistics. In 2006 in South Korea, 57 percent of music sales were digital, compared to only 10 percent in the United States, and of the digital sales made, 45 percent were to cell phones.[103]

## Japan

Japan has the fastest average broadband rate in the world, an average of 63.6 Mbps. As part of NTT's Next Generation Network, 75 percent of homes in NTT's East territory subscribe to fiber-to-home service at a blistering speed of 100 Mbps, almost 50 times the average speed in the U.S. At 70 cents per 1 Mbps, Japanese have the cheapest broadband service in the world (the United States rate is $4.90). From 2000–2005, the average monthly rate in Japan for broadband fell 47 percent. As in South Korea, cell phones act as an electronic wallet, being used to pay for goods at retail stores, to get money from an ATM, to get soft drinks from vending machines, and to pay for train tickets, to name only a few applications.

The combination of Japan's fast broadband rates, and unlimited data transmission packages for cell phones has affected not only the distribution of copyrighted works, but their creation. Japan is front and center in the democratization brought about by innovation,[104] most vividly seen in the *keitai shosetsu*, cell phone novels. The phenomenon of *keitai shosetsu* illustrates the effect that changes in innovation policy can have. As explained in a January 2008 *New York Times* story:

> The cellphone novel was born in 2000 after a home-page-making Web site, Maho no i-rando, realized that many users were writing novels on their blogs; it tinkered with its software to allow users to upload works in progress and readers to comment, creating the serialized cellphone novel. But the number of users uploading novels began booming only two to three years ago, and the number of novels listed on the site reached one million last month, according to Maho no i-rando ["Magic Island"].
>
> *The boom appeared to have been fueled by a development having nothing to do with culture or novels but by cellphone companies' decision*

*to offer unlimited transmission of packet data, like text-messaging, as
part of flat monthly rates. The largest provider, Docomo, began offering
this service in mid-2004.*

"Their cellphone bills were easily reaching $1,000, so many people
experienced what they called 'packet death,' and you wouldn't hear
from them for a while," said Shigeru Matsushima, an editor who over-
sees the book uploading site at Starts Publishing, a leader in repub-
lishing cellphone novels.[105]

Japanese youth had been reading novels on cellphones for some time,
but it is the change in service plans and the simplification of Japanese
characters via special software developed for cellphones that led them to
become novelists: unlike the complicated *kanji* used in writing long-
hand, cellphone software permits push button writing. The special features of cellphone writing in Japanese has had an important impact on
the composition of cellphone novels. One of the successful cellphone
novelists, Rin, explained:

You're not trying to pack the screen. . . . You're changing the line in the
middle of sentences, so where you cut the sentence is an essential
part. If you've got a very quiet scene, you lose a lot more of those
returns and spaces. When a couple is fighting, you'll cram the words
together and make the screen very crowded.[106]

The aesthetic developed for cellphones was then adopted for hardcopy
publication of them:

Printed, the books announce themselves as untraditional, with hori-
zontal lines that read right to left, as on the phone. . . . Other conven-
tions established on the screen are faithfully replicated in print. Often,
the ink is colored or gray; black text is thought to be too imposing.
"Some publishers removed the [space bar] returns, but those books
didn't sell well," a representative of Goma Books said. "You need to
keep that flow."[107]

The new format and way of writing reached a new generation that was
not reading traditional books. Sales of traditional books declined by

20 percent in the last eleven years. Rin, the cellphone novelist, explained that traditional novels left members of her generation "cold." Her generation, she said, "[doesn't] read works by professional writers because their sentences are too difficult to understand, their expressions are intentionally wordy, and the stories are not familiar to them."[108] This is a large market to ignore, and a market that was plugged into its cellphones: 82 percent of Japanese youth between 10 and 29 have cellphones, in a country where there has been wireless Internet connections for 10 years.[109] Cellphone novels are uploaded to websites such as Magic Island for free, but this doesn't mean money is not ultimately made. In 2007, four of the top five hardcopy books had been cellphone novels; one, "The Red Thread," sold 1.8 million copies in a country where traditional novels are lucky to sell a few thousand copies. On top of spectacular hard copy sales, cellphone novels have also been made in motion pictures and manga (comics).

Why, one might ask, would those who have read a novel for free, on a cellphone, buy a hardcopy? The answer to this question is found in what those in Silicon Valley and other places have been saying for years, but which corporate copyright owners reject as an article of faith: the interactive nature of the Internet creates a bond between those who start the conversation going—either in a blog (the launching point for cellphone novels) or any other Web site where people are encouraged to participate. Unlike the passive consumer idealized by corporate copyright owners (because they will passively buy whatever corporations decide they should buy), many people find greater satisfaction by participating, even for free, witness for example, Wikipedia. In the case of cellphone novels, the editor of Rin's best-selling novel explained:

> It might seem strange that young readers are going out and buying the book after they've already read the story on their mob'ie. Often it's because they email suggestions and criticisms to the au' nor on the novel website as the story is unfolding, so they feel like they've contributed to the final product, and they want a hardcopy keepsake of it.[110]

Japan reveals the win-win situation that can occur when government takes innovation policy seriously and where publishers go with the technology and youth, rather than declare war on them as is the case in the United States.

## 🎜 Conclusion

The Copyright Wars must be understood as archetypal responses of businesses that are inherently non-innovative and that rely on the innovation of others to succeed. I cannot think of a single significant innovation in either the creation or distribution of works of authorship that owes its origins to the copyright industries. Being forced to rely on others' innovation creates a great sense of insecurity that is reflected in efforts to control innovators and consumers. Copyright owners live in perpetual fear, but it is a fear that is self-imposed.

This fear is manifested in a refusal to engage in the type of creative destruction that is essential for survival and renewal in a capitalist society, and in congenital marketing myopia. The ascent of lawyers as the heads of many entertainment companies is both a sign of those companies' lack of commitment to business innovation and a symptom of why the Copyright Wars exist: litigation is not a business model but instead is reflective of the failure of a business model.

Lawyers, adversarial by nature and training, typically seek to get ahead by besting others rather than looking internally for the source of success. Given the large number of lawyers who run entertainment companies, it should not be surprising that litigation is viewed as a business model, occasionally openly so.

By contrast, innovation, and therefore business success, is driven by an internal dynamic, not an external one, and certainly not by litigation as a business model. Those who focus on competitors, or as in the Copyright Wars, on conjured up enemies, are simply blaming others for their own failure to innovate, their own failure to have a clear internal focus. The problems in the Copyright Wars are not caused by technologies or by consumers acting badly, and they cannot therefore be solved by laws, and certainly not by more draconian laws. The problems—such as the decline in sales of CDs and DVDs—are the result of the copyright industries' many and considerable failures to focus on satisfying consumers' desires as opposed to stifling those desires out of a woefully misguided view that copyright equals control and that control equals profits.

The choice of whether to break with this view, decisively, and not merely for public relations consumption, is entirely up to copyright owners, but the time for doing so is short, and the opportunities are diminishing.

In other areas where a government monopoly, created to serve the public interest, is blatantly abused over a long period of time, it is taken away.

# Notes

## 🏵 Introduction

1. Hans-Georg Gadamer, *Truth and Method* 546 (Continuum Press, 2d revised edition 2004).
2. George Orwell, *Politics and the English Language* (1946), *available at*: http://www.mtholyoke.edu/acad/intrel/orwel146.htm.
3. *Sarl Louis Feraud Int'l v. Viewfinder, Inc.,* 406 F. Supp. 2d 274, 281 (S.D.N.Y. 2005), affirmed on this point, vacated and remanded on other grounds, 489 F.3d 474, 480 n.3 (2d Cir. 2007). *See generally* the excellent treatment by William Landes & Richard Posner, *The Economic Structure of Intellectual Property Law* (Belknap Press, Harvard University 2003).
4. Lord Macaulay's speech was all the more significant because he was one of the most famous historians, essayists, and poets of his day. He was a man of letters in every sense of that term in Victorian England, and thus the impact of his speech carried weight beyond his famous rhetorical skills. *See* http://en.wikipedia.org/wiki/Thomas_Babbington_Macaulay.
5. At the time, the term of copyright in the United Kingdom was the life of the author if this was longer than the 14 plus 14-year term established in the 1710 Statute of Anne. The bill proposed increasing the term to life of the author plus 60 years. *See* 2 William Patry, *Patry on Copyright* § 7:4, at 7–12 (Thomson/West 2007, semi-annual supplements).
6. *Available at*: http://yarchive.net/macaulay/copyright.html. The following year (1842) the proponents were forced to accept Macaulay's proposed amendment of a set term of 42 years from publication or life of the author plus 7 years, whichever was longer. In offering his proposal, Macaulay delivered a second speech that is only slightly less revered than the first. The second speech too is *available at*: http://yarchive.net/macaulay/copyright.html. The whole saga is discussed in detail in, 1 William Patry, *Patry on Copyright* § 1:15 (Thomson/West 2007 [with twice-a-year supplements]).

   The Paley referred to by Lord Macaulay is William Paley (1743–1805). *See* http://en.wikipedia.org/wiki/William_Paley. Paley's 1785 collection of essays, *Moral and Political Philosophy,* was enormously popular and influential. *See* David Roberts, *The Social Conscience of the Early Victorians* 117 (Stanford University Press 2002).

7. Those taking this approach who do not believe in a divine entity—or think that such an entity would not be concerned about copyright—believe that copyright is a "natural right," a right whose origins lie outside of legal enactment, and whose origins are much in the eye of the beholder. Such rights are, however, always enforced by legal enactments, fatally undercutting the natural rights claim. For a further discussion of the natural rights theory, *see* Chapter 4.

8. *See* Chapter 7.

9. Note the early association of copyright debates with metaphoric military skirmishes.

10. Describing the Internet as a "place" is to use an inaccurate metaphor. *See* Jack Goldsmith and Timothy Wu, *Who Controls the Internet?: Illusions of a Borderless World* (Oxford University Press 2006).

11. Theodore Levitt, *The Marketing Imagination* 5 (Free Press 1983, expanded edition 1986).

12. *Id.* at 6.

13. Theodore Levitt, "Marketing Myopia," *Harvard Business Review* 6 (1960, special September–October 1975 edition).

14. The era ended because of antitrust cases that required the studios to divest themselves of their interest in theaters and because of the advent of television.

15. Submitted to the United States House of Representatives Committee on Appropriations, Subcommittee on Commerce, Justice, State, and related agencies, April 23, 2002, *available at*: http://www.politechbot.com/docs/valenti.movies.testimony.042302.doc.

16. 249 U.S. 47 (1919).

17. 249 U.S. at 52.

18. *See* http://www.firstmonday.org/Issues/issue8_7/logie/.

19. *See* Lisa Gitelman, *Media, Materiality, and the Measure of the Digital; Or, the case of Sheet Music and the Problem of Piano Rolls*, in *Memory Bytes* 199 (Lauren Rabinovitz & Abraham Geil eds., Duke University Press 2004).

20. *Available at*: http://www.explorepahistory.com/odocument.php?docId=418.

21. *New York Times*, July 19, 1933, quoted in Michael Lesk, *Chicken Little and the Recorded Music Crisis*, IEEE Computer Soc'ty, Sept./Oct. 2003, at 73.

22. *See* Michelle Maiese, *Dehumanization, available at*: http://www.beyondintractability. org/essay/dehumanization/.

23. Yehuda Amichai, quoted in Arnold Modell, *Imagination and the Meaningful Brain* 1 (MIT Press 2006).

24. *See e.g.*, Alice Deignan, *Corpus Linguistics and Metaphor*, in *The Cambridge Handbook of Metaphor and Thought* 280, 290 ("Metaphor is ideological") (Raymond Gibbs ed., Cambridge University Press 2008); Veronica Koller, *"A Shotgun Wedding": Concurrence of War and Marriage Metaphors in Merger and Acquisitions Discourse*, 17 Metaphor & Symbol 179–203 (2003).

25. Taken from George Lakoff & Mark Johnson, *Metaphors We Live By* 4 (University of Chicago Press 2003) (1980).

26. *Id.*

27. For a Web site that attempts to track down the origins of this saying, *see* http://www.guardian.co.uk/notesandqueries/query/0,5753,-21510,00.html.

28. Speech delivered in Philadelphia, Pennsylvania, January 17, 2008. At the time of the speech, he was President-elect Obama. The reference to better angels is from the concluding paragraph of Abraham Lincoln's first inaugural address, delivered on March 4, 1861, and *available at*: http://www.bartleby.com/124/pres31.html. Lincoln was referring to the tensions between the North and the South that led to the Secession. The final paragraph of the address reads:

> We are not enemies, but friends. We must not be enemies. Though passion may have strained it must not break our bonds of affection. The mystic chords of memory, stretching from every battlefield and patriot grave to every living heart and hearthstone all over this broad land, will yet swell the chorus of the Union, when again touched, as surely they will be, by the better angels of our nature.

## 𝄞 Chapter 1  How the Copyright Wars Are Being Fought and Why

1. Nevertheless, *see* the introduction for a brief explanation, as well as *Commentary: Are the Copyright Wars Chilling Innovation?*, Bus. Wk., Oct. 11, 2004, *available at*: http://www.businessweek.com/magazine/content/04_41/b3903473.htm; Scott Carlson, *In the Copyright Wars, This Scholar Sides with the Anarchists*, Chron. Higher Educ., Nov. 19, 2004, *available at*: http://connect.educause.edu/Library/Abstract/IntheCopyrightWarsThisSch/35930; Peter Yu, *The Escalating Copyright Wars* (2006), *available at*: http://papers.ssrn.com/s013/papers.cfm?abstract_id=436693; and, generally, Matthew Rimmer, *Digital Copyright and the Consumer Revolution: Hands Off My ipod* (Edward Elgar Publishing 2007).

2. *See* Speech of Edgar Bronfman, Jr., Nov. 2007, to the GSMA Mobile Asia Congress in Macau, http://www.pcpro.co.uk/macuser/news/138990/music-boss-we-were-wrong-to-go-to-war-with-consumers.html. *See also* Bennett Lincoff, *Common Sense, Accommodation and Sound Policy for the Digital Marketplace*, 2 J. Int'l Media & Ent. L. 1, 16 (2007): "By its refusal to meet consumer demand, the music industry has relegated consumers to unlicensed services. In turn, the industry used technological measures in an effort to disrupt these services. For example, it seeds them with adware and spyware."

3. *See* page below in this chapter "The Copyright Wars and the Great Cultural Revolution" for a more recent statement by Mr. Bronfman casting some doubt on his 2007 remarks.

4. As explained by Wikipedia, Napster arose this way:

> Shawn Fanning along with two friends he'd met online, Jordan Ritter, a fellow Bostonian, and Sean Parker, from Virginia, first released the original Napster in June of 1999. Fanning wanted an easier method of finding music than by searching IRC or Lycos. John Fanning of Hull, Massachusetts, who is Shawn's uncle ran all aspects of the company's operations for the first year from their office on Nantucket beach. The final agreement gave Shawn 30% control of

the company, with the rest going to his uncle. It was the first of the massively popular peer-to-peer file sharing systems, although it was not fully peer-to-peer since it used central servers to maintain lists of connected systems and the files they provided, while actual transactions were conducted directly between machines. This is very similar to how instant messaging systems work. Although there were already networks that facilitated the sharing of files across the Internet, such as IRC, Hotline, and USENET, Napster specialized exclusively in music in the form of MP3 files and presented a friendly user-interface. The result was a system whose popularity generated an enormous selection of music to download.

*Available at*: http://en.wikipedia.org/wiki/Napster. *See also* Joseph Menn, *All the Rave: The Rise and Fall of Shawn Fanning's Napster* (Amazon Remainders Account, Apr. 8, 2003), available in a Kindle edition.

5. *See* Charles C. Mann, *The Heavenly Jukebox*, The Atlantic Monthly, Sept. 2000, *available at*: http://www.theatlantic.com/issues/2000/09/mann.htm.
6. *See* http://www.hinduonnet.com/2001/02/22/stories/01220004.htm.
7. *See* the discussion of the negotiations in Steve Knopper, *Appetite for Self-Destruction: The Spectacular Crash of the Record Industry in the Digital Age* 138–143 (Free Press 2009).
8. *See* Brian Hiatt & Evan Serpick, *The Record Industry's Decline*, Rolling Stone, June 28, 2007, *available at*: http://www.rollingstone.com/news/story/15137581/the_record_industrys_decline.
9. Knopper at 22–23.
10. John Battelle, *The Search* 84 (Penguin 2005).
11. *Id.* at 84.
12. Quoted in Randall Stross, *Planet Google* 5 (2008).
13. Robert Guth, Microsoft Bid to Beat Google Builds on a History of Misses, *Wall St. J.* January 16, 2009, page A1. This opportunity arose out of Microsoft's acquisition in 1998, of a company called LinkExchange.
14. Knopper at 106.
15. Dan Ariely, *Predictable Irrationality*, ch. 8 (Harper 2008).
16. Wired Mag., Nov. 7, 2007, *available at*: http://www.wired.com/entertainment/music/magazine/15–12/mf_morris?currentPage=all.
17. Speech at an April 4, 2004, Future of Entertainment conference at Stanford University, quoted in Andrew Currah, *Hollywood Versus the Internet: The Media and Entertainment Industries in a Digital and Networked Economy*, 6 J. Econ. Geogr. 439, 459 (2006).
18. Professor Clayton Christensen's well-known book *The Innovator's Dilemma* (Collins Business Essentials 2002) (1997), details this phenomenon. *See also* his later book with Michael Raynor, *The Innovator's Solution* 32–71 (Harvard Business School Press 2003).
19. Quoted in Robin Gerber, *Barbie and Ruth* 143 (Collins Business Essentials 2009).
20. Theodore Levitt, "Marketing Myopia," *Harvard Business Review* 6 (1960, special September–October 1975 edition).

21. John Seely Brown and John Hagel III, "From push to pull: The next frontier of innovation," *The McKinsey Quarterly*, August 2005, *available at*: http://www.mckinseyquarterly.com/From_push_to_pull_The_next_frontier_of_innovation_1642.

22. *Id.*

23. *Id.*

24. Ironically Napster was recently resurrected in name as a purchase and subscription service after it as acquired in a bankruptcy sale. *See* http://en.wikipedia.org/wiki/Napster_%28pay_service%29.

25. The service was originally founded by RealNetworks, which later sold its share to a private equity group, Baker Capital, *see* http://www.realnetworks.com/company/press/releases/2005/real_musicnet.html.

26. For example, Steve Knopper quotes statements that Sony engaged in negotiations with MusicNet about licensing Sony's content (otherwise available only on PressPlay), but that the negotiations "never felt productive. We were going through the motions and had little chance of anything happening." Steve Knopper, *Appetite for Self-Destruction: The Spectacular Crash of the Record Industry in the Digital Age* 144 (Free Press 2009).

27. Quoted in Steven Levy, *The Perfect Thing: How the iPod Shuffles Commerce, Culture, and Coolness* 146 (Simon & Schuster 2007) (2006).

28. Free Press.

29. Knopper at 141.

30. In re Napster, Inc. Copyright Litigation, Case No. C MDL-00-1369 MHP (unpublished opinion issued on April 26, 2000), page 3, *available at*: https://www.eff.org/deep-links/2006/04/did-emi-and-umg-lie-antitrust-investigators.

31. *Id.* at 7.

32. In re Napster, Inc. Copyright Litigation, 2007 WL 844551 (March 20, 2007) (unpublished).

33. Quoted in http://en.wikipedia.org/wiki/Santangelo_v._RIAA#cite_note-8.

34. Mike Musgrove, "Recording Industry to Hot Music Trader," *Washington Post*, Nation column, June 26, 2003.

35. http://en.wikipedia.org/wiki/Cultural_Revolution.

36. One possibility would be exclusive or favorable content deals, but these deals would presumably be conditioned on implementing graduated response.

37. Robert Andrews, *Virgin Scraps Legal P2P Music Plans After Labels Get Jitters*, Paid Content website, January 23, 2009, *available at*: http://www.paidcontent.co.uk/entry/419-virgin-scraps-legal-p2p-music-plans-after-labels-get-jitters/.

38. *Id.*

39. Quoted in *id.*

40. Andrew Orlowski, *Virgin puts 'legal P2P' plans on ice: Historic deal consigned to history*, The Register, January 23, 2009, *available at*: http://www.theregister.co.uk/2009/01/23/virgin_puts_legal_p2p_on_ice/.

41. *See* in particular Michael Piatek, Tadayoshi Kohno, Arvind Krishnamurthy, "Challenges and Directions for Monitoring P2P File Sharing Networks—or—Why

My Printer Received a DMCA Takedown Notice." This article explains the difference between direct and indirect detection of infringing use via BitTorrent:

- *Indirect detection* of infringing users relies on the set of peers returned by the coordinating tracker only, treating this list as authoritative as to whether or not

IPs are actually exchanging data within the swarm.

- *Direct detection* involves connecting to a peer reported by the tracker and then exchanging data with that peer.

Direct detection has relatively high resource requirements . . .

42. *See* http://www.laquadrature.net/fr/suede-rejet-riposte-graduee.
43. This topic is explored in Chapter 6. *See also* Neil Netanel, *Why has Copyright Expanded? Analysis and Critique*, in *6 Directions in Copyright Law* (Fiona Macmillan ed. Edward Elgar Publ. 2008).
44. *See* Mark Johnson, *The Body in the Mind*, at xi–xii (University of Chicago Press 1987).
45. Steven Pinker, *The Stuff of Thought: Language as a Window into Human Nature* 4 (Penguin Books 2007). *See also id.* at 243–245. The leading discussion of the issue is Amos Tversky & Daniel Kahnemann, *The Framing of Decisions and the Psychology of Choice*, 211 Science 453 (1981).
46. For an early examination of framing, *see* Erving Goffman, *Frame Analysis: An Essay on the Organization of Experience* (Northeastern University Press 1986) (1974).
47. Quoted in Scott Plous, *The Psychology of Judgment and Decision Making* 67–68 (McGraw-Hill 1993).
48. There are many important differences between the movie industry at the time of block booking and the later album-focused record industry. The motion picture industry, for example, in this period consisted mostly of captive circuits, and copies of motion pictures were leased, not sold. The point I am making in the text is that the Supreme Court recognized the ill effects that tying has on the quality of the products produced and on the public. One effect of record companies being able to force consumers to buy 10 lousy songs on an album is that there is little incentive to develop consistently high-quality songs.
49. From by J. A. Aberdeen, *The Root of All Evil in the Motion Picture Industry, available at*: http://www.cobbles.com/simpp_archive/blockbook_intro.htm.
50. *United States v. Paramount Pictures*, 334 U.S. 131, 157, 158 (1948).
51. Source: Wikipedia, *List of highest-grossing films, available at*: http://en.wikipedia.org/wiki/List_of_highest-grossing_films.
52. *See* Video Business website, January 22, 2009, *available at*: http://www.video-business.com/article/CA6631456.html.
53. *See Games versus Music: The Stats: ERA Yearbook 2008, available at*: http://www.mcvuk.com/interviews/217/Games-vs-Music-the-stats.
54. *David Byrne's Survival Strategies for Emerging Artists—and Megastars*, Wired Mag., Dec. 18, 2007, *available at*: http://www.wired.com/print/entertainment/music/magazine/16–01/ff_byrne.

55. Quoted in Brian Hiatt and & Evan Serpick, *The Record Industry's Decline*, Rolling Stone, June 28, 2007, *available at*: http://www.rollingstone.com/news/story/15137581/the_record_industrys_decline.

56. Steve Knopper, *Appetite for Self-Destruction: The Spectacular Crash of the Record Industry in the Digital Age* 33 (Free Press 2009).

57. Steven Levy, *The Perfect Thing: How the iPod Shuffles Commerce, Culture, and Coolness* 166–167 (Simon & Schuster 2007).

58. *Available at*: http://www.billboard.biz/bbbiz/content_display/magazine/upfront/e3icd8f44807b52b1a668d4afff3b2063af

59. Mr. Jobs had resisted the move to what is called "variable pricing" beginning in 2005, when he stated:

    > We're trying to compete with piracy. We're trying to pull people away from piracy and say, "You can buy these songs legally for a fair price." If the price goes up people will go back to piracy, then everybody loses. . . .
    >
    > If they want to raise the prices it just means they're getting a little greedy.

    *Available at*: http://www.afterdawn.com/news/archive/6844.cfm.

60. Games versus Music: The Stats: ERA Yearbook 2008, *available at*: http://www.mcvuk.com/interviews/217/Games-vs-Music-the.stats.

61. Brian Garrity, *Changing His Tune: Bronfman Eyes More Cash in Video Game Deals*, N.Y. Post, Aug. 8, 2008, at 35.

62. Michael Pachter, quoted in Ryan Nakashima, "Boon in video games helps original artists," Associated Press, December 22, 2008, *available at*: http://www.mlive.com/videogames/index.ssf/2008/12/boom_in_music_video_games_help.html.

63. http://www.msnbc.msn.com/id/21324512/.

64. *Available at*: http://www.msnbc.msn.com/id/21269633/.

65. It is also entirely possible that Mr. Bronfman suffers from an acute case of what economist Joseph Stiglitz has called the "human sociability" characteristic: "[T]here is convincing evidence that individuals' perceptions of whether they are fairly treated affects their work effort; fairness is largely a social concept—one compares one's wages with others in one's orbit." *See* Joseph Stiglitz, "The Invisible Hand and Modern Welfare Economics," reproduced in *Information, Strategy and Public Policy* 12, 28 (David Vines and Andrew Stevenson eds. Blackwell 1991).Mr. Bronfman may feel that it is "unfair" that others should making more money than he is, a feeling which would, if true, go a long way toward explaining the false moralizing that one encounters in so many of his and other entertainment executives' carping about others.

66. Dan Ariely, *Predictably Irrational: The Hidden Forces That Shape Our Decisions* 61 (HarperCollins 2008).

67. *See* below "Copyright, Innovation, and Joseph Schumpeter's Creative Destruction."

68. Theodore Levitt, *Marketing Myopia*, Harvard Business Review 2 (1960, special September–October 1975 edition).

69. *Id.* at 2–3. In 1960, box office receipts had fallen from $1 billion in 1959 to $984 million, a decline that continued until 1964.

70. *Id.* at 4.

71. *Id.* at 11.

72. *Id.* at 3.

73. Interview *available at*: http://www.youtube.com/watch?v=XY89F7EQUh8.

74. *Id.* at 7.

75. Dean Marks & Bruce Turnball, *Technical Protection Measure: The Intersection of Technology, Law and Commercial Licenses*, Dec. 3, 1999, at 16, *available at*: http://www.wipo.int/edocs/mdocs/copyright/en/wct_wppt_imp/wct_wppt_imp_3.pdf.

76. *Id.* at 11.

77. *See* http://en.wikipedia.org/wiki/End-to-end_principle.

78. Andrew Currah, *Hollywood, the Internet and the World: Geography of Disruptive Innovation*, 14 Industry & Innovation 359, 371 (2007).

79. Quoted in Andrew Currah, *Hollywood, the Internet and the World: A Geography of Disruptive Innovation*, 14 Industry & Innovation 359, 374 (2007).

80. Andrew Currah, *Hollywood Versus the Internet: The Media and Entertainment Industries in a Digital and Networked Economy*, 6 J. Econ. Geogr. 439, 461–462 (2006).

81. Quoted in Peter Dekom & Peter Sealey, *Not on My Watch: Hollywood vs. the Future* 157 (2003, New Millennium Press).

82. John Holt, *Teach Your Own* 166 (De Capo Press 2003).

83. Theodore Levitt, *Marketing Myopia*, Harvard Business Review 2 (1960, Special September–October 1975 edition).

84. *Hollywood Versus the Internet: The Media and Entertainment Industries in a Digital and Networked Economy*, 6 J. Econ. Geogr. 439, 456–457 (2006).

85. *See e.g., Moral Panics Over Contemporary Children and Youth* (Charles Krinsky ed. Ashgate Publications 2008); Bernard Schlissel, *Blaming Children: Youth Crime, Moral Panics and the Politics of Hate* (Fernwood Publishers 1997); John Springhall, *Youth, Popular Culture and Moral Panics: Penny Gaffs to Gangsta Rap 1830–1996* (Palgrave Macmillan 1999).

86. 580 U.S. 559, 580 (1996).

87. *Id.* at 575, note 24.

88. *Defendant's Opposition to Motion to Dismiss Counterclaims 2, Sony BMG Music Entm't et al. v. Joel Tenenbaum, U.S.D., Mass.*, Civil Action No. 1:07-cv-11446-NG, submitted Oct. 27, 2008.

89. The same metaphors have been employed in other countries, especially in Europe; my reference to America here should not be regarded as limiting the issues to the United States.

90. *See* Chapter 8.

91. Act of October 13, 2008, S. 3325, Pub. L. No. 110-403, 110th Cong., 2d Sess.

92. *Available at*: http://leahy.senate.gov/press/200807/072408a.html.

93. *Available at*: http://www.edn.com/index.asp?layout=article&articleid=CA6488501.

94. Quoted in Julian Sanchez, 750,000 Lost Jobs? The Dodgy Digits Behind the War on Piracy, Oct. 7, 2008, *available at*: http://arstechnica.com/articles/culture/dodgy-digits-behind-the-war-on-piracy.ars.

95. March 5, 2008, letter from R. Bruce Josten, sent to Congressmen Howard Berman and Howard Coble, *available at*: http://www.uschamber.com/issues/letters/2008/080305_pro_ip_act.htm.

96. *U.S. Customs Announces International Counterfeit Case Involving Caterpillar Heavy Equipment*, May 29, 2002, *available at*: http://www.cbp.gov/xp/cgov/newsroom/news_releases/archives/legacy/2002/52002/05292002.xml.

97. Julian Sanchez, *750,000 Lost Jobs? The Dodgy Digits Behind the War on Piracy*, Oct. 7, 2008, *available at*: http://arstechnica.com/articles/culture/dodgy-digits-behind-the-war-on-piracy.ars. David Kravets of the Wired blog also wrote about the issue, *see* David Kravets, *Fiction or Fiction: 750,000 American Jobs Lost to IP Piracy*, Oct. 3, 2008, *available at*: http://blog.wired.com/27bstroke6/2008/10/fiction-or-fict.html.

98. Julian Sanchez, *750,000 Lost Jobs? The Dodgy Digits Behind the War on Piracy*, Oct. 7, 2008, *available at*: http://arstechnica.com/articles/culture/dodgy-digits-behind-the-war-on-piracy.ars.

99. Julian Sanchez, *750,000 Lost Jobs? The Dodgy Digits Behind the War on Piracy*, Oct. 7, 2008, *available at*: http://arstechnica.com/articles/culture/dodgy-digits-behind-the-war-on-piracy.ars.

100. *Id.*

101. *See* Anne Broache & Declan McCullagh, *Democrats: Colleges Must Police Copyright, or Else*, CNET, Nov. 9, 2007, *available at*: http://news.cnet.com/Democrats-Colleges-must-police-copyright,-or-else/2100-1028_3-6217943.html -. Ken Fisher, *Congressman Hollywood: Universities a Wretched Hive of Scum and Villainy*, Mar. 9, 2007, *available at*: http://arstechnica.com/news.ars/post/20070309-senator-hollywood-universities-a-wretched-hive-of-scum-and-villainy.html.

102. http://strategis.ic.gc.ca/epic/site/ippd-dppi.nsf/en/ip01462e.html. A 2009 Dutch study found an overall favorable impact. *See Economic and Cultural Effects of file sharing on music, film and games*, TNO Information and Communication Technology, Feb. 18, 2004, *available at*: http://www.iviz.nl/publicaties/vaneijk/Ups_And_Downs_authorised_translation.pdf.

103. The Higher Education Opportunity Act of 2008, H.R. 4147, Act of August 14, 2008, Pub. L. No. 110-315, 110th Cong., 2d Sess., 122 Statutes at Large 3078.

104. *See* Kenneth Green, *The Costs of P2P Compliance*, The Campus Computing Project, Oct. 2008, at 9.

105. I do not assert that creative destruction is at the root of *all* issues surrounding copyright, only those that are involved with what I am calling the Copyright Wars. For a full discussion of the more general issues, *see* William Landes & Richard Posner, *The Economic Structure of Intellectual Property Law* (Belknap Press, Harvard University 2003).

106. In his book *The Innovator's Dilemma*, at xv, xvii–xix, 180–182, Professor Christensen draws a distinction between what he calls disruptive and sustaining innovations. Sustaining technologies, which he regards as constituting the most frequent types of technological advances, improve the performance of existing products. Disruptive technologies, by contrast, result in worse product

performance at least in the near term, yet are the type of innovations most likely to cause market leaders to ultimately fail.

107. Joseph Schumpeter, *Capitalism, Socialism and Democracy* 83 (Harper & Brothers 3d ed. 1950, 2006 paperback) (1942).

108. *Id.* at 82. *See also* his earlier article, *The Instability of Capitalism* 38 Econ. J. 361–336 (September 1928), edited by John Maynard Keynes. The essay is reproduced in *Joseph A. Schumpeter: Essays on Entrepreneur, Innovation, Business Cycles, and the Evolution of Capitalism* 47–72 (Richard Clemence ed. 1951, Addison-Wesley).

109. Joseph Schumpeter, 2 *Business Cycles: A Theoretical, Historical, and Statistical Analysis of the Capitalist Process* 1033 (McGraw-Hill 1939).

110. Clayton Christensen & Michael Raynor, *The Innovator's Solution* 43 (Harvard Business School Press 2003).

111. Thomas McGraw, *Prophet of Innovation: Joseph Schumpeter and Creative Destruction* 256 (Belknap Press, Harvard University 2007).

112. Andrew Currah, *Hollywood, the Internet and the World: A Geography of Disruptive Innovation*, 14 Industry & Innovation 359 at 364 (2007).

113. *Testimony before the U.S. Senate Foreign Relations Committee on WIPO Copyright Treaties Implementation Act and the Online Copyright Liability Limitation Act*, 105th Cong., 2d Sess. (1998).

114. John Cantwell, *Innovation and Competitiveness*, in *The Oxford Handbook of Innovation* (John Fagerberg et al. eds., Oxford University Press 2006).

115. Google purchased YouTube in October 2006. For convenience sake, I refer only to YouTube.

116. *See* http://www.latimes.com/technology/la-fi-myspace3–2008nov03,1,1003794.story.

117. *See* David King, *Making Money on YouTube with Content ID*, Aug. 27, 2008, *available at*: http://googleblog.blogspot.com/2008/08/making-money-on-youtube-with-content-id.html.

118. A report on Commissioner Reding's remarks is *available at*: http://euobserver.com/9/26903.

119. Charles Clark, *The Answer to the Machine is in the Machine and Other Writings* (2006, Jon Bing and & Thomas Drier eds., Institutt for Rettsinformatikk 2006).

120. http://en.wikipedia.org/wiki/Moore%27s_law.

121. Red Herring, *Forget Moore's Law*, Feb. 9, 2003, *available at*: http://www.redherring.com/Home/10203.

122. Clayton Christensen, *The Innovator's Dilemma* xviii (Collins Business Essentials 1997, 2002). Professor Christensen explains his concept in much more detail in Clayton Christensen & Michael Raynor, *The Innovator's Solution* 32–71 (Harvard Business School Press 2003).

123. *See* data compiled by Andrew Curran, *Hollywood Versus the Internet: The Media and Entertainment Industries in a Digital and Networked Economy*, 6 J. Econ. Geogr. 439, 452–454 (2006).

124. *See* Andrew Currah, *Hollywood, the Internet and the World: A Geography of Disruptive Innovation*, 14 Industry & Innovation 359, 364 (2007).

125. Quoted in http://publishing2.com/2008/11/10/the-market-and-the-internet-dont-care-if-you-make-money/, November 10, 2008.

## 𝓦 Chapter 2 The Role of Metaphors in Understanding

1. If this were a comedy routine, chicken would be the punch line. Although it is exceedingly rare for lawyers to try stand-up, the chicken theme has been used in the legal literature. In the esoteric field of choice of law, where courts must determine which of two state's or two country's potentially applicable laws should be used to decide a dispute, Professor David Cavers related the story of his son encountering tuna fish for the first time; when told that it wasn't chicken, the reply was that it was "fish made of chicken." David Cavers, *The Choice of Law: Selected Essays 1933–1983*, at 46–47 (1985). *But see* Harold Maier, *Baseball and Chicken Salad: A Realistic Look at Choice of Law*, 44 Vand. L. Rev. 827, 842–843 (1991).

2. Wikipedia has the following entry on "Tastes Like Chicken":

   > When trying to describe the flavor of meat the listener has never eaten, a common declaration is that it tastes like chicken. The expression has been used so often that it has become somewhat of a cliché. As a result, the phrase also sometimes gets used for incongruous humor, by being deployed for foods or situations to which it has no real relevance.
   >
   > The expression has made its way into popular culture in a variety of contexts. The phrase has made modern appearances in the media, such as in *The Lion King, Six Days Seven Nights, The Matrix, Surf's Up* and the initial season of the reality television show *Survivor*.
   >
   > As an explanation of why unusual meats would taste more like chicken than common alternatives such as beef or pork, different possibilities have been offered. One suggestion is that chicken has a bland taste because fat contributes more flavor than muscle (especially in the case of a lean cut such as a skinless chicken breast), making it a generic choice for comparison. Also, chicken reportedly has lower levels of glutamates that contribute to the "savory" aspect of taste sometimes known as umami; processing or tenderizing other meats would also lower glutamate levels and make them taste more like chicken.
   >
   > Another suggestion, made by Joe Staton of the Museum of Comparative Zoology, is that meat flavors are fixed based on the evolutionary origin of the animal. Accordingly, birds (the most numerous form of meat by type) would naturally taste more like chicken than mammals. Furthermore, based on evidence for dinosaurs as the ancestors of birds, reptile meat might also taste somewhat like chicken. Seafood, however, would logically have a more

distinctive flavor. Staton's lighthearted study of the question was published in the *Annals of Improbable Research.*

*See* http://en.wikipedia.org/wiki/Tastes_like_chicken.

3. Sam Glucksberg, *Understanding Figurative Language: From Metaphors to Idioms* 41 (Oxford University Press 2001). *See also id.* at 7, and C. Cacciari & Sam Glucksberg, *Understanding Figurative Language,* in *Handbook of Psycholinguistics* 447 (Morton Ann Gernsbacher ed. Academic Press 1994); Morton Ann Gernsbacher, Boaz Keysar, Rachel Robertson, & Necia Werner, *The Role of Suppression and Enhancement in Understanding Metaphors,* 45 J. Memory & Language 433 (2001); Morton Ann Gernsbacher & Rachel Robertson, *The Role of Suppression in Figurative Language Comprehension,* 31 J. Pragmatics 1619 (1999). Professor Glucksberg has also quoted this amusing passage from Richard Russo's 1998 novel, *Straight Man:*

> Student: "I like the clouds. . . . They're like a metaphor."
> Professor: "They *are* a metaphor. . . . If they were *like* a metaphor, [t]hey'd be, like, a simile."—?

4. The distinction between simile and metaphor is the subject of dispute among scholars and has been since at least Aristotle's time. Aristotle treated simile as a poetic device and regarded it as a type of metaphor. *See On Rhetoric* 205 (George Kennedy trans., 2d ed. Oxford University Press 2007): "A simile is also a metaphor; for there is little difference: when the poet says, 'He rushed as a lion: it is simile, but 'The lion rushed' [with lion referring to a man] would be a metaphor. . . ." *See also id.* at 218 ("A simile is, as we said earlier, a metaphor differing by what is put first." *See also* Glucksberg at 29. Some scholars have misdescribed Aristotle's views by inverting them. *See e.g.,* John Searle, *Metaphor,* in *Metaphor and Thought* 95 (Andrew Ortony ed. 2d ed. Cambridge University Press 1993) (describing Aristotle as taking the view that "all metaphor is really literal simile with 'like' or 'as' deleted and the respect of the similarity left unspecified"); Andrew Goatly, *The Language of Metaphors* 118–119, 183–186 (Routledge 1997) (adopting comparison theory metaphor as an elliptical simile). *Cf.* Andrew Ortony, *Similarity in Similes and Metaphors, id.* at 344 (rejecting Searle's view of metaphor); Sam Glucksberg & Boaz Keysar, *How Metaphors Work, id.* at 422–423 ("Metaphors are not understood by transforming them into similes. Instead they are intended as class-inclusion statements and are understood as such. When metaphors are expressed as comparisons, that is, as similes, they are interpreted as implicit category statements, rather than the other way around. The grouping that is created by the metaphor induces the similarity relation, and so the grouping is prior.") (*see also id.* at 406–407); Sam Glucksberg & Catrinel Haught, *On the Relationship Between metaphor and Simile: When Comparison Fails,* 21 Mind & Language 360 (2005); Sam Glucksberg & Boaz Keysar, *Understanding Metaphorical Comparisons: Beyond Similarity,* 97 Psychol. Rev. 3 (1990). Lakoff & Johnson's *Metaphors We Live By* 153–155 (University of Chicago Press 1980, 2003), also rejects the comparison theory for metaphors.

A third category is metonymy, e.g., "she's just a pretty face." In metonymy, one characteristic is reductively associated with an entire person or thing. *See Metaphor and Metonymy at the Crossroads: A Cognitive Perspective* (Antonio Barcelona ed. Mouton de Gruyter 2003); *Metaphor and Metonymy in Comparison and Contrast* (René Driven & Ralf Pörings eds., Mouton de Gruyter 2003).

5. There is no uniformity on this point. *See* the previous endnote. Historically many have believed that metaphors are a form of simile, and some believe that metaphors are processed as similes. Under this approach, when someone says "lawyers are sharks," it is processed as "lawyers are like sharks."

6. Walter Kintsch, *How the Mind Computes the Meaning of Metaphor* in *The Cambridge Handbook of Metaphor and Thought* 129, 135 (Raymond Gibbs ed. Cambridge University Press 2008).

7. *See also* Glucksberg & Keysar, *Understanding Metaphorical Comparisons: Beyond Similarity*, 97 Psychological Review 3, 15–16 (1997) (suggesting that metaphor is used rather than simile when a specific, forceful assertion is made, rather than a more general, hedged assertion).

8. Paul Ricoeur has suggested that the term "metaphor" is itself a metaphor. *See* Paul Ricoeur, *The Metaphorical Process as Cognition, Imagination, and Feeling* 5 Critical Inquiry 143, 145 (1978). *See also* Richard Boyd, *Metaphor and Theory Change: What is "metaphor" a metaphor for?*, in *Metaphor and Thought* 481 (Andrew Ortony ed. 2d ed. Cambridge University Press 1993). Steven Pinker appears to agree as to some metaphors, *see The Stuff of Thought: Language as a Window into Human Nature*, Chapter 5, *The Metaphor Metaphor"* (Penguin 2007), but his discussion is so inaccurate as to cognitive linguist George Lakoff's views, and his own positions are so inconsistent that it is hard to know what he thinks other than that he dislikes Lakoff. In the end, however, even he concludes: "Still, I think that metaphor really is a key to explaining thought and language." *Id.* at 176.

9. For a discussion of the metaphor "Juliet is the Sun," *see* Samuel Guttenplan, *Objects of Metaphor*, ch. 1 (Oxford University Press 2005).

10. For Aristotle's views on similes (Greek: *eikon*), *see On Rhetoric* 205 (George Kennedy translation, 2d ed. Oxford University Press 2007). *See also* the excellent series of articles in *Metaphor, Allegory, and the Classical Tradition* (G.R. Boys-Stones ed. Oxford University Press 2003). The most extensive view of Aristotle's views on metaphors and similes is by Paul Ricoeur, *The Rule of Metaphor* (Robert Czerny trans., University of Toronto Press 2006).

11. Aristotle, *Poetics* 1457b, reprinted in 2 *The Complete Works of Aristotle* 2332 (J. Barnes ed. 1984). Roman orators Quintilian, *De Institutione Oratorico* 803 (H. E. Butler trans.), and Cicero, *De Oratore* 155 (E. W. Sutton & H. Rackham trans.), admired their figurative elegance. John Locke (*An Essay Concerning Human Understanding* 327), by contrast, expressed highly negative views on figurative language:

> If we would speak of things as they are, we must allow that all the art of rhetoric, besides order and clearness, all the artificial and figurative application of words eloquence hath invented, are for nothing else but to insinuate wrong

ideas, move the passions, and thereby mislead the judgment, and so indeed are perfect cheat; and therefore however laudable or allowable oratory may render them in harangues and popular addresses, they are certainly, in all discourses that pretend to inform or instruct, wholly to be avoided and, where truth and knowledge are concerned, cannot but be thought a great fault either of the language or person who makes use of them.

12. I.A. Richards, *The Philosophy of Rhetoric* 90 (1936).
13. *See* George Lakoff & Mark Turner, *More than Cool Reason: A Field Guide to Poetic Metaphor* (University of Chicago Press 1989); Yeshayahu Shen, *The Cambridge Handbook of Metaphor,* ch. 17, *Metaphor and Poetic Figures* (Raymond Gibbs ed. Cambridge University Press 2008); David Punter, *Metaphor* 12–25 (Routledge 2007).
14. *See* Andrew Ortony, *Why Metaphors Are Necessary and Not Just Nice*, 25 Educa. Theory 45 (Apr. 2, 2007).
15. Arnold Modell, *Emotional Memory, Metaphor, and Meaning*, 5 Psychoanalytic Inquiry 555, 562 (2005).
16. Sam Glucksberg, *Beyond the Literal in Understanding Figurative Language: From Metaphors to Idioms,* ch. 2 (Oxford University Press 2001).
17. *Id.* at 17. *See also* Raluca Budiu & John R. Anderson, *Word Learning in Context: Metaphors and Neologisms* (Carnegie Mellon University, Aug. 2001).
18. Professor Glucksberg makes a further point in this respect, distinguishing between literal meaning and literal interpretation:

> If literal meanings always require additional work to arrive at literal interpretation, then there is no reason to claim that literal meanings have priority. Instead, the claim would have to be literal interpretations. If this is the case, then the priority of the literal would be not a natural consequence of how the language processor works but instead a consequence of a bias or preference for literal interpretations as a default strategy.

19. *See* Raluca Budiu & John R. *Anderson, Integration of Background Knowledge in Language Processing: A Unified Theory of Metaphor Understanding, Moses, Illusions and Text Memory, available at*: http://repository.cmu.edu/cgi/viewcontent.cgi?article=1054&context=psychology.
20. *See* http://en.wikipedia.org/wiki/I._A._Richards.
21. I.A. Richards, *The Philosophy of Rhetoric* (Oxford University Press 1936).
22. *Id.* at 94.
23. *Id.*
24. *Id.* at 96. For further discussions of Professor Richards' tenor and vehicle approach, *see e.g.,* Manuel Bilsky, *I. A. Richards' Theory of Metaphor*, 50 Modern Philology 130 (Nov. 1952); David Douglass, *Issues in the Use of I. A. Richards' Tenor-Vehicle Model of Metaphor*, W. J. Comm. (Oct. 2000); Matthew McGlone & D. Manfredi, *Topic-Vehicle Interaction in Metaphor Comprehension*, 29 Memory & Cognition 1209 (2001). Paul Ricoeur has written: "The relationship between the vehicle and the tenor is not like the relationship of one idea to another, but like that of an image

to an abstract meaning," The Rule of Metaphor 207 (Robert Czerny translator, 2006 paperback edition, University of Toronto Press).

25. Max Black, *Models and Metaphors: Studies in Language and Philosophy* 44 (Cornell University Press 1962).

26. *Id.* at 40.

27. Colin Turbayne, *The Myth of Metaphor* 14–15 (University of South Carolina Press 1962).

28. *Id.* at 42.

29. *Id.* at 3.

30. *Id.* at 23.

31. *Id.* at 3.

32. *See*, in particular, John R. Andersen's oft-cited article, *A Spreading Theory of Activation*, 22 J. Verbal Learning & Verbal Behav. (1983), and his recent book *How Can the Human Mind Occur in the Physical Universe?* (Oxford University Press 2007).

33. *A Spreading Theory of Activation*, at 21. George Lakoff believes that a physical change in the brain occurs after repetition, George Lakoff, *Whose Freedom? The Battle over America's Important Idea* (Picador 2006):

> When a word or phrase is repeated over and over for a long period of time, the neural circuits that compute its meaning are activated repeatedly in the brain. As the neurons in those circuits fire, the synapses connecting the neurons in the circuits get stronger and the circuits may eventually become permanent, which happens when you learn the meaning of any word in your fixed vocabulary. Learning a word physically changes your brain, and the meaning of that word becomes physically instantiated in your brain.

For a neurological explanation of how metaphors are processed, *see* Seana Coulson, *The Cambridge Handbook on Metaphor and Thought*, ch. 10, *Metaphor Comprehension and the Brain*, at 177–194 (Raymond Gibbs ed. Cambridge University Press 2008).

34. Max Sutherland & Alice Sylvester, *Advertising and the Mind of the Consumer* 9 (Allen & Unwin 2000).

35. Frank Luntz, *Words That Work* 29 (Hyperion, updated paperback edition 2008).

36. *Id.* at 61, citing Charles Osgood et al. *The Measurement of Meaning* (University of Illinois 1957).

37. Drew Westen, *The Political Brain: The Role of Emotion in Deciding the Fate of the Nation* 85 (Public Affairs Press 2007).

38. *See* Chapters 7 and 8.

39. Patricia Loughlan, *"You Wouldn't Steal a Car . . .": Intellectual Property and the Language of Theft*, 29 Eur. Intell. Prop. Rev. 401, 401 (2007).

40. *See also* Nigel Hollis, *Foreword* to Erik du Plessis, *The Advertised Mind*, at xvi (Millward Brown 2006).

41. *Id.* at 4–5. For those looking for a detailed discussion of the possible definitions of what constitutes emotion and how to understand it, *see* Jerome Kagan, *What Is Emotion?: History, Measures, and Meanings* (Yale University Press 2007); Keith

Oakley & Jennifer Jenkins, *Understanding Emotions* (Oxford University Press 1995).

42. *See* Patricia Loughlan, *Pirates, Parasites, Reapers, Sowers, Fruits, Foxes. . . . The Metaphors of Intellectual Property*, 28 Sydney L. Rev. 210, 216 (2006), from which these examples are derived.

43. *See also* George Lakoff & Mark Turner, *More Than Cool Reason: A Field Guide to Poetic Metaphor* (1989).

44. I use the term "cognitive process" in the way used by Lakoff and Johnson, "any mental operations and structures that are involved in language, meaning, perception, conceptual systems and reason." George Lakoff & Mark Johnson, *Philosophy in the Flesh* 12 (Basic Books 1999).

45. *Id.* at 94.

46. William Croft & Alan Cruse, *Cognitive Linguistics* 197 (Cambridge University Press 2004). Not all metaphors are expressed linguistically, *see* Zoltán Kövesces, *Nonlinguistic Realizations of Conceptual Metaphors* in *Metaphor: A Practical Introduction* (Oxford University Press 2002).

47. *Philosophy in the Flesh* at 126. Not all scholars of metaphor agree with this statement; some follow the "comparison theory" of metaphor in which metaphor is treated as a paraphrased statement of similarity or analogy, and as therefore an elliptical form of simile. *See* Andrew Goatly, *The Language of Metaphors* 118–119 (Routledge 1997); George A. Miller, *Images and Models, Similes and Metaphors*, in *Metaphor and Thought* 357–400 (Andrew Ortony ed. 1993). *But see* John Searle, "Metaphor" in *id.* at 91–102 (examining weaknesses in comparison theory).

48. Paul Ricoeur, *The Metaphorical Process as Cognition, Imagination, and Feeling*, 5 Critical Inquiry 143, 145 (1978).

49. Lakoff & Johnson at 147–155, 245.

50. Other attempts have been successful, most infamously in Judge Kevin Duffy's opinion in *Grand Upright Music Ltd. v. Warner Bros. Records, Inc.*, 780 F. Supp. 182, 183 (S.D.N.Y. 1991), which began:

> "Thou shalt not steal" has been an admonition followed since the dawn of civilization. Unfortunately, in the modern world of business this admonition is not always followed. Indeed, the defendants in this action for copyright infringement would have this court believe that stealing is rampant in the music business and, for that reason, their conduct here should be excused. The conduct of the defendants herein, however, violates not only the Seventh Commandment, but also the copyright laws of this country.

The case involved sampling of music and had a disastrous impact on hip hop music. *See* Daphne Keller, *The Musician as Thief*, in *Sound Unbound* 135 (Paul Miller ed. MIT Press 2008).

51. This supports research done by Professor Morton Ann Gernsbacher and her colleagues that some metaphoric understanding occurs through the creation of ad hoc categories. Under this approach, when we use a metaphor, the metaphoric vehicle (sharks) are *seen* as a category of things that are ruthless. When we say that lawyers are sharks, the metaphor is understood as an assertion that lawyers

are members of the class of ruthless things: Through the metaphor lawyers become a superordinate category of ruthless things. *See* Morton Ann Gernsbacher, Boaz Keysar, Rachel Robertson, and Necia Werner, *The Role of Suppression and Enhancement in Understanding Metaphors*, 45 Journal of Memory and Language 433 (2001).

52. *See* testimony of Jack Valenti before the Senate Foreign Relations Committee on June 9, 2004: "What we often refer to as 'piracy' is more clearly and accurately defined as 'outright thievery,'" *available at*: http://foreign.senate.gov/testimony/ 2004/ValentiTestimony040609.pdf.

53. *See* Martin Stefik, Introduction to *Internet Dreams: Archetypes, Myths, and Metaphors*, at xvi (Martin Stefik ed. 1996, 2001 3d prtg.).

54. *See id.*, ch. 3, *Human Associative Memory.*

55. George Lakoff & Mark Johnson, *Philosophy in the Flesh* 12 (Basic Books 1999). *Cf.* Arnold Modell's expansion of Lakoff & Johnson's approach, *Imagination and the Meaningful Brain* 47–48 (MIT Press 2006).

56. *Id.* at 11.

57. *See* Brian Nosek & Jeffrey Hansen, *The Associations in Our Heads Belong to Us: Searching for Attitudes and Knowledge in Implicit Evaluation*, 22 Cognition & Emotion 553–594 (2008).

58. *See* M. Marschak & R. Hunt, *On Memory for Metaphor*, 13 Memory & Cognition 413 (1985).

59. *Modell* at 68.

60. *See* Brian Bowdle & Dedre Gentner, *The Career of Metaphor*, 112 Psychol. Rev. 193 (2005). "Mapping" is itself a metaphor and is used in many fields, including law. *See* Stephen Waddams, *Dimensions of Private Law: Categories and Concepts in Anglo-American Legal Reasoning*, "Introduction: The Mapping of Legal Concepts" and "Conclusion: The Concept of Legal Mapping" (Cambridge University Press 2003).

61. These terms are those used first by George Lakoff and Mark Johnson. *See also* Giles Fauconnier, *Mappings in Thought and Language* 1 (Cambridge University Press 1997). Professor Fauconnier points out a fundamental circularity in efforts to understand how this process works: We produce our account of language and thought by relying on language and thought. *Id.* at 3.

62. *Internet Dreams: Archetypes, Myths, and Metaphors* 356 (Martin Stefik ed.).

63. Those who are interested in detailed, specific examples of how this occurs should read Eva Kittay, *Metaphor: Its Cognitive Force and Linguistic Structure*, ch. 7, *Semantic Fields and the Structure of Metaphor* (Clarendon Press, Oxford University 1987), and Andrew Goatly, *The Language of Metaphors* (Routledge 1997) at ch. 4, *How Different Kinds of Metaphors Work.*

64. *See generally* Alan Baddeley, *Working Memory, Thought, and Action* (Oxford University Press 2007); *The Oxford Handbook of Memory* (Endel Tulving ed. Oxford University Press 2000). Short-term memory is said to last only 15–30 seconds, *see The Britannica Guide to the Brain* 115 (2008). I do not distinguish here between episodic and semantic memory, nor their relationship. *See generally,* Endel Tulving, *Episodic and Semantic Memory*, in *Organization of Memory* (Endel

Tulving & William Donaldson eds., Academic Press 1972). Episodic memory is memory of specific events; semantic memory is memory of learned events, for example, Abraham Lincoln was the sixteenth president of the United States.

65. Quoted in Peter Dekom and Peter Sealey, *Not on My Watch: Hollywood vs. the Future* 42 (New Millennium Press 2003).

66. *See* Zoltán Kövecses, *Metaphor, and Emotion: Language, Culture, and Body in Human Feeling* (Cambridge University Press 2000); Zoltán Kövesces, Gary Palmer, René Dirven, *Language and Emotion: The Interplay of Conceptualism with Psychology and Culture*, in *Metaphor and Metonymy in Comparison and Contrast* 133 (René Dirven & Ralf Pörings eds., 2003, Mouton de Gruyter publisher); George Lakoff and &Mark Johnson, *Philosophy in the Flesh* 4 (Basic Books 1999) (stating that "Reason is emotionally engaged.").

67. Drew Westen, *The Political Brain: The Role of Emotion in Deciding the Fate of the Nation* 318 (Public Affairs Press 2007).

68. 5 Critical Inquiry 143 (1978).

69. *Id.* at 156. *See also* Charles Peirce Saunders' remark that "A feeling is merely the quality of a mental sign," quoted in *Modell* at 131, and C.F. Delaney, *Peirce's Account of Mental Activity*, 41 Synthese 25 (1979).

70. *See* http://en.wikipedia.org/wiki/George_Campbell_(Presbyterian_minister).

71. George Campbell, *The Philosophy of Rhetoric* 72 (L. Blitzer ed. Southern Illinois University Press 1988 ed.).

72. *Id.*

73. *See* James Dillard & Anneloes Meijindes, *Persuasion and the Structure of Affect*, in *The Persuasion Handbook: Developments in Theory and Practice* 309 (James Dillard & Michael Pfau eds., Sage 2002).

74. *The Cognitive-Emotional Fugue*, in *Emotions, Cognition & Behavior* 264 (Carroll Izard, Jerome Kagan, & Robert Zajonic eds., Cambridge University Press 1984). For examples of emotional metaphors in psychological states, *see* James Averill, "Inner feelings, works of the flesh, the beast within, diseases of the mind, driving force, and putting on a show: six metaphors of emotion and their theoretical extensions," in *Metaphors in the History of Psychology* 104 (David Leary ed. Cambridge University Press 1990).

75. *Modell* at 144.

76. *Id.* at 145.

77. Erik du Plessis, *The Advertised Mind* 4 (2006 Millward Brown 2006).

78. *Id.* at xii.

79. Robin Nabi, *Discrete Emotions and Persuasion*, in *The Persuasion Handbook: Developments in Theory and Practice* 289, 299 (James Dillard & Michael Pfau eds., Sage 2002). *See also* Robin Nabi, *A Cognitive Functional Model for the Effects of Discrete Negative Emotions on Information Processing, Attitude Change and Recall*, 9 Commun. Theory 292 (2006); Robin Nabi, *Exploring the Framing Effects of Emotion*, 30 Commun. Res. 224 (2003).

80. Susan Fisk & Shelley Taylor, *Social Cognition* (2d ed. McGraw-Hill 1991) (1984).

81. http://en.wikipedia.org/wiki/Cognitive_miser.

82. *The Social Psychology of Stereotyping and Group Life* 10 (Russell Spears et al. eds., Blackwell 1997).

83. *See* the two classic collections of essays, *Judgment Under Uncertainty: Heuristics and Biases* (Daniel Kahneman, Paul Slovic, & Amos Tversky eds., 22d prtg. Cambridge University Press 2006) (1982); *Heuristics and Biases: The Psychology of Intuitive Judgment* (Thomas Gilovich, Dale Griffin, & Daniel Kahneman eds., Cambridge University Press 2002). For another collection of essays with a generally (and sometimes excessively) positive attitude toward heuristics, *see Heuristics and the Law* (Gerd Gigerenzer & Christoph Engel eds., MIT Press 2006).

84. In the case of courts, we must be careful to distinguish between courts' written opinions and the reasoning used to come to a result. Courts and Congress stand very differently in this respect. Congress's job is to respond to political pressure, and in responding it need not explain its actions, certainly not publicly. Not so with judges, who are often tasked with interpreting the work of others, principally statutes and the decisions of prior judges. Judge Richard Posner, in a review of a book by Anthony Amsterdam and Jerome Bruner criticized the authors for thinking that

> judicial decisions and other human actions are determined by unconscious mental processes that trigger and guide the evaluation of our perceptions. In their view, we do not reason to conclusions, we jump to them, or rather, we are jumped to them by the promptings of our mental furnitures.
>
> ....
>
> They merely assume that causation in judicial decision-making runs from categorization, narrative, rhetoric, and culture to judicial case outcome, rather than vice versa. They do not consider the possibility that judges reason to the outcome and then, when it comes time to write the opinion explaining and justifying their conclusion, resort to categorization, narrative, rhetoric, and cultural cues, either in a conscious effort to make the opinion more persuasive or in unconscious conformity to the customs and usages that define advocacy prose, which is what a judicial opinion is.

Posner, *The Law of the Beholder*, review of Anthony G. Amsterdam & Jerome Bruner, *Minding the Law*, New Republic 49 (Oct. 16, 2000).

## 𝍑 Chapter 3  Metaphors and the Law

1. [2001] F.S.R. 11, ¶ 26 (H.L. Nov. 23, 2000). *See also* Isaiah Berlin, *The Hedgehog and the Fox: An Essay on Tolstoy's View of History* (1953):

> There is a line among the fragments of the Greek poet Archilochus which says: 'The fox knows many things, but the hedgehog knows one big thing.' Scholars have differed about the correct interpretation of these dark words, which may mean no more than that the fox, for all his cunning, is defeated by the hedgehog's one defense. But, taken figuratively, the words can be made to yield a sense in which they mark one of the deepest differences which divide writers and thinkers, and, it may be, human beings in general. For there exists a great

chasm between those, on one side, who relate everything to a single central vision, one system less or more coherent or articulate, in terms of which they understand, think and feel-a single, universal, organizing principle in terms of which alone all that they are and say has significance-and, on the other side, those who pursue many ends, often unrelated and even contradictory, connected, if at all, only in some de facto way, for some psychological or physiological cause, related by no moral or aesthetic principle; these last lead lives, perform acts, and entertain ideas that are centrifugal rather than centripetal, their thought is scattered or diffused, moving on many levels, seizing upon the essence of a vast variety of experiences and objects for what they are in themselves, without consciously or unconsciously, *see*king to fit them into, or exclude them from, any one unchanging, all-embracing, sometimes self-contradictory and incomplete, at times fanatical, unitary inner vision. The first kind of intellectual and artistic personality belongs to the hedgehogs, the second to the foxes; and without insisting on a rigid classification, we may, without too much fear of contradiction, say that, in this sense, Dante belongs to the first category, Shakespeare to the second; Plato, Lucretius, Pascal, Hegel, Dostoevsky, Nietzsche, Ibsen, Proust are, in varying degrees, hedgehogs; Herodotus, Aristotle, Montaigne, Erasmus, Molière, Goethe, Pushkin, Balzak, Joyce are foxes.

2. *L. Wooley Jewellers Ltd. v. A&A Jewellery Ltd.* (No. 2), [2004] FSR 47, at 934. Whether Judge Fysh's effusion was attributable to his having been boxed around the ears by Judge Hoffman when appearing as counsel in *Designer's Guild*, I leave to others. Judge Fysh's reference to a sibyl is, presumably to the *Sibylline Books*, a collection of oracular utterances, that began in the sixth century B.C.E. in Greece. *See* http://en.wikipedia.org/wiki/Sibylline_Books.

3. *See* Ronan Deazley, *Copyright in the House of Lords: Recent Cases, Judicial Reasoning and Academic Writing*, 2 Intell. Prop. Q. 121, 132 (2004):

> It is here that Lord Hoffmann's enigmatic allusion to hedgehogs and foxes comes properly into its own.
>
> . . .
>
> Transported to the context of the decision in *Designers*, for Lord Hoffmann "the more abstract and simple the copied idea, the less likely it is to constitute a substantial part." That is, copyright is about protecting the detail within which a basic idea is presented; the more and more of the details that you take from another's work, the greater the chances are that you are taking too much. This is why, in Lord Hoffmann's opinion, "[c]opyright law protects foxes better than hedgehogs."

Mark Chacksfield wrote:

> In all, Lord Hoffmann's subtle restatement of the law would appear to be sound, both logically and legally. But where does all this leave foxes and hedgehogs?

It is perhaps better to read this statement not as a direct reference to the relatively well known quote from the Greek poet Archilochus ("The Fox knows many things, but the Hedgehog knows one big thing"), but rather to the famous essay of another Oxford academic, Isaiah Berlin ("The Hedgehog and the Fox"). The Hedgehogs and Foxes contemplated by Isaiah Berlin represent the two ends of the spectrum of academic historians. On the one hand the "Hedgehogs" perceive that the tides of history are directed by grand unifying forces, which act above and beyond the elements of any particular situation. On the other, the "Foxes" subscribe to the belief that the devil is in the detail, and that history is driven by the combined weight of the minutiae. It is a comparison of the importance of trivia against the abstraction of grand ideas, and the core concept is that without the detail there is nothing to be abstracted from history. Perhaps, in another sense, the same is true of art.

Mark Chacksfield, *The Hedgehog and the Fox, a Substantial Part of Copyright*, 23 Eur. Intell. Prop. Rev. 259, 261–262 (2005). *See also* criticism in Michael Spence & Timothy Endicott, *Vagueness in the Scope of Copyright*, 121 L. Q. Rev. 657, 672 (2005). This and other metaphors are discussed in Patricia Loughlan, *Pirates, Parasites, Reapers, Sowers, Fruits, Foxes. . . . The Metaphors of Intellectual Property*, 28 Sydney Law Review 210 (2006).

4. Quoted in Robert Tsai, *Fire, Metaphor, and Constitutional Myth-Making*, 93 Georgetown L. J. 181, 186 (2004).

5. *Berkey v. Third Avenue Railway Co.*, 244 N.Y. 84, 94 (1926). To the same effect are the remarks of Justice Gummow of the Australian High Court, *see Commonwealth of Australia v. Yamirr*, [2001] 208 C.L.R. 1, 68; *Truth About Motorways v. Macquarie Infrastructure Mgt. Ltd.*, [2000] 200 C.L.R. 591, 625.

6. Loughlan, 28 Sydney Law Review at 215–216.

7. *See* R. Tourangeau & R. Sternberg, *Aptness in Metaphor*, 13 Cognitive Psychol. 203 (1981).

8. *See* http://en.wikipedia.org/wiki/Henry_Temple,_3rd_Viscount_Palmerston.

9. Quoted in Philip Guedella, *Palmerston* 226 (1927). Karl Marx wrote a desultory biography of Palmerston, published originally in pieces, and then ultimately published by Eleanor Marx as a whole in 1899, *The Story and Life of Lord Palmerston*. International Publishers put out an edition of the work in 1969.

10. George Lakoff, *Metaphor and War: The Metaphor System Used to Justify War in the Gulf, pt. I*, paper presented Jan. 30, 1991, Alumni House, U.C. Berkeley, *available at*: http://www.arieverhagen.nl/11-sept-01/Lakoff_1991.html.

11. Arturo Rosenbluth & Norbert Wiener, quoted in Arnold Modell, at 7.

12. *See* Steven Winter, *What is the "Color" of Law?* in *The Cambridge Handbook of Metaphor and Thought*, ch. 20 (Raymond Gibbs ed. Cambridge University Press 2008).

13. A metaphor meaning the legal principle is foundational and undisputed.

14. *See* William Patry, 2 *Patry on Copyright*, ch. 4, § 4:31 (Thomson/West 2007, 2008, 2009 supplements).

15. Clothing your thoughts is of course a metaphor.

16. *Peter Pan Fabrics, Inc. v. Martin Weiner Corp.*, 274 F.2d 487, 489 (2d Cir. 1960).
17. *Holmes v. Hurst*, 174 U.S. 82, 86 (1899).
18. 17 Parl. Hist. Eng. cols. 992–1001 (Hansard ed. 1813).
19. 4 Burr. 2303, 98 E.R. 201 (K.B. 1769).
20. Letter from Thomas Jefferson to Isaac McPherson, August 13, 1814, in *The Complete Jefferson* 1011, 1015 (Saul Padover, ed. 1943). For a good review of the letter, *see* James Boyle, *The Public Domain: Enclosing the Commons of the Mind* 17–21 (Yale University Press 2009).
21. *See* Zoltán Kövesces, *Metaphor: A Practical Introduction* 74, 205, 234 (Oxford University Press 2002).
22. *Holmes v. Hurst,* 174 U.S. 82, 86 (1899):

    > The right thus secured by the copyright act is not a right to the use of certain words, because they are the common property of the human race, and as little susceptible of private appropriation as air or sunlight; nor is it the right to ideas alone, since in the absence of means of communicating them they are of value to no one but the author. But the right is to that arrangement of words which the author has selected to express his ideas.

23. *See* Justice Thompson's dissent in *Wheaton v. Peters*, 33 U.S. 591, 673 (1834):

    > Nothing can be an object of property which has not a corporal substance. The property claimed is all ideal; a set of ideas which have no bounds or marks whatever-nothing that is capable of a visible possession-nothing that can sustain any one of the qualities or incidents of property. Their whole existence is in the mind alone. Incapable of any other modes of acquisition or enjoyment than by mental possession or apprehension; safe and invulnerable from their own immateriality, no trespass can reach them, no tort affect them; no fraud or violence diminish or damage them. Yet these are the phantoms which the author would grasp and confine to himself; and these are what the defendant is charged with having robbed the plaintiff of.

24. *See* further discussion in Chapter 5.

## ✎ Chapter 4　The Mythical Origins of Copyright and Three Favorite Copyright Metaphors

1. *See* a review of the various theories in David McGowan, *Copyright Noncons-equentialism*, 69 Mo. L. Rev. 1 (2004).
2. *See* Samuel Trosow, *The Illusive Search for Justificatory Theories: Copyright, Commodification and Capital*, 16 Canadian J. L. & Jurisprudence 217 (July 2003).
3. Joanne Wright, *Origin Stories in Political Thought: Discourses on Gender, Power and Citizenship* 9–10 (2004), quoted in Jessica Sibley, *The Mythical Beginnings of Intellectual Property*, 15 Geo. Mason L. Rev. 319 (2008).
4. *See* Majid Yar, *The Rhetorics and Myths of Anti-Piracy Campaigns: Criminalization, Moral Pedagogy and Capitalist Property Relations in the Classroom*, 10 New Media

Soc'ty 605 (2008), *available at*: http://nms.sagepub.com/cgi/content/abstract/10/4/605.

5. James K. Galbraith, *The Predator State* xii (Free Press 2008).

6. This rationale is also frequently coupled with concerns about the "public goods" problem. Judge Posner and Professor Landes have noted that the "very term 'public good' is misleading. . . . It sounds like a good produced by the government as opposed to the private sector." William Landes & Richard Posner, *The Economic Structure of Intellectual Property Law* 14 (Harvard University Press, Belknap 2003). Instead, by "public good," economists mean that "consumption of it by one person does not reduce its consumption by another." *Id.*

7. *Id.* at 20–21.

8. *See* Brief of George Akerlof et al. *Eldred v. Ashcroft,* May 20, 2006, *available at*: http://cyber.law.harvard.edu/openlaw/eldredvashcroft/supct/amici/economists.pdf; 2002 Westlaw 1041846.

9. Mark Lemley, *Ex Ante Versus Ex Post Facto Justifications for Intellectual Property,* *supra* at 7.

10. Sir Hugh Laddie, *The Insatiable Appetite for Intellectual Property,* unpublished lecture delivered on December 4, 2007, University College London. All quotes are from this lecture.

11. Joseph Stiglitz, *Economic Foundations of Intellectual Property Rights,* 57 Duke L. J. 1693, 1710 (2008).

12. *See* 1 *Patry on Copyright,* Chapter 3, Part II (Thomson/West 2007, semi-annual supplements).

13. *Meshwerks, Inc. v. Toyota Motor Sales U.S.A., Inc.,* 528 F.3d 1258, 1268 (10th Cir. 2008).

14. *Rockford Map Publishers, Inc. v. Directory Service Co.,* 768 F.2d 145, 148–149 (7th Cir. 1985).

15. *Feist Publications, Inc. v. Rural Telephone Service Co.,* 499 U.S. 340 (1991).

16. *See* http://en.wikipedia.org/wiki/Lake_Wobegon.

17. Paul Goldstein, *Copyright's Highway: From Gutenberg to the Celestial Jukebox* 76 (1994). Professor Mark Rose, in *Mothers and Authors: Johnson v. Calvert and the New Children of Our Imagination,* 22 Critical Inquiry 613, 629, 631 (1996), correctly takes Professor Goldstein to task for these remarks.

18. http://en.wikipedia.org/wiki/Aaron_Copland.

19. *Id.*

20. *See* http://en.wikipedia.org/wiki/Appalachian_Spring. National Public Radio devoted one of its "Milestones of the Millennium" programs to *Appalachian Spring* on November 29, 2004; the program, *available at*: http://www.npr.org/programs/specials/milestones/991027.motm.apspring.html, contains a careful analysis of the music and all of its prior sources and influences.

21. *See* http://www.literarytraveler.com/authors/fitzgerald_hemingway_sunalsorises.aspx.

22. *See* http://en.wikipedia.org/wiki/Citizen_Kane:

> The principal source for the story of Citizen Kane was the life of media tycoon William Randolph Hearst, and the film is *seen* by critics as a fictionalized,

unrelentingly hostile parody of Hearst. Hearst often entertained Hollywood celebrities at Hearst Castle (just north of San Luis Obispo, California)—but only as long as they revealed secrets that would be published the following week in the Hearst newspapers. This quid pro quo resulted in Hearst drawing wide resentment from many actors and directors in Hollywood, and Citizen Kane was seen by many as payback for Hearst's exploits. Welles was also inspired by other figures of the day, and the film even contains autobiographical elements.

"Citizen Kane" is in part based on the life of Samuel Insull and his wife Gladys. Playwright Herman J. Mankiewicz based Susan Alexander's catastrophic operatic debut in "Citizen Kane" on Gladys Wallis Insull's New York role as Lady Teazle in a charity revival of "A School for Scandal." The review of Susan Alexander's debut in Kane echoes Mankiewicz's actual 1925 review of Gladys Insull. His 1925 review began: "As Lady Teazle, Mrs. Insull is as pretty as she is diminutive; with a clear smile and dainty gestures. There is a charming grace in her bearing that makes for excellent deportment. But Lady Teazle seems much too innocent to lend credit to her part in the play."

I do not mean to slight Welles' brilliance as a filmmaker, which is precisely why Citizen Kane is a classic.

23. *Wheaton v. Peters*, 33 U.S. 591 (1834).

24. *See* http://www.phrases.org.uk/meanings/254050.html.

25. The most comprehensive examination of these records is found in William Maher, *Copyright Term, Retrospective Extension, and the Copyright Law of 1790 in Historical Perspective*, 49 J. Copyright Soc'ty U.S.A. 1021 (2002). Mr. Maher conducted an extensive review of the records and corrected errors found in an earlier, oft-cited study, *Federal Copyright Records 1790–1800* (James Gilreath & Elizabeth Wills 1987). *See also* Christopher Sprigman, *Reforma(aliz)ing Copyright*, 57 Stan. L. Rev. 485 (2004).

26. For works published after December 31, 1977, there is a single term of protection with no renewal.

27. Assuming for U.S. works that they were timely renewed. There is no such requirement for foreign works.

28. Landes & Posner at 237.

29. *See* http://www.copyright.gov/orphan/comments/reply/OWR0116-Interaction Law.pdf.

30. Barbara Ringer, *Renewal of Copyright*, Copyright Office Study No. 31, at 221 (1960).

31. Feminist legal writers have used the personhood metaphor in arguing for copyright rights believed to be more sympathetic to women writers. *See e.g.*, *Symposium on Feminism and Dualism in Intellectual Property*, 15 Am. U. J. Gender Soc. Pol'y & L. (2007); Malla Pollack, *Towards a Feminist Theory of the Public Domain, or Rejecting the Gendered Scope of United States Copyrightable and Patentable Subject Matter*, 2 Wm. & Mary J. Women & L. 603 (2006). *See also* Christine Battersby, *Gender and Genius: Toward a Feminist Aesthetic* (1989), and Richard Swartz, *Patrimony and the Figuration of Authorship in the Eighteenth-Century Literary Property Debates*, 7 Works & Days 2 (1989) for a discussion of the gendering of authors as males.

32. *See* Mark Rose, *Mothers and Authors:* Johnson v. Calvert *and the New Children of Our Imagination*, 22 Critical Inquiry 613, 622 (1996). Professor Rose also provides the following other references for the trope of the book as a child: Terry Castle, *Lab'ring Bards: Birth Topoi and the English Poetics 1660–1820*, 78 J. Eng. & Germanic Philol. 193 (Apr. 1979); Elizabeth Sacks, *Shakespeare's Image of Pregnancy* (1980); Susan Friedman, *Creativity and the Childbirth Metaphor: Gender Difference in Literary Discourse*, in *Speaking of Gender* 73 (Elaine Showalter ed. 1989); Mark Rose, *From Paternity to Property: The Remetamorphization of Writing* (unpublished 1996).

33. Miguel de Cervantes Saaverdra, *The Adventures of Don Quixote* 41 (Walter Starkie trans.), declaring that is book is not "the handsomest, the liveliest, and the wisest" child.

34. *See* Mark Rose, *Copyright and its Metaphors*, 50 UCLA L. Rev. 1, 3–4 (2002).

35. James Joyce, Letter to Nora Barnacle, dated August 12, 1912, in 2 *Letters of James Joyce* 41 (Stuart Gilbert & Richard Ellmann eds., 1957–1966), quoted in Mark Rose, *supra, Mothers and Authors*, 22 Critical Inquiry, at 622.

36. Less pleasant to present sensibilities, Mr. Defoe also wrote that the unauthorized use of authors' works was "every jot as unjust as lying with their Wives, breaking-up their Homes." *See* Mark Rose, *Authors and Owners: The Invention of Copyright* 39 (1993).

37. *See* Walter Pagel, *Medieval and Renaissance Contributions to Knowledge of the Brain and Its Functions*, reprinted in *The History and Philosophy of the Brain and its Function* 95 (Poynter ed. 1958).

38. As is often the case in the eighteenth and nineteenth centuries, the person employing the metaphor was a man; hence, paternity rather maternity was the appropriate description. *See* Rose, 50 UC L. Rev., at 4–5 for a discussion of this point, as well as Rose, *supra, Mothers and Authors*; Christine Battersby, *Gender and Genius: Toward a Feminist Aesthetic* (1989); Susan Friedman, *Creativity and the Childbirth Metaphor: Gender Difference in Literary Discourse*, 13 Feminist Stud. 49 (Spring 1987).

39. Quoted in William Fisher, *Property and Contract on the Internet*, 73 Chicago-Kent L. Rev. 1203, 1221–1222 n. 48 (1998).

40. *Moore v. Regents of the University of California*, 793 F.2d 479 (1990). The physician was held to have a fiduciary duty to obtain patients' informed consent to engage in personal interests unrelated to the patient's health.

41. *See* http://en.wikipedia.org/wiki/Ecclesiastes.

42. *The Metsudah Five Megillos* 48 (1995).

43. *See* William Patry, *Patry on Copyright*, ch. 2.

44. Hans-Georg Gadamer, *Truth and Method* 291 (Continuum Press, 2004 revised edition).

45. *Available at*: http://www.bartleby.com/200/sw4.html.

46. *See* Honey Meconi, *Early Music Borrowing* (2004).

47. *See* Zorach & Rodini, *Paper Museums: The Reproductive Print in Europe, 1500–1800* (2005); Lisa Pon, *Raphael, Dürer, and Marcantonio Raimondi: Copying and the Italian Renaissance Print* (2004).

48. Benjamin Kaplan, *An Unhurried View of Copyright* 23 (1967).

49. Richard Posner, *Law and Literature* 397 (1998). *See also id.* at 398–400, giving other examples.

50. Northrop Frye, *Anatomy of Criticism: Four Essays* 96–97 (Princeton University Press 1957).

51. Harold Bloom, *The Anxiety of Influence: A Theory of Poetry* 5 (2d ed. 1997).

52. Hugh Laddie, *Copyright: Over-Strength, Over-Regulated, Over-Rated*, 18 Eur. Intell. Prop. Rev. 253, 259 (1996).

53. Eric Sundquist, *King's Dream* 96 (Yale University Press 2009). *See also* Drew Hanssen, *The Dream: Martin Luther King, Jr., and the Speech That Inspired a Nation* (Harper 2005); Keith Miller, *The Voice of Deliverance: The Language of Martin Luther King, Jr., and Its Sources* (University of Georgia Press 1998).

54. Sundquist, *King's Dream* at 97, note *. This habit extended also to his dissertation at Boston University. King's unacknowledged appropriation from others, even in the I Had a Dream speech did not stop him from suing others for copyright infringement for making and selling unauthorized copies of the speech, *see King v. Mister Maestro, Inc.*, 224 F. Supp. 101 (S.D.N.Y. 1963), a practice his estate has continued with great vigor, *see e.g., Estate of Martin Luther King, Jr., Inc. v. CBS,* Inc., 194 F.3d 121 (11th Cir. 1999).

55. Quoted in Arleen Croce, *Balanchine Said*, New Yorker Magazine, Jan. 26, 2009 at p. 38.

56. *Id.* at 36.

57. Continuing the metaphor.

58. *Law and Literature Id.,* at 396.

59. *See* William Patry, 4 *Patry on Copyright* § 10:139 (Thomson/West, 2007–2009).

60. *Bridgeport Music, Inc. v. Dimension Films,* 410 F.3d 792 (6th Cir. 2005).

61. *See, Sarl Louis Feraud Int'l v. Viewfinder, Inc.,* 406 F. Supp. 2d 274, 281 (S.D.N.Y. 2005), affirmed on this point, vacated and remanded on other grounds, 489 F.3d 474, 480 n.3 (2d Cir. 2007), quoted in the introduction.

62. Andrew Currah, *Hollywood Versus the Internet: The Media and Entertainment Industries in a Digital and Networked Economy*, 6 J. Econ. Geogr. 439, 440 (2006).

63. *See* Mihir Desai et al. *The Strategy and Sources of Motion Picture of Motion Picture Finance*, Harv. Bus. Rev. Online, Nov. 14, 2002, *available at*: http://harvardbusinessonline.hbsp.harvard.edu/b01/en/common/item_detail.jhtml?id=203007.

64. By contrast, some civil law countries have moral rights that recognize authors' personal ties with their works, but even in these countries economic rights are generally alienable.

65. *Report of the Register of Copyrights on Orphan Works* 1 (Jan. 2006), *available at*: http://copyright.gov/orphan/.

66. George Taylor & Michael Madison, *Metaphor, Objects, and Commodities*, 54 Clev. St. L. Rev. 141, 161 (2006).

67. Mark Lemley, *Property, Intellectual Property, and Free Riding*, 83 Tex. L. Rev. 1031, 1031 (2005).

68. *Id.* at 8. Professor Lemley's insight stands in contrast to another academic who circularly concluded: "Free-riding . . . may be a pejorative description of copying, but it still copying." Jane Ginsburg, *Copyright, Common Law, and Sui Generis Protection of Databases in United States and Abroad*, 66 U. Cin. L. Rev. 151, 1562 (1997). But if the copying is of unprotectible material (e.g., facts from databases), there is no free riding.

69. Benjamin Kaplan, *An Unhurried View of Copyright* 2 (1967).

70. Mark Rose, *Copyright and Its Metaphors*, 50 U. Cal. L. Rev. 1, 6 (2002).

71. Quoted in Robert Friedel, *A Culture of Improvement: Technology and the Western Millennium* 111 (2007, MIT Press). For a discussion of the Venetian privileges regarding manuscripts and graphic works, *see* 1 *Patry on Copyright*, § 1:2.

72. 4 Burr. 2303, 98 Eng. Rep. 201 (K.B. 1769). As noted in the text, *Millar* was reversed five years later by the House of Lords in *Donaldson v. Beckett*, 4 Burr. 2408, 98 Eng. Rep. 257 (H.L. 1774). *See* 1 *Patry on Copyright*, § 1:9.

73. The term was 14 years from publication with the possibility of a second, 14-year renewal term. *See* 1 *Patry on Copyright*, §§ 1:6–1:11.

74. 33 U.S. (8 Pet.) 591 (1834).

75. 4 Burr. 2334–35; 98 Eng. Rep. 218.

76. 4 Burr. 2354; 98 Eng. Rep. 228.

77. 4 Burr. 2359; 98 Eng. Rep. 231.

78. 4 Burr. 2360; 98 Eng. Rep. 231–232.

79. Under modern ethics laws, Lord Mansfield would have recused himself—that is, declined to hear the case—because he had been a partisan in the matter before joining the bench. His views from the bench, although entirely genuine, were completely aligned with those of his former clients. The bench and bar were a more intimate affair in those days, and no one thought Judge Mansfield's conduct in any way inappropriate. A sense of propriety did play a role at the next stage of the Copyright Wars, for when the issue went to the House of Lords five years later in *Donaldson v. Beckett*, Lord Mansfield, as a peer, believed it inappropriate to participate in deliberations over an issue he had heard as a judge, and so recused himself.

80. 4 Burr. 2398; 98 Eng. Rep. 252.

81. 4 Burr. 2408, 98 Eng. Rep. 257 (H.L. 1774).

82. 17 *Cobbett's Parliamentary History of England* (1806–1820).

83. H.R. Rep. No. 2222, S. Rep. 1108, 60th Cong., 2d Sess. 7 (1909). For those attentive to the question of the authority of such legislative history, *see* 1 *Patry on Copyright*, ch. 2, it should be noted that both the House and Senate committees issued an identical report.

84. 499 U.S. 340 (1991).

85. 499 U.S. 349. In 1918, in an unfair competition case, the Supreme Court had held that defendant was wrongly "endeavoring to reap where it has not sown," and was appropriating to himself the harvest of those who have not sown, *International News Service v. Associated Press*, 248 U.S. 215, 250 (1918). *INS* was later abrogated for creating a discredited form of federal common law, and in any event equivalent state law unfair competition is preempted by the Copyright Act. *See* 1 *Patry on Copyright*, § 18:39.

86. In a wonderfully written article, Professor Patricia Loughlan of the University of Sydney Law Faculty argued:

> Because the boundaries of intellectual property protection are never finally fixed, those boundaries are always a matter of contested political choice in which persuasion and rhetoric of this kind (and, of course, other kinds) can have substantive effect.

Patricia Loughlan, *Pirates, Reapers, Sowers, Fruits, Foxes . . . The Metaphors of Intelelctual Property*, 28 Sydney L. Rev. 211, 213 (2006).

87. Quoted and discussed in Arthur J. Jacobson, *The Conscience of the King: Equity as Reconciliation in Shakespeare's Last Play*, *available at*: http://papers.ssrn.com/sol3/papers.cfm?abstract_id=994366.

88. [2001] All E.R. 700.

89. [2001] All E.R. 701.

90. Prime Minister's Science and Engineering Council, 2 *The Role of Intellectual Property in Innovation: Perspectives* 61 (1993).

91. Sefer Vayikra, Parsha Kedoshim (19:9), translation *The JPS Commentary, Leviticus* 127 (The Jewish Publication Society 1989).

92. Sefer Shemot, Parsha Mishpatim (23:10–11), translation *The JPS Commentary, Exodus* 143 (The Jewish Publication Society 1991). *See also* repetition of the requirement in Sefer Vayikra, Parsha Behar (25:1–7; 25:20–22); Sefer Devarim (Numbers), Parsha Re'eh (15:1–6), Parsha Vayeilech (31:10–13).

93. Quoted in David Micklethwait, *Noah Webster and the American Dictionary* 212 (2005).

94. *See* http://en.wikipedia.org/wiki/Thomas_Dilworth.

95. Bill Bryson, *The Mother Tongue: English and How It Got That Way* 154–155 (1999).

96. *See* http://en.wikipedia.org/wiki/Thomas_Dyche.

97. *Micklethwait* at 24–26.

98. The origins of this saying, and its phrasing, have been the subject of much scholarly interest, regardless of one's height. The most extensive look at the quote is by Robert K. Merton in a 1965 book called, appropriately, *On the Shoulders of Giants*. A 1991 reprint, called the *Post-Italianate Edition*, has a "Shandean Postscript" and a foreword by Umberto Eco.

99. *Nash v. CBS, Inc.*, 899 F.2d 1537, 1542 (7th Cir. 1990).

100. Jurists with a particular fondness for alliteration involving the letter P will, on occasion, also throw in "poachers" and "predators."

101. The term "thief" is sometimes associated with the term "plagiarist," because of the shared association with the Latin *plagiarius*, an abductor, and *plagiare*, to steal. There is, however, no law against plagiarism. Because the term has not been used in the Copyright Wars, I do not explore it here. For a short introduction to the subject *see* Judge Richard's *The Little Book of Plagiarism* (Pantheon Books 2007). Francisco Javier Cabrera Blázquez, an Analyst in the Department of Legal Information at the European Audiovisual Observatory has written in a May 2005 article, *Plagiarism: An Original Sin?*, *available at*: http://72.14.205.104/

search?q=cache:b75F009ehewJ:www.obs.coe.int/online_publication/expert/
plagiarism.pdf.en+martial+plagiarism&hl=en&ct=clnk&cd=1&gl=us.

The word comes originally from the Latin *plagium*, which was the Roman Law term for the kidnapping of children or slaves. The Latin poet and epigrammatist Martial (Marcus Valerius Martialis, ca. AD 40—ca. AD 104) used the word for the first time in a metaphorical way to mock his rival Fidentinus, who allegedly recited the former's poems in public as if they were his own. Martial viewed his works as similar to freed slaves being enslaved again by his rival poet. Martial indeed considered his rival's behaviour as shameful, but nevertheless Roman Law knew no such concept as plagiarism in the contemporary sense of the word.

102.  *See generally,* John Logie, *Peers, Pirates, & Persuasion: Rhetoric in the Peer-to-Peer Debates*, ch. 4 (2006); Patricia Loughlan, *"You Wouldn't Steal a Car...," Intellectual Property and the Language of Theft*, 29 Eur. Intell. Prop. Rev. 401, 401 (2007).

103.  Quoted in Peter Dekom and Peter Sealey, *Not on My Watch: Hollywood vs. the Future* 42 (New Millennium Press 2003).

104.  Quoted in Patricia Loughlan, *"You Wouldn't Steal a Car...," Intellectual Property and the Language of Theft*, 29 Eur. Intell. Prop. Rev. 401, 403 (2007).

105.  Stephen Waddams, *Dimensions in Private Law: Categories and Concepts in Anglo-American Legal Reasoning* 175–176 (Cambridge University Press 2003), quoted in *Network Ten Pty v. Ten Channel Nine Pty Ltd.,* [2004] 218 C.L.R. 373, HCA [14–15] (High Court of Australia); *Lambretta Clothing Company Limited v. Teddy Smith (UK) Ltd.* [2004] EWCA Civ. 886 [37] (Civ. App.).

106.  Karl Wallace, *Francis Bacon on Communication and Rhetoric: Or the Art of Applying Reason to Imagination for the Better Moving of the Will,* 19 Phil. 175 (1944).

107.  29 Hansard 2139 (H.C., Aug. 17, 1911). Thanks to Kim Weatherall for providing me with this source.

108.  For a short biographical entry on Mr. Booth, *see* Michael Stenton & Stephen Lees, 2 *Who's Who of British Members of Parliament 1886–1918*, at 38 (1978).

109.  In the end the term "infringing" was substituted.

110.  29 Hansard 2139–2140 (H.C., Aug. 17, 1911) (remarks of Mr. Booth).

111.  Paul Gilbert, *Historiography of the Golden Era of Anglo-American Piracy in the Atlantic 1680–1730,* July 6, 2006, *available at*: http://www.piratesinfo.com/cpi_Historiography_of_the_Golden_Era_of_Anglo-American_Piracy_in_the_Atlantic_1680–1730_514.asp.

112.  Hyperion Books, 2002. *See also* Marcus Rediker, *Villains of All Nations: Atlantic Pirates in the Golden Age* (Beacon Press 2004); Robert Ritchie, *Captain Kidd and the War Against the Pirates* (Harvard University Press).

113.  Patrick Pringle, *Jolly Roger and the Great Age of Piracy* 150 (Dover Publications 2001).

114.  David Cordingly, *Under the Black Flag: The Romance and the Reality of Life Among the Pirates,* at xiii-xiv (Random House Trade Paperback 1996). The grandfather of all histories of pirates is Captain Charles Johnson's 1724, *A General History of the Robberies and Murders of the Most Notorious Pyrates*, available in a 2002 edition

with an introduction by Mr. Cordingly, published by Lyons Press. *See also* this entry on Wikipedia (*available at*: http://en.wikipedia.org/wiki/Piracy):

> In the popular modern imagination, pirates of the classical period were rebellious, clever teams who operated outside the restricting bureaucracy of modern life. Pirates were also depicted as always raising their Jolly Roger-flag when preparing to hijack a vessel. The Jolly Roger is the traditional name for the flags of European and American pirates and a symbol for piracy that has been adopted by film-makers and toy manufacturers.
>
> In reality, many pirates ate poorly, did not become fabulously wealthy, and died young. Unlike traditional Western societies of the time, many pirate crews operated as limited democracies. Both the captain and the quartermaster were elected by the crew, they in turn appointed the other ship's officers. The captain of a pirate ship was often a fierce fighter in whom the men could place their trust, rather than a more traditional authority figure sanctioned by an elite. However, when not in battle, the quartermaster usually had the real authority. Many groups of pirates shared in whatever they seized; pirates injured in battle might be afforded special compensation similar to medical insurance. Often all of these terms were agreed upon and written down by the pirates, but these articles could also be used as incriminating proof that they were outlaws. Pirates readily accepted outcasts from traditional societies, perhaps easily recognizing kindred spirits, and they were known to welcome them into the pirate fold. For example as many as 40% of the pirate vessels crews were slaves "liberated" from captured slavers.

115. S. Rep. No. 622, 50th Cong., 1st Sess. 2 (1888). *See also* Catherine Seville, The Internationalization at Copyright Law: Books, Buccaneers and the Black Flag in the Nineteenth Century (2006); Catherine Seville, From Pirates to Eagles: America's Changing View of Copyright, 29 Eur. Intell. Prop. Rev. 406 (2007).

116. Peter Drahos with John Braithwaite, *Information Feudalism: Who Owns the Knowledge Economy?* 32 (2002).

117. 473 U.S. 207, 216–18 (1985).

118. The Barbary Coast was comprised of the semiautonomous North African city-states of Algiers, Tunis, and Tunis. Some pirates also operated out of Solè and ports in Morocco. *See* C.S. Forester's popular *The Barbary Pirates* (1975); Alieen Weintraub, *The Barbarossa Brothers: 16th Century Pirates of the Barbary Coast* (2002). The United States had frequent run-ins with the Barbary Coast pirates, reflected in the opening of the Marine Corps hymn "to the shores of Tripoli." In 1785, the United States paid $60,000 as a ransom for captured crews over the objection of Thomas Jefferson, who correctly argued it would only lead to further demands. Eventual ransom and tribute payments amounted to 20% of the 1800 government's revenue. When Jefferson became president in 1801, he refused a demand from the pasha of Tripoli, leading to the first Barbary Coast War (1801–1805), settled in part by payment by the United States for $60,000.

A secondary Barbary Coast War occurred in 1815, as a result of the United States' weakened state after the 1812 war with Britain. Commodores Stephen Decatur and William Bainbridge forced a treaty with the Dey of Algiers. Eventually Algeria and Tunis became colonies of France, and Tripoli became a part of the Ottoman Empire, and then a colony of Italy.

119. 898 F. Supp. 586, 595 (M.D. Tenn. 1995).

120. *Illustro Systems Int'l, LLC v. IBM,* 2007 WL 1321825, at *13 (N.D. Tex. May 4, 2007) (citing this author's criticism of the *Curb* decision in 7 *Patry on Copyright* § 25:87).

121. Benjamin N. Cardozo, *The Nature of the Judicial Process* 140–141 (Kessinger Publishing, 2008 reprint of 1921 edition).

122. *See* Peter Shawn Taylor, *On Canadian Copyright Pirates, Past and Present,* National Post, Full Comment column, June 5, 2008, *available at*: http://network. nationalpost.com/np/blogs/fullcomment/archive/2008/06/05/peter-shawn-taylor-on-canadian-copyright-pirates-past-and-present.aspx.

　　Mr. Taylor also notes that Twain's ploy did not work: "To his chagrin, the federal Minister of Agriculture (Ottawa boasted a leaner and more versatile cabinet back then) turned down Twain's application. Canadian copyright was available only to permanent residents, not visitors. The humourist was not amused." Professor Catherine Seville has done a great deal of research on this period, and with respect to Twain in particular. *See e.g.,* Catherine Seville, *Authors as Copyright Campaigners: Mark Twain's Legacy,* 55 J. Copyright Soc'ty USA 283 (2008); Catherine Seville, *The Internationalization at Copyright Law: Books, Buccaneers and the Black Flag in the Nineteenth Century* (2006); Catherine Seville, *From Pirates to Eagles: America's Changing View of Copyright,* 29 Eur. Intell. Prop. Rev. 406 (2007).

123. *Copyright Issues Presented by Digital Audio Tape,* 100th Cong., 1st Sess., Apr. 2, 1987, S. Serial No. J-100-13, House Serial No. 6.

124. *Id.* at 36.

125. *Id.* at 4.

126. *See* John Philip Sousa, *The Menace of Mechanical Music,* originally published in 8 Appleton's Mag. 278–84 (1906), reprinted at http://www27.brinkster.com/ phonozoic/menace.htm.

127. *See* http://en.wikipedia.org/wiki/Bogeyman.

128. *Id.*

129. *Hearing* at 39.

130. *Id.*

131. *Hearing* at 40.

132. *See* David Kravets, *Recording Industry Decries AM-FM Broadcasting as "A Form of Piracy,"* Wired Mag. (June 23, 2008), *available at*: http://blog.wired.com/ 27bstroke6/2008/06/recording-indus.html.

## ℳ Chapter 5  Property as Social Relationships

1.  Benjamin Franklin, *Queries and Remarks Respecting Alterations in the Constitution of Pennsylvania* (1789), in 10 *The Writings of Benjamin Franklin* 54, 59 (Albert H. Smyth ed. 1907).
2.  Letter from Thomas Jefferson to Isaac McPherson (Aug. 13, 1813), in 13 *The Writings of Thomas Jefferson* 334 (Andrew A. Lipscomb & Albert Ellery Bergh eds., 1905).
3.  Jeremy Bentham, "Principles of the Civil Code," 1 *The Works of Jeremy Bentham*, John Bowring ed. 1843).
4.  This sentence is paraphrased from Singer at 8.
5.  *See e.g.*, Abraham Bell & Gideon Parchomovsky, *A Theory of Property*, 90 Cornell L. Rev. 531, 552 (2005).
6.  In turn defining what is a "property" right would take a book in itself and would in any event not be free from dispute. One excellent look at the issue is provided by Laura Underkuffler in *The Idea of Property: Its Meaning and Power*, chs. 1 & 8 (Oxford University Press 2003).
7.  As compared, say to a bailee or trustee.
8.  Joseph Singer, *Entitlement: The Paradoxes of Property* 3 (Yale University Press 2000). Professor Singer, it should be noted, does not agree with the statement.
9.  James Galbraith, *The Predator State* 16 (Free Press 2008).
10. http://em.wikipedia.org/wiki/Market_fundamentalism.
11. Joseph Stiglitz, "The Invisible Hand and Modern Welfare Economics," reproduced in *Information, Strategy and Public Policy* 12 (David Vines and Andrew Stevenson eds. Blackwell 1991). *See also* Joseph Stiglitz, *Economic Foundations of Intellectual Property Rights*, 57 Duke L. J. 1693, 1693 (2008).
12. Stiglitz, *Economics Foundations of Intellectual Property Rights, id.*
13. The Federalist Papers, 270–271 (Rossiter ed. Longman 1998), emphasis added.
14. *See* Edward C. Walterscheid, *The Nature of the Intellectual Property Clause: A Study in Historical Perspective* 203 (William S. Hein & Company 2002).
15. John Maynard Keynes, *The End of Laissez-Faire* 39 (Hogarth Press 1926).
16. Keynes' remarks were published in 1926, three years before the "Black Tuesday" stock market crash on October 29, 1929.
17. I do not let Mr. Greenspan off the hook because he was not part of the Administration.
18. Quoted in Mike McIntire, *Bail-out is a No-Strings Windfall to Bankers, if Not Borrowers*, N.Y. Times, January 18, 2009, p. A1.
19. *Available at*: http://oversight.house.gov/story.asp?ID=2256.
20. Mr. Wilson's actual testimony was more nuanced than the popular version of his testimony given in the text. During the hearings, he was asked whether, as Secretary of Defense he could make a decision adverse to the interests of General Motors. He stated he could, but added that he could not conceive of such a conflict

"because for years I thought what was good for the country was good for General Motors and vice versa."

21. January 17, 2009 speech in Philadelphia Pennsylvania, *available at*: http://content. usatoday.com/communities/theoval/post/2009/01/61522608/1.

22. Laura Underkuffler, *The Idea of Property* 54 (2003).

23. Singer at 28.

24. *Id.* at 31.

25. Introduction to *Early Modern Conceptions of Property* 3 (John Brewer & Susan Staves eds., Routledge 1996).

26. *See e.g., Kelo v. City of New London*, 545 U.S. 469 (2005), discussed at http://en. wikipedia.org/wiki/Kelo_v._City_of_New_London.

27. Laura Underkuffler, *Property as Constitutional Myth: Utilities and Dangers*, 92 Cornell L. Rev. 1239, 1248 (2007).

28. For a discussion of early American cases on the taking of patents, *see* Adam Mossoff, *Patents as Constitutional Private Property: The Historical Protection of Patents Under the Takings Clause*, 87 Boston U.L. Rev. 689 (2007).

29. Augustine Birrell, *Seven Lectures on the Law and History of Copyright in Books* 11–13 (1899).

30. Blackstone lived from 1723 to 1780, *see* http://en.wikipedia.org/wiki/William_ Blackstone.

31. *See* http://en.wikipedia.org/wiki/Commentaries_on_the_Laws_of_England.

32. 2 William Blackstone, *Commentaries on the Laws of England* 2 (facsimile edition 1979) (1765–1769).

33. Wikipedia states with considerable understatement: "The Commentaries were influential largely because they were in fact readable, and because they met a need. The work is as much an apologia for the legal system of the time as it is an explanation; even when the law was obscure, Blackstone sought to make it *seem* rational, just, and inevitable that things should be how they were." *See* http://en. wikipedia.org/wiki/Commentaries_on_the_Laws_of_England.

34. Robert Gordon, *Paradoxical Property*, reproduced in *Early Modern Conceptions of Property* 95, 97 (John Brewer & Susan Staves eds., Routledge 1996). *See also* Carol Rose, *Canons of Property Talk, Or Blackstone's Anxiety*, 108 Yale L.J. 601, 631 (1998) (describing the sole despotic dominion description as a caricature of the actual rights rather than as descriptive).

35. Carol Rose, *Canons of Property Talk, Or, Blackstone's*, 108 Yale L.J. 601 (1998).

36. 2 William Blackstone, *Commentaries on the Laws of England* 2 (facsimile edition 1979) (1765–1769).

37. Augustine Birrell, *Seven Lectures on the Law and History of Copyright in Books* 11–13 (1899).

38. 2 Blackstone, at *7.

39. 2 Blackstone, at *8; Rose, 108 Yale L.J. at 607.

40. *Rose,* 108 Yale L.J. at 608.

41. Mark *Lemley, Property, Intellectual Property, and Free Riding,* 83 Tex. L. Rev. 1031 (2005).

## 🎞 Chapter 6  Why Classifying Copyright as Property Is Important in the Copyright Wars

1. Singer at 7.
2. *Id.* at 8.
3. *Home Recording of Copyrighted Works: Hearings on H.R. 4783 et al. Before the Subcommittee on Courts, Civil Liberties, and the Administration of Justice of the Committee on the Judiciary of the U.S. House of Representatives*, 97th Cong., 2d Sess. 65 (1982).
4. There are currently seven compulsory licenses: Sections 111 (cable television retransmission right); 112(3) (transmitting organizations using sound recordings); 114 (sound recordings); 115 (nondramatic musical works); 116 (jukeboxes); 118 (public broadcasting organizations); and 119 (satellite retransmissions of television programming). Aside from compulsory licenses, there are other provisions in the Copyright Act that permit third parties to use copyrighted works without permission and without payment. There is also the fair use privilege in Section 107, and exemptions from liability in Sections 108 (library and archival photocopying); 109 (resale of lawfully made copies); 110 (classroom and other public performances); 112 (ephemeral copies by broadcasters); 113 (pictorial, graphic, and sculptural works); 117 (backup copies of computer programs); 120 (certain uses of architectural works); 121 (copying for the blind and other people with disabilities); and 122 (secondary transmissions by satellite carriers within local markets).
5. Benjamin Kaplan, *An Unhurried View of Copyright* 74 (Columbia University Press 1967).
6. As Professor Mark Lemley has noted: "The rise of property rhetoric in intellectual property cases is closely identified not with common law property rules in general, but with a particular economic view of property rights." Mark Lemley, *Property, Intellectual Property, and Free Riding*, 83 Tex. L. Rev. 1034 (2005). That economic view is one in which everything should be owned; everything should be owned because of the belief that private ownership will result in the maximum efficient use. This belief is in turn based on the assumption that there are never any transaction costs, and all people will act perfectly rationally. Needless to say, reality is quite different.
7. For a discussion of Canadian law, *see* Daniel Gervais, *The Purpose of Copyright Law in Canada*, 2 U. Ottawa L. & Tech. J. 315 (2005).
8. *See* William Patry, *Patry on Copyright*, ch. 1, (2007, 2008 supplements); Simon Stern, *Tom Jones and the Economies of Copyright*, 9 Eighteenth-Century Fiction 429 (July 1997).
9. Augustine Birrell, *Seven Lectures on the Law and History of Copyright in Books* 11–13 (1899); Ronan Deazley, *On the Origin of Copyright* (Hart Publishing 2004); Ronan Deazley, *Rethinking Copyright* (Edward Elgar 2006).
10. *Cf.* Frank Easterbrook, *Intellectual Property Is Still Property*, 13 Harv. J. L. & Pub. Pol'y 108 (1990).
11. Lofft 775, 775–76 (1774).

12. 1 Russell Sanjek, *American Popular Music and Its Business: The Beginning to 1790*, at 204–205 (1988). *See also* John Feather, *A History of British Publishing* 53–55, 81 (2d ed. 2006); Catherine Seville, Literary Reform in Early Victorian England 101 (Cambridge University Press 1999), and generally, Tredwell, *London Trade Publishers 1675–1750*, 4 Library (16th Ser.) 99 (1982).

13. As noted in a brief online biographical entry on Donaldson:

> Alexander Donaldson made a substantial fortune in the printing and publishing business and, when he died, left his entire estate, worth about £210,000, to found Donaldson's Hospital—a hospital for the education and care of poor and deaf children, which opened in 1851. Today it still functions as a special care institution for deaf children, and has recently been used as a stand-in for Hogwarts in the Harry Potter movies.

http://www.jamesboswell.info/People/biography-4.php.

14. Both *Millar v. Taylor*, 4 Burr. 2303, 98 Eng. Rep. 201 (K.B. 1769).

15. 3 Commentaries 329, quoted in David Lieberman, "Property, commerce, and the common law: Attitudes to legal change in the eighteenth century," in *Early Modern Conceptions of Property* 145, 149 (John Brewer & Susan Staves eds., Routledge 1995).

16. 1 Russell Sanjek, *American Popular Music and Its Business: The Beginning to 1790*, at 205 (1988). *See also* Seville, *Literary Copyright Reform in Early Victorian England* at 102–103.

17. *See* Benjamin Kaplan, *An Unhurried View of Copyright* 13 (1967): "The fact that publishers, not authors, were at bar, was passed over in silence, as usual."

18. *See* William Patry, 2 *Patry on Copyright* §§ 5:92–5:93 (2007, biannual supplements).

19. The labels would rely either on boilerplate language in contracts or, in the absence of such language in arguments, that the recordings were created at their instance and expense.

20. Steve Knopper, *Appetite for Self-Destruction: The Spectacular Crash of the Record Industry in the Digital Age* 32 (Free Press 2009).

21. Chart provided by MCPS/PRS Alliance, and reproduced in *Gowers Review of Intellectual Property* at p.55, H.M.S. Treasury, November 2006, *available at*: http://www.ipo.gov.uk/policy/policy-issues/policy-issues-gowers.htm.

22. *Id.*

23. *Id.* at 56.

24. *Available at*: http://www.ft.com/cms/s/0/8ca0a7c6-cadd-11dd-87d7-000077b07658.html?nclick_check=1.

25. *Available at*: http://www.huffingtonpost.com/2008/09/30/two-minute-obama-ad-blast_n_130507.html. *See also* John Talbott, *Obamanomics: How Bottom-Up Economic Prosperity Will Replace Trickle-Down Economics* (Seven Stories Press July 2008).

26. Mark Lemley, *Book Review*, 75 Tex. L. Rev. 873, 902 (1997).

27. *See* William Patry, 3 *Patry on Copyright*, § 9:5 (2007, 2008 supplements).

28. *See* Stephen Waddams, Introduction *The Mapping of Legal Concepts* and Conclusion *The Concept of Legal Mapping in Dimensions of Private Law: Categories and Concepts in Anglo-American Legal Reasoning* (Cambridge University Press 2003); Shyamkrishna Balganesh, *Demystifying the Right to Exclude: Of Property, Inviolability, and Automatic Injunctions,* 1 Harv. J. L. & Pub. Pol'y 593 (2008); Lee Anne Fennell, *Property and Half-Torts,* 116 Yale L.J. 1400 (2007); Shyamkrishna Balganesh, *Property Along the Tort Spectrum: Trespass to Chattels and the Anglo-American Doctrinal Divergence,* 35 Common L. World Rev. (June 2006).

29. *See e.g., eBay Inc. v. MercExchange L.L.C.,* 547 U.S. 388, 392 (1990), citing 35 U.S.C. 261.

30. 85 Harv. L. Rev. 1089 (1972).

31. For an excellent discussion of the article as applied to information, *see* Mark Lemley & Philip Weiser, *Should Property or Liability Rules Govern Information?,* 84 Tex. L. Rev., No. 4 (Mar. 2007).

32. Stephen Munzer, *A Theory of Property* 24 (Cambridge University Press 1990).

33. *Id.* at 97.

34. Joseph Singer, *The Ownership Society and Takings of Property: Castles, Investments, and Just Obligations,* 30 Harv. Envtl. L. Rev. 309, 332 (2006).

35. *Id.* at 334.

36. *Fox Film Corporation v. Doyal,* 286 U.S. 123, 127 (1932). *See also United States v. Paramount Pictures, Inc.,* 334 U.S. 131, 158 (1948); *Sony Corp. of America v. Universal City Studios, Inc.,* 464 U.S. 417, 429 (1984).

37. Singer at 3.

38. *Id.* at 4.

39. Susan Sell, *The Globalization of Intellectual Property Rights* 51 (2003, Cambridge University Press 2003).

40. Such as educational uses, parody, satire, fair use, and fair dealing.

41. *Available at*: http://yarchive.net/macaulay/copyright.htmlhttp://yarchive.net/macaulay/copyright.html. The following year (, 1842), the proponents were forced to accept Macaulay's proposed amendment of a set term of 42 years from publication or life of the author plus 7 years, whichever was longer. In offering his proposal, Macaulay delivered a second speech that is only slightly less revered than the first. The second speech too is *available at*: http://yarchive.net/macaulay/copyright.htmlhttp://yarchive.net/macaulay/copyright.html. The whole saga is discussed in detail at in, 1 William Patry, 1 *Patry on Copyright* § 1:15 (Thomson/West 2007 [with twice-a-year supplements, Thomson/West]).

     The Paley referred to by Lord Macaulay is William Paley (1743–1805). *See* http://en.wikipedia.org/wiki/William_Paley. Paley's 1785 collection of essays, *Moral and Political Philosophy* was enormously popular and influential. *See* David Roberts, *The Social Conscience of the Early Victorians* 117 (2002, Stanford University Press 2002).

42. Sam Ricketson, *WIPO Study on Limitations and Exceptions of Copyright Related Rights in the Digital Environment* 4, Standing Committee on Copyright and Related Rights, 9th Sess., Geneva, June 23 to June 27, 2003, SCCR/9/7 (Apr. 5, 2003).

Professor Ricketson's view was challenged by three prominent European experts in a July 17, 2008, declaration for "A Balanced Interpretation of the 'Three-Step' Test in Copyright Law," *available at*: http://www.ip.mpg.de/ww/en/pub/news/declaration_on_the_three_step_.cfm.

43. It should be noted that Professor Ricketson was referring principally to the civil law tradition.

44. Pierre Leval, *Toward a Fair Use Standard*, 103 Harv. L. Rev. 1105, 1110 (1990).

45. [2004] 1 S.C.R. 339, 2004 SCC 13, ¶ 48.

46. Statement of Marybeth Peters, the Register of Copyrights, before the Subcommittee on Courts and Intellectual Property, Committee on the Judiciary, United States House of Representatives, 106th Cong, 2nd Sess. June 15, 2000, "Copyrighted Broadcast Programming on the Internet," *available at*: http://www.copyright.gov/docs/regstat61500.html. *See also* 65 Fed. Reg. 77292, 77297 (Dec. 11, 2000); 57 Fed. Reg. 3284, 3293, Jan. 29, 1992); 49 Fed. Reg. 14944, 14950 Apr. 16, 1984).

47. *See* discussion in Chapter 5.

48. 489 U.S. 141 (1989).

49. *Id.* at 146.

50. 499 U.S. 340 (1991).

51. *Id.* at 349.

52. 510 U.S. 517 (1994).

53. *Id.* at 525–527.

54. *See e.g.*, William Wordsworth's repeated references to enclosure and unauthorized appropriation in Tilar Mazzeo, *Plagiarism and Literary Property in the Romantic Era*, ch. 6 (University of Pennsylvania Press 2007).

55. Frank Luntz, *Words That Work* 92 (Hyperion 2008).

56. The article was originally published in 1 J. Econ. Behav. & Org. 39, 44 (1980) and is reproduced in *Choices, Values and Frames* 269 (Daniel Kahneman & Amos Tversky eds., 8th prtg. Cambridge University Press 2000). *See also* Daniel Kahneman, Jack Knetsch, & Richard Thaler, *The Endowment Effect, Loss Aversion, and Status Quo Bias*, reproduced *id.* at 159, originally published in 5 J. Econ. Persp. 193 (1991); George Lowenstein & Daniel Kahneman, Explaining the Endowment Effect (1991) (unpublished working paper, Dpt. Soc. & Decision Sci., Carnegie Mellon U.).

57. *Id.* at 274. (The jargon in behavioral economics refers to a Willingness to Accept versus a Willingess to Pay.)

58. *Cf.* Michael Hanemann, *Willingness to Pay and Willingness to Accept: How Much Can They Differ?*, 81 Am. Econ. Rev. 636 (1991), attempting to integrate, somewhat findings of endowment effect to neoclassical economics. By contrast, Herbert Hovenkamp was one of the most trenchant critics of neoclassical economics in light of the findings of behavioral economics, *see* Herbert Hovenkamp, *Legal Policy and the Endowment Effect*, 20 J. Legal Stud. 263 (1991). *See also* Daniel Kahneman, J. L. Knetsch, & R. H. Thaler, *Experimental Tests of the Endowment Effect and the Coase Theorem*, 98 J. Pol. Econ. 1325 (1990).

59. Law professor Russell Korobkin has cautioned that the endowment effect is not constant across all fact settings. It *seems* to be the strongest when the value of the item to be acquired or sold is of uncertain value, and the weakest or nonexistent when the value is certain. *See* Russell Korobkin, *The Endowment Effect and Legal Analysis*, 97 Nw. U. L. Rev. 1127, 1229, 1232–1242 (2003).

60. Dan Ariely, *Predictably Irrational* (HarperCollins 2008).

61. *Id.* ch. 7.

62. Russell Korobkin, *The Endowment Effect and Legal Analysis*, 97 Nw U. L. Rev. 1127, 1236 (2003).

63. *Id.* at 1238.

64. Oliver Wendell Holmes Jr., *The Path of the Law*, 10 Harv. L. Rev. 457, 457–58 (1897).

## ✐ Chapter 7  Moral Panics, Folk Devils, and Fear as a Tactical Weapon

1. *See* further discussion of these metaphors in Chapter 4.

2. A third edition was published in 2002 in paperback by Routledge, reprinted twice in 2004, and once in 2005. The book had been his doctoral thesis and was written in 1967 through 1969. Professor Cohen acknowledges that he derived the term "moral panic" from Jock Young's *The Role of the Police as Amplifiers of Deviancy, Negotiators of Reality and Translators of Fantasy*, contained in a book Cohen edited, *Images of Deviance* 37 (Harmondsworth, Penguin 1971). Cohen has also acknowledged that his work "was informed by the sixties fusion of labeling theory, cultural politics and critical sociology. Today's students of moral panics do not have to engage with this theoretical mix-up. They can go straight into the literature on social constructionism and claims-making." *Folk Devils and Moral Panics*, at xxii. *See also* Chas Critcher, *Critical Readings: Moral Panics and the Media* (Open University Press 2006); Chas Critcher, *Moral Panics and the Media* (Open University Press 2003).

3. *See* John Springhall, *Youth, Popular Culture and Moral Panics: Penny Gaffs to Gangsta-Rap, 1830–1996* (St. Martin's Press 1998). The 1981 song "Rumble in Brighton" by the Stray Cats was inspired by such events.

4. http://en.wikipedia.org/wiki/Mods_and_Rockers. There was a Mods and Rockers film festival in June to July 2008, at Grauman's Egyptian Theater in Hollywood. *See* http://www.modsandrockers.com/.

5. The original group consisted of Jack Ely (vocalist/rhythm guitar), Lynn Easton (drummer), Mike Mitchell (guitar), Don Gallucci (piano), and Bob Nordby (bass guitar). *See* http://en.wikipedia.org/wiki/The_Kingsmen. The story is told in David Marsh's 2004 book, *Louie Louie: The History and Mythology of the World's Most Famous Rock 'n Roll Song; Including the Full Details of Its Torture and Persecution at the Hands . . . Introducing for the First Time Anywhere, the Actual Dirty Lyrics*. (The book was published in a second edition by the University of

Michigan Press in 2004.) The drummer on the recording, Dick Peterson, published a book in 2006, *Louie Louie: Me Gotta Go Now* (Jim Ojala ed. Thalian Press). There are also a number of Web sites devoted to the song. *See* http://louielouieweb. tripod.com/default.htm (a site that aggregates links to Louie Louie Web sites); http://www.louielouie.net/, and http://www.xs4all.nl/~tdg/.

6. As sung by the Kingsmen, the lyrics were:

> *Louie, Louie*
> *Oh no, me gotta go.*
> *Yeah, yeah, yeah, yeah, yeah, said, ah*
> *Louie, Louie*
> *Oh, baby, me gotta go.*
>
> *A fine little girl she waits for me*
> *Me catch a ship for cross the sea.*
> *Me sail that ship all alone*
> *Me never think how I make it home.*
>
> *Ah, Louie, Louie*
> *No, no, no, no, me gotta go.*
> *Oh, no.*
> *Said, Louie, Louie*
> *Oh, baby, said we gotta go.*
> *(indistinct yell in the background)*
>
> *Three nights and days I sail the sea*
> *Think of girl, oh, constantly.*
> *Ah, on that ship I dream she there*
> *I smell the rose, ah, in her hair.*
>
> *Ah, Louie, Louie*
> *Oh, no, sayin' we gotta go.*
> *Yeah, yeah, yeah, yeah, yeah, but, ah,*
> *Louie, Louie*
> *Oh, baby, said, we gotta go.*
> *[Yelled] Okay, let's give it to 'em*
> *right now! [instrumental]*
>
> *Me see Jamaica, ah, moon above.*
> *It won't be long, me see me love.*
> *Take her in my arms again,*
> *I got her; I'll never leave again.*
>
> *Ah, Louie, Louie*
> *Oh, no, sayin' me gotta go.*
> *Yeah, yeah, yeah, yeah, yeah,*
> *But, ah, Louie, Louie*
> *Oh, baby, said, ah, we gotta go.*

> *I said we gotta go now,*
>
> *Let's get on outta here.*
>
> *[Yelled] Let's go.*

7. *See Peterson v. Highland Music, Inc.*, 140 F.3d 1313 (9th Cir. 1998).

8. Marsh at 39–40. According to http://www.louielouie.net/03-richardberry.htm, Berry, an African American, later recovered some funds for his rights, perhaps as a result of the termination of transfer provisions in 17 USC § 304(c)(6). Other sources have put the amount Berry received at approximately $2 million. He died in his sleep in January 1997.

9. http://en.wikipedia.org/wiki/Moral_panic.

10. *See e.g.*, David Hajdu, *The Ten Cent Plague: The Comic Book Scare and How it Changed America* (Farrar, Straus, & Giroux 2008); Amy Nyberg, *Seal of Approval: The History of the Comics Code* (University Press of Mississippi 1998).

11. *See* Majid Yar, *The Rhetorics and Myths of Anti-Piracy Campaigns: Criminalization, Moral Pedagogy and Capitalist Property Relations in the Classroom*, 10 New Media Society 605 (2008), *available at*: http://nms.sagepub.com/cgi/content/abstract/10/4/605.

12. Published by St. Martin's Press, 1998.

13. *Youth, Popular Culture and Moral Panics: Penny Gaffs to Gangsta-Rap, 1830–1996* at 7.

14. Adapted from Richard Griffiths, "Deviance in the Media: The Presentation of Folk Devils, Moral and Synthetic Panics," Mar. 27, 2002, for the course Sociology of Media, University of Auckland, New Zealand, Faculty of Arts, citing Moral Panics and Folk Devils at 23 (original 1980 ed.).

15. Moral Panics and Folk Devils at xxviii.

16. *Id.* at viii.

17. This refers to Joseph Goebbels' January 12, 1941, remarks about the British, as set forth in *Die Zeit ohne Beispiel* [The Time without Example]:

> Die Engländer gehen nach dem Prinzip vor, wenn du lügst, dann lüge gründlich, und vor allem bleibe bei dem, was du gelogen hast! Sie bleiben also bei ihren Schwindeleien, selbst auf die Gefahr hin, sich damit lächerlich zu machen.
>
> [The English follow the principle that when one lies, one should lie big, and stick to it. They keep up their lies, even at the risk of looking ridiculous.]

George Orwell also used the Big Lie in his novel *1984*:

> To tell deliberate lies while genuinely believing in them, to forget any fact that has become inconvenient, and then when it becomes necessary again, to draw it back from oblivion for just so long as it is needed.

*See generally* http://en.wikipedia.org/wiki/The_Big_Lie (from which the above was taken).

18. Moral Panics and Folk Devils at xxviii; Moral Panics and the Media 2. *See also* Critcher, *Critical Readings*: Moral Panics and the Media (Open University Press

2006); Kenneth Thompson, *Moral Panics* (Routledge 1998); *Behaving Badly: Social Panics and Moral Outrage—Victorian and Modern Parallels* (Judith Rowbotham & Kim Stevenson eds., Ashgate Publications 2003).

19. Critcher, Moral Panics and the Media, at 3.

20. *Testimony before the U.S. Senate Foreign Relations Committee on WIPO Copyright Treaties Implementation Act and the Online Copyright Liability Limitation Act,* 105th Cong., 2d Sess. (1998).

21. Quote in Tarleton Gillespie, *Wired Shut: Copyright and the Shape of Digital Culture* 123 (2007).

22. *Id.* at 124.

23. *See* February 14, 2008, testimony of Congressman William D. Delahunt, on *Hearing on Design Law: Are Special Provisions Needed to Protect Unique Industries?, Before the Subcommittee on Courts, the Internet, and Intellectual Property of the Committee on the Judiciary, U.S. House of Representatives.*

24. *Available at*: http://www.nytimes.com/2007/08/30/opinion/30thomas.html?_r= 1&em&ex=1188619200&en=1c36b305564f7dcc&ei=5087%0A&oref=slogin.

25. *See* http://www.infoworld.com/article/03/03/13/HNfilefund_1.html. In March 2009, the Rand Corporation debased itself by issuing a report funded by the British motion picture industry, a report that has all the integrity of the industry's "piracy" statistics. *See* Rand Corporation, *Film Piracy, Organized Crime*, and Terrorism (Gregory Treverton et al., authors)

26. http://en.wikipedia.org/wiki/Folk_devil

27. *Moral Panics and Folks Devils* at 4. *See also* Erich Goode & Nachman Ben-Yehuda, *Moral Panics: The Social Construction of Deviance* (Wiley Blackwell 1994); Howard Becker, *Outsiders: Studies in the Sociology of Deviance* (Free Press 1977) (1963).

## 🕮 Chapter 8  Copyright Owners and Moral Panics

1. Speech of President-elect Barack Obama, Speech delivered in Philadelphia, Pennsylvania, January 17, 2008. The reference to better angels is from the concluding paragraph of Abraham Lincoln's first inaugural address, delivered on March 4, 1861, and *available at*: http://www.bartleby.com/124/pres31.html. Lincoln was referring to the tensions between the North and the South that had led to Secession. The concluding paragraph reads:

> We are not enemies, but friends. We must not be enemies. Though passion may have strained it must not break our bonds of affection. The mystic chords of memory, stretching from every battlefield and patriot grave to every living heart and hearthstone all over this broad land, will yet swell the chorus of the Union, when again touched, as surely they will be, by the better angels of our nature.

2. Critcher, Moral Panics at 4.

3. Rose McDermott, James Fowler, & Oleg Smirnov, *On the Evolutionary Origin of Prospect Theory Preferences*, 70 J. Pol. 335 (Apr. 2008).

4. That the scope of copyrights has expanded dramatically in the last three decades is uncontested. The scope of copyrights has expanded in every way imaginable: the number and type of works protected; the automatic, formality-free nature of protection, the term of protection, and the remedies provided for infringement. For a very informative look at the issue, *see* Netanel, *Why Has Copyright Expanded? Analysis and Critique*, UCLA L. Sch., Pub. Pol'y & Legal Theory Res. Paper Ser., Res. Paper No. 07-34, in *6 New Directions in Copyright Law* (Fiona Macmillan ed. Edward Elgar 2008), and in his book *Copyright's Paradox* (Oxford University Press 2008).

5. Along with other quotes, *available at*: http://en.wikiquote.org/wiki/Jack_Valenti.

6. *See* http://en.wikipedia.org/wiki/Jack_Valenti.

7. *See* Richard Lanham, *A Handlist of Rhetorical Terms* 38 (2d ed. 1991).

8. Jack Valenti, *Speak Up with Confidence: How to Prepare, Learn, and Deliver Effective Speeches* 51 (Hyperion 2002) (1982).

9. Modell, *Emotional Memory, Metaphor, and Meaning*, 5 Psychoanalytic Inquiry 555, 556 (2005).

10. Jack Valenti, *Speak Up with Confidence* at 52.

11. Richard Lanham, *A Handlist of Rhetorical Terms* 45 (2d ed. University of California Press 1991).

12. *Id.* at 46.

13. *See* Wikipedia (http://en.wikipedia.org/wiki/Suspension_of_disbelief) on the general concept:

> Suspension of disbelief or "Willing Suspension of Disbelief" is an aesthetic theory intended to characterize people's relationships to art. It was coined by the poet and aesthetic philosopher Samuel Taylor Coleridge in 1817. It refers to the willingness of a person to accept as true the premises of a work of fiction, even if they are fantastic or impossible. It also refers to the willingness of the audience to overlook the limitations of a medium, so that these do not interfere with the acceptance of those premises. According to the theory, suspension of disbelief is a quid pro quo: the audience tacitly agrees to provisionally suspend their judgment in exchange for the promise of entertainment.

14. Quoted in Scott Kirsner, *Inventing the Movies* 9 (CinemaTech Books 2008).

15. *Id.* at 9–10.

16. *United States v. Motion Picture Patents Co.*, 225 F. 800, 802 (E.D. Pa. 1915).

17. *Home Recording of Copyrighted Works: Hearing on H.R. 4783 et al. before the Subcommittee on Courts, Civil Liberties, and the Administration of Justice of the Committee on the Judiciary of the U.S. House of Representatives*, 97th Cong., Sess. 8. The full quote is reproduced below.

18. Laureen Snider, *Theft of Time: Disciplining Through Science and Law*, 40 Osgoode Hall L. J. 89, 90 n. 2 (2002), quoted in Patricia Loughlan, *"You Wouldn't Steal a Car...": Intellectual Property and the Language of Theft*, 29 Eur. Intell. Prop. Rev. 401, 403 (2007).

19. *The Rhetorics and Myths of Anti-Piracy Campaigns: Criminalization, Moral Pedagogy and Capitalist Property Relations in the Classroom*, 10 New Media Society 605 (2008), *available at*: http://nms.sagepub.com/cgi/content/abstract/10/4/605.

20. *Available at*: http://cryptome.info/0001/hrcw-hear.htm.
21. James Lardner, *Fast Forward: Hollywood, the Japanese, and the VCR Wars* 10 (1987).
22. Steve Knopper, *Appetite for Self-Destruction: The Spectacular Crash of the Record Industry in the Digital Age* 28 note * (Free Press 2009).
23. *Id.*
24. Bragging rights to being the first VCR varies according to one's definition of what made one a VCR. The Rewind Museum Web site has this discussion:

> Sony claims the 1st ever videocassette recorder, was the VP 1100, (invented by Sony in 1971), however, this was a playback machine (as was the VR-1000) and actually the first record / playback machine was the Sony VO 1600. The Umatic system used the 3/4 inch tape UMATIC video system. UMATIC was the very first video cassette system. . . . There were three Umatic units released, we believe, by Sony in 1971. They were the VP-1100, the VP-1000 and the VO-1600. The VO-1600 having more features including record. It was Sony's intention that this would be the worlds first domestic video cassette recorder. It was a "VCR" that is to say record and playback, not just playback. It was a full VCR. Before 1971 all video recorders were reel to reel machines. Let us consider the criteria for a consumer domestic VCR. The VO-1600 was in a wood "domestic" cabinet. It had UHF and VHF TV tuners. TV tuners would generally only go into domestic equipment as recording studios would normally only require AV in and out for cameras, or copying, not recording from TV. It had a crude counter but crucially it did not have a timer and it was very expensive. It was therefore left to Philips with the n1500 in 1972 to claim the title "first ever domestic VCR" for four main reasons:
>
> 1. The N1500 included an analogue timer.
> 2. At about £650 it was affordable.
> 3. The N1500 used smaller cassettes with 1/2 inch tape. The VO 1600 used large cassettes with 3/4 inch tape. This meant that the Sony was capable of higher quality but even in the earlier days of reel to reel video, 3/4 inch tape was associated with professional formats and not domestic formats.
> 4. Most importantly the VO-1600 was bought by professionals and not by consumers, the Philips was bought by consumers and used in the home.
>
> It therefore follows that no matter what a manufacturers intentions might be, the consumer decides for themselves. There are therefore strong arguments for agreeing that the Philips N1500 was the first domestic VCR in 1972, but the Sony VO-1600 takes the accolade as the world's first video cassette recorder in 1971.

In his book *Fast Forward*, James Lardner notes that MCA's executives had a Sony U-matic that they used for informal screenings of movies. *Fast Forward* at 21. *See also* 73, 89–91 for further discussion of the U-Matic.
25. Pictures of the early Betamax machines can be seen at http://www.rewindmuseum.com/betamax.htm.
26. Sony of course lost the Betamax versus VHS format wars, but at the time other manufacturers, including Toshiba and Sanyo, were making licensed Betamax machines.
27. A term attributed to Akio Morita.

28. *Id.* at 21–22.

29. *Id.* at 28. NBC's affiliate RCA had a laser disc player called "SelectaVision" in development, as did Magnavox, called, grandly, Magnavision. *See id.* at 79.

30. *Id.* at 33–34.

31. Larnder at 36.

32. *Id.* at 98.

33. For an excellent review of the relationship between advertising, the VCR, and the DVR, *see* Randall Picker, *The Digital Video Recorder: Unbundling Advertising and Content*, 71 U. Chic. L. Rev. 205 (2004).

34. Quoted in Scott Kirsner, *Inventing the Movies* 57 (CinemaTech Books 2008).

35. *Id.* at 319.

36. *Id.* at 320.

37. *Home Recording of Copyrighted Works: Hearing on H.R. 4783 et al. before the Subcommittee on Courts, Civil Liberties, and the Administration of Justice of the Committee on the Judiciary of the U.S. House of Representatives*, 97th Cong., Sess. 8–10. The House subcommittee held hearings on the issue an amazing seven days: April 12–14, June 24, August 11, and September 22–23. The Senate held two days of hearings in 1981 and 1982, on November 30, 1981, and on April 22, 1982—*Copyright Infringements (Audio and Video Recorders): Hearings on S. 1758 Before the Senate Judiciary Committee*, 97th Cong., 1st & 2d Sess. The Senate held another one-day hearing on October 25, 1983—*Video and Audio Home Taping: Hearing on S. 31 and S. 175 Before the Subcommittee on Patents, Copyrights and Trademarks of the Senate Committee on the Judiciary*, 98th Cong., 1st Sess.; and held a one-day hearing in 1986—*Home Video Recording: Hearing Before the Senate Judiciary Committee*, 99th Cong., 2d Sess.

38. 659 F.2d 693 (9th Cir. 1981).

39. 480 F. Supp. 429 (C.D. Cal. 1979).

40. 464 U.S. 417 (1984). The Court had heard argument first on January 18, 1983, and again on October 3, 1983. For a discussion of the case throughout the various levels, *see* William Patry, 4 *Patry on Copyright*, ch. 10, §§ 10:83–10:86 (2007, 2008 supplements).

41. *Audio and Video Rental: Hearing on S. 32 and S. 33 before the Subcommittee on Patents, Copyrights and Trademarks of the Committee on the Judiciary, U.S. Senate*, 98th Cong., 1st Sess. S. 32 concerned record rental and in an amended form, legislation barring record rental was passed in 1984. *See* 1 *Patry on Copyright*, ch. 1, § 1:86.

42. 4 *Patry on Copyright*, ch. 13, §§ 13:13–13:25.

43. *Senate Hearing* at 11.

44. *Id.* testimony of Register of Copyrights David Ladd.

45. Quoted in Laurel Leff, *Firms renting videocassettes worry studios*, Wall Street Journal, March 27, 1981.

46. *Id.*

47. *Id.* at 48.

48. *Id.* at 51, emphasis in original.

49. Quoted in Scott Kirsner, *Inventing Movies* at 59.

50. A description of the suit and links to the court papers *available at*: http://www. eff.org/deeplinks/2008/10/hollywood-menaces-dvd-rental-kiosks.

51. *Available at*: http://www.eff.org/files/Redbox%20v%20Universal_Complaint.pdf.

52. *Available at*: http://www.eff.org/files/Redbox%20v%20Universal_Complaint.pdf.

53. The studios' efforts to control home viewing through the "broadcast flag" is beyond the scope of this book, but is ably covered in chapter 7 of Tarleton Gillespie's 2007 book *Wired Shut* (MIT Press), and in Susan Crawford, *The Biology of the Broadcast Flag*, 25 Hastings Comm. & The Law Entm't J. 603 (2004).

54. 17 U.S.C. § 1201(a) (1)(A).

55. 17 U.S.C. § 1201(a) (2).

56. Fred von Lohmann, *Movie Studios Sue to Stop Loading of DVDs onto iPods Deeplink*, Nov. 16, 2006, *available at*: http://www.eff.org/deeplinks/2006/11/ movie-studios-sue-stop-loading-dvds-ipods.

57. *See* Brad Stone, *Wal-Mart Plans to Test Online Films*, N.Y. Times, Nov. 29, 2006, *available at*: http://www.nytimes.com/2006/11/29/technology/29bitt.html?_ r=1&oref=slogin.

58. *See* Dean Marks and Bruce Turnball, *Technical Protection Measure: The Intersection of Technology, Law and Commercial Licenses*, December 3, 1999, annex C, *available at*: http://www.wipo.int/edocs/mdocs/copyright/en/wct_wppt_imp/ wct_wppt_imp_3.pdf.

59. http://www.eff.org/deeplinks/2009/01/apple-shows-us-drms-true-colors.

60. *See* Jane Ginsburg, *Putting Cars on the "Information Superhighway": Authors, Exploiters, and Copyright on Cyberspace*, 95 Colum. L. Rev. 1466 (1995).

61. *Id.*

62. *See* http://en.wikipedia.org/wiki/Corporatism.

63. Tarleton Gillespie, *Wired Shut: copyright and the shape of digital culture* 275 (2007, MIT Press). *See also* Christopher May, *Digital Righted Management: The Problems of Expanding Ownership Rights* (Chados Publishing 2007).

64. *Id.* at 278.

65. Dean Marks & Bruce Turnball, *Technical Protection Measure: The Intersection of Technology, Law and Commercial Licenses*, December 3, 1999, *available at*: http:// www.wipo.int/edocs/mdocs/copyright/en/wct_wppt_imp/wct_wppt_imp_3. pdf.

66. Tarleton Gillespie, *Wired Shut: Copyright and the Shape of Digital Culture* 170 (MIT Press 2007).

67. *Id.* at 181–184.

68. *Id.* at 9. There are now DVRs, which as the name indicates, do record. *See* http://en.wikipedia.org/wiki/Digital_video_recorder.

69. *Sony Corporation of America v. Universal City Studios, Inc.*, 464 U.S. 417 (1984). *See* James Lardner, *Fast Forward: Hollywood, the Japanese, and the VCR Wars* 10 (1987) for an excellent account of the litigation.

70. Bennett Lincoff, *Common Sense, Accommodation and Sound Policy for the Digital Music Marketplace*, 2 J. Int'l Media & Ent. L. 1, 13–14 (2007).

71. Gillespie at 171.

72. *See* http://en.wikipedia.org/wiki/DeCSS.

73. The encryption locks used for DVD and other consumer electronics devices, of course, have nothing to do with the Internet.
74. Quoted in Gillespie at 190.
75. *Digital Europe: The Internet megatrends that will shape tomorrow's Europe," speech delivered by Viviane Reding on November 13, 2008, before the Digital Internet Foundation.*
76. There are two definitions of "service provider." The definitions are contained in 17 U.S.C. § 512(k).
77. *See* http://arstechnica.com/news.ars/post/20070830-viacom-caught-in-copyright-infringement-loop.html.
78. *See* http://www.eff.org/press/archives/2004/09/30.
79. *See* http://arstechnica.com/news.ars/post/20070322-dmca-takedown-backlash-eff-sues-viacom-over-colbert-parody-clip.html.
80. *See* http://www.eff.org/cases/lenz-v-universal.
81. *See* http://bits.blogs.nytimes.com/2008/10/14/mccain-fights-for-right-to-remix-on-youtube/.

## ✇ Chapter 9  How Innovation Occurs: Creative Destruction and Disruptive Technologies

1. *See* http://en.wikipedia.org/wiki/Robert_Solow.
2. His prize lecture is *available at*: http://ca.geocities.com/econ_0909meet/solow-lecture.html.
3. In 1987 Solow took a dim view of computers as an aid to productivity. As noted by Wikipedia (http://en.wikipedia.org/wiki/Productivity_paradox):

    The productivity paradox (also known as the Solow paradox or sometimes the Solow computer paradox) is the theory that computers have contributed negligibly to productivity, and is often summarized with Robert Solow's 1987 quip, "You can *see* the computer age everywhere but in the productivity statistics." The paradox has been defined as the "discrepancy between measures of investment in information technology and measures of output at the national level."

    Since 1987, others have found a "significant positive relationship between information technology (IT) investments and productivity in a series of studies," *see* Erik Brynjolfsson & Lorin M. Hitt, *Computing Productivity: Firm Level Evidence* and the papers cited therein. Others have attacked the basis for the alleged paradox and noted, "Even before the mid-1990s, ICT [information and communication technology] had a much bigger impact on growth than steam and at least a similar impact to that of electricity in a similar early phase," Nicholas Craft, *The Solow Paradox in Historical Perspective,* London Sch. Econ., (Nov. 2001), *available at*: http://www.j-bradford-delong.net/articles_of_the_month/pdf/Newsolow.pdf; Robert Atkinson & Andrew McKay, *Digital Prosperity* 15 (Mar. 2007, ITIF). In any event, since the advent of the World Wide Web in 1992, the critical contribution to information technologies to productivity is unchallenged.

4. Viviane Reding, *Digital Europe: The Internet megatrends that will shape toward tomorrow's Europe*, Speech delivered on November 13, 2008 to the European Internet Foundation.

5. Robert Atkinson & Andrew McKay, *Digital Prosperity* 10 (ITIF Mar. 2007).

6. *Boosting Productivity, Innovation, and Growth Through a National Innovation Foundation*, App. A (Brookings Institute, Apr. 2008). *See also Digital Prosperity* at 12–20 for an explanation of why productivity growth is the key to increasing the standard of living.

7. Robert Atkinson & Andrew McKay, *Digital Prosperity* 11 (ITIF Mar. 2007).

8. *Id.* at Robert Atkinson and Andrew McKay, *Digital Prosperity* 34 (March 2007, ITIF).

9. *Id.* at 4, quoting Paul Romer, *Implementing a National Technology Strategy with Self-Organizing Industry Boards*, in 2 *Brookings Papers on Economic Activity, Macroeconomics 1993*, at 345 (Martin Bailey et al. eds., Brookings Institute 1993).

10. *Id.* at 3; Robert Atkinson & Andrew McKay, *Digital Prosperity* 1; Larry Downes & Chunka Mui, *Unleashing the Killer App: Digital Strategies for Market Dominance* 73 (Harvard Business School Press 1998).

11. *See* http://www.garlic-central.com/vampires.html.

12. *Boosting Productivity, Innovation, and Growth Through a National Innovation Foundation* 18 (Brookings Institute, Apr. 2008).

13. Jan Fagerberg, *Innovation: A Guide to the Literature*, in *The Oxford Handbook of Innovation* 1, 20 (Jan Fagerberg et al. eds., Oxford University Press 2006).

14. Michael Cieply, *Jitters are Setting In for States Giving Big Incentives to Lure Film Producers*, N.Y. Times, Sunday Oct. 12, 2008, front section page 26. *See also*, Peter Sanders, *Lawmakers Weigh Hollywood Tax Break*, Wall St. J., Wednesday, Feb. 18, 2009, Section A, page 4.

15. Tom Bell, *Authors' Welfare: Copyright as a Statutory Mechanism for Redistributing Rights*, 69 Brooklyn L. Rev. 229 (2003).

16. Joseph Schumpeter, *Capitalism, Socialism and Democracy* 83 (Harper & Brothers 1942, 3d ed. 1950, 2006 paperback).

17. *Id.* at 82. *See also* his earlier article, "The Instability of Capitalism" published in 38 Economic Journal 361–366 (Sept. 1928), edited by John Maynard Keynes. The essay is reproduced in *Joseph A. Schumpeter: Essays on Entrepreneur, Innovation, Business Cycles, and the Evolution of Capitalism* 47–72 (Richard Clemence ed. Addison-Wesley 1951).

18. Schumpeter, 2 *Business Cycles: A Theoretical, Historical, and Statistical Analysis of the Capitalist Process* 1033.

19. Thomas McGraw, *Prophet of Innovation: Joseph Schumpeter and Creative Destruction* 256 (Belknap Press, Harvard University 2007).

20. J.S. Metcalfe, *Knowledge of growth and growth of knowledge*, 12 J. Evolutionary Econ. 3, 8 (2002).

21. Theodore Levitt, "Marketing and Corporate Purpose," in Theodore Levitt *The Marketing Imagination* 9 (Free Press 1983, 1986 edition).

22. *Id.* at xviii.

23. Scott Kirsner, *Inventing Movies* 199–200 (CinemaTech Books 2008).

24. *See* Peter Dekom & Peter Sealey, *Not On My Watch: Hollywood vs. the Future* 5–6 (New Millennium Press 2003): "Most of Hollywood is *about titles*, reporting structures and clear lines of power. Hollywood is governed from the top down, with lots of middle managers to filter, summarize, and often distort information flow. In the Internet era of personalization and customization, the new economy is bottom-up directed: The consumer is boss . . . ."

25. *See* http://www.grameen-info.org.

26. *See* his 2008 book *Creating a World Without Poverty: Social Business and the Future of Capitalism.*

27. *See* http://www.grameen-info.org/Media/mediadetailGE.html.

28. *Boosting Productivity, Innovation, and Growth Through a National Innovation Foundation* 5 (Brookings Institute, Apr. 2008).

29. Introduction to Henry Chesbrough, *Open Innovation and the New Imperative for Creating and Profiting from Technology*, at ix (Harvard Business School Press 2006). *See also Open Innovation: Researching a New Paradigm* (Henry Chesbrough, Wim Vanhaverbeke, & Joel West eds., Oxford University Press 2006). *See also* Dr. Brown's book with Paul Duguid, *The Social Life of Information* (Harvard Business School Press 2002).

30. *See* Mr. Brown's in-depth discussion of this in John *See*ley Brown & Paul Duguid, *The Social Life of Information* 150–161 (Harvard Business School Press 2002).

31. *Open Innovation and the New Imperative for Creating and Profiting from Technology* at 77–78.

32. *Id.* at 79.

33. *Id.* at xxx.

34. Joseph Schumpeter, *The Theory of Economic Development* 86 (Harvard University Press 1934).

35. Andrew Currah, Hollywood *Versus* the Internet: *The Media* and *Entertainment Industries* in a *Digital* and *Networked Economy*, 6 J. of Econ. Geogr. 439, 462 (2006).

36. Joseph Schumpeter, *The Tendencies of Our Social Structure* (1928; Florian Miller trans.), quoted in Thomas McGraw, *Prophet of Innovation: Joseph Schumpeter and Creative Destruction* 163 (Belknap Press, Harvard University 2007).

37. Dec. 15, 1959, published by the RAND Corp., P-1856-Rc, *available at*: http://www.rand.org/pubs/papers/2006/P1856.pdf.

38. Don Topscott & Anthony Williams, *Wikinomics* 174 (Portfolio hardcover ed. 2008).

39. *See* http://www.imdb.com/title/tt0120885/.

40. John Naughton, *A Brief History of the Future* 107 (1999). *See also* Katie Hafner & Matthew Lyon, *Where Wizards Stay Up Late* 52–66 (1996).

41. However AT&T's views about the Internet may have evolved since the 1960s, it should be pointed out that it has been an opponent of network neutrality (but *see* http://www.savetheinternet.com/=wu), and a strong advocate of ISP monitoring of customers, *see* http://arstechnica.com/news.ars/post/20070613-att-willing-to-spy-for-nsa-mpaa-and-riaa.html. The Electronic Frontier Foundation filed a class-action lawsuit against AT&T for "violating the law and the privacy of its customers by collaborating with the National Security Agency

(NSA) in its massive and illegal domestic spying program to wiretap and data-mine Americans' communications." *See* http://www.eff.org/nsa/faq#39.

42. Wikipedia (http://en.wikipedia.org/wiki/Internet#The_name_Internet) has the following entry on the name "Internet":

> Historically, Internet and internet have had different meanings, with internet meaning "an interconnected set of distinct networks," and Internet referring to the worldwide, publicly available IP internet. Under this distinction, the Internet is the familiar network through which websites exist; however, an internet can exist between any two remote locations. Any group of distinct networks connected together is an internet; each of these networks may or may not be part of the Internet. The distinction was evident in many RFCs, books, and articles from the 1980s and early 1990s (some of which, such as RFC 1918, refer to "internets" in the plural), but has recently fallen into disuse. Instead, the term intranet is generally used for private networks, whether they are connected to the Internet or not.

43. He did not sit for a PhD but was subsequently knighted. *See* http://en.wikipedia.org/wiki/Tim_Berners-Lee. For convenience, I refer to him as "Mr."

44. *See* Tim Berners-Lee, *Weaving the Web: The Original Design and Ultimate Destiny of the World Wide Web* 123 (HarperBusiness 2000).

45. He is now Vice President and Chief Internet Evangelist at Google Inc.

46. *U.S. Senate Committee on Commerce, Science, and Transportation Hearing on "Network Neutrality,"* February 7, 2006, *available at*: http://74.125.45.104/search?q=cache:u10LVoYCEYkJ:commerce.senate.gov/pdf/cerf-020706.pdf+vint+cerf+Internet+open&hl=en&ct=clnk&cd=1&gl=us&client=firefox-a.

47. Tim Berners-Lee, *Weaving the Web: The Original Design and Ultimate Destiny of the World Wide Web* 4 (HarperBusiness 2000). Dr. Berners-Lee readily acknowledges that many others "contributed essential ingredients," *id.* at 2, most importantly Robert Cailliau, with whom he worked at CERN, a name derived from the former Counseil Européen pour la Recherche Nucléaire. *Id.* at 4, note 1.

48. *Id.* at 36.

49. *See* http://en.wikipedia.org/wiki/Gopher_(computer).

50. *Weaving the Web* at 72–74. The press release announcing the decision was issued on April 30, 1993 and is *available at*: http://tenyears-www.web.cern.ch/tenyears-www/Declaration/Page1.html.

51. *Id.* at 140.

52. *Id.* at 140–141.

53. Marisa Peacock, *Reuters Lab Opens Content Through API* (May 15, 2008), *available at*: http://www.cmswire.com/cms/web-publishing/reuters-lab-opens-content-through-api-002660.php.

54. *See*
http://www.guardian.co.uk/media/pda/2007/dec/14/thenutshellabeginnersguide.

55. *New York Times' Derek Gottfrid and NPR's Dan Jacobson Discuss APIs* (July 25, 2008), Webmonkey Website, *available at*: http://www.webmonkey.com/blog/New_York_Times__Derek_Gottfrid_and_NPR_s_Dan_Jacobson_Discuss_APIs.

56. *Id.* remarks of Dan Jacobson.

57. Approximately 1700 of these.

58. Approximately 5000 of these. Outside the United States, equivalent companies are AP subscribers, paying a fee for the use of AP material.

59. Reproduced in *Intellectual Property Stories* 11 (Thomson/West 2005).

60. *Id.*

61. *Id.* at 15

62. *Id.*

63. *Id.*

64. The book is available for free online at http://www.teleread.org/brasscheck.htm.

65. *See* William Patry, 2 *Patry on Copyright* § 4:14 (2007, 2009 supplement).

66. Marcus Errico, *The Evolution of the Summary News Lead,* http://www.scripps. ohiou.edu/mediahistory/mhmjour1–1.htm.

67. *Available at:* http://www.ap.org/pages/about/whatsnew/documents/Curley_ ACAP.pdf.

68. In 2006, AP sued Google over its news search service. The parties settled.

69. *Available at:* http://www.ap.org/pages/about/whatsnew/documents/Curley_ ACAP.pdf.

70. This fact was acknowledged in the speech, but nevertheless search engines still erroneously described it as free-riding.

71. For a genuine examination of the issue, *see* Mark Lemley, *Property, Intellectual Property, and Free Riding,* 83 Tex. L. Rev. 1031 (2005).

72. *See Harper & Row, Publishers, Inc. v. Nation Enterprises,* 471 U.S. 539, 547 (1985); William Patry 2 *Patry on Copyright* § 4:9 (2007, 2008, 2009 supplements, Thomson/ West).

73. 1 *Patry on Copyright* § 4.2

74. *See* http://license.icopyright.net/user/offer.act?gid=3&inprocess=t&sid=36&tag =3.5721%3Ficx_id%3DD91BPUSG0&urs=WEBPAGE&urt=http%3A%2F%2Fhos ted.ap.org%2Fdynamic%2Fstories%2FA%2FAP_BLOGGERS%3FSITE%3DRIPRJ %26SECTION%3DHOME%26TEMPLATE%3DDEFAULT.

75. *See* 4 *Patry on Copyright* § 4.2 for an explanation of the *de minimis* doctrine in copyright.

76. It is also known as the Robot exclusion standard or Robots Exclusion Protocol, *see* http://en.wikipedia.org/wiki/Robots_Exclusion_Standard. Other complimentary metatag tools include NoArchive, and Sitemaps.

77. robots-request@nexor.co.uk.

78. *See* http://www.seoconsultants.com/meta-tags/robots/googlebot.asp.

79. *Field v. Google Inc.,* 412 F.2d 1106, 1116 (D. Nev. 2006).

80. *See* http://en.wikipedia.org/wiki/Automated_Content_Access_Protocol.

81. One writer lamented: "In the interests of fairness I tried to find a positive article about ACAP, but there's absolutely nothing." *Available at:* http://new-media. lazaruscorporation.co.uk/2007/12/04/automated-content-access-protocol-acap/.

82. http://blogs.telegraph.co.uk/technology/iandouglas/dec2007/acap.htm.

83. *Id.* Jan. 23, 2008.

84. http://new-media.lazaruscorporation.co.uk/2007/12/04/automated-content-access-protocol-acap/.

85. *See* http://people-press.org/report/479/internet-overtakes-newspapers-as-news-source. Television remains the lead source.

86. There is no non-broadband access in South Korea.

87. Unless otherwise indicated, all figures in this section are from the 2008 Information Technology & Innovation Foundation's 2008 Broadband rankings.

88. Mbps stands for megabits per second. An Mbps is a unit of data transfer rate equal to 1,000,000 bits per second. *See* http://en.wikipedia.org/wiki/Mbps#Megabit_per_second.

89. *See id.* A large part of the reason for the slow speed in the United States is that cable accounts for 12 subscribers per 100 inhabitants, DSL accounts for 10 subscribers per 100 inhabitants, and fiber only 0.6 subscribers per 100 inhabitants. Thirteen of the fourteen countries ahead of the United States in house-hold broadband penetration use DSL for the majority of their broadband connections.

90. *Speed Matter: A Report on Internet Speeds in All 50 States* at 2, *available at*: www.speedmatters.org.

91. *Id.* at 2.

92. Tomi Ahonen & Jim O'Reilly, *Digital Korea* 97 (Futuretext 2008).

93. *Id.*

94. *See Digital Korea* at 204–205. *Lineage* is another popular game, although less popular than *Kart Rider*.

95. *Digital Korea* at 202.

96. http://en.wikipedia.org/wiki/Cyworld.

97. Tomi Ahonen and Jim O'Reilly, *Digital Korea* 35 (2008, Futuretext).

98. DMB stands for Digital Media Broadcasting. *See* http://en.wikipedia.org/wiki/Digital_Multimedia_Broadcast.

99. *Digital Korea* at 79.

100. http://news.cnet.com/South-Korea-leads-the-way/2009–1034_3–5261393.html.

101. http://www.ifpi.org/content/library/DMR2008.pdf, at 3.

102. Quoted at http://euobserver.com/9/26903.

103. *Digital Korea* at 162.

104. *See e.g.*, Eric von Hippel, *Democratizing Innovation* (2005, MIT Press).

105. Norimitsu Onishi, "Thumbs Race as Japan's Best Sellers Go Cellular," *available at*: http://www.nytimes.com/2008/01/20/world/asia/20japan.html.

106. Quoted in Dana Goodyear, "I ♥ Novels," New Yorker Magazine, December 22 & 29, 2008 issue, at page 65.

107. *Id.* at 66.

108. Norimitsu Onishi, "Thumbs Race as Japan's Best Sellers Go Cellular," *available at*: http://www.nytimes.com/2008/01/20/world/asia/20japan.html.

109. "I ♥ Novels" at 65.

110. Justin Norrie, "In Japan, cellular storytelling is all the rage," Sydney Morning Herald, December 3, 2007.

# Index